SONGS OF MYSELF

SONGS OF MYSELF

EPISODES

FROM THE

EDGE OF

ADULTHOOD

EDITED BY DIANE SCHARPER

FOREWORD BY JUDITH PATERSON

WOODHOLME
HOUSE
PUBLISHERS

BALTIMORE, MARYLAND

Printed and bound in the United States of America.

1 2 3 4 5   07 06 05 04 03 02 01 00 99 98

Library of Congress Cataloging-in-Publication Data

Songs of myself : episodes from the edge of adulthood / edited by
  Diane Scharper
        p.   cm.
    Includes bibliographical references (p.   ).
    ISBN 1-891521-00-4 (alk. paper)
    1. College students' writings, American—Maryland—Towson.
  2. College students—Maryland—Towson—Literary collections.
  3. Young adults—Maryland—Towson—Literary collections. 4. College
  students—Maryland—Towson—Biography. 5. Young adults—Maryland—
  Towson—Biography. 6. Autobiographies. I. Scharper, Diane, 1942- .

      PS508.C6S66   1998
      810.8'09283'0975271—dc21   97-51152
                                                             CIP

Excerpts of "Song of Myself" taken from Whitman, Walt. "Song of Myself." *Leaves of Grass*, with an introduction by Gay Wilson Allen. (New York: A Mentor Book—New American Library, 1959).

Woodholme House Publishers
1829 Reisterstown Road
Suite 130
Baltimore, Maryland 21208
Fax: (410) 653-7904
Orders: 1-800-488-0051

Cover design: Anna Burgard
Book design: Lance Simons
Cover photograph: Jimmy Serkoch

In loving memory
of my mother,
Constance K. Waesche, 1911-1996

I am of

old and young,

of the foolish

as much as the wise,

Regardless

of others, ever regardful of others,

Maternal

as well as

paternal,

a child

as well as

a man,

Stuff'd with the stuff that is coarse,

and stuff'd with the stuff that is fine...

And of these one and all I weave the song of myself...

CONTENTS

FOREWORD

I have been teaching writing and literature to college students for almost three decades now. When I started out in 1970, teaching at the Montgomery, Alabama, branch campus of Auburn University, I was a part-time graduate student and full-time wife and mother of two small children. I held an undergraduate degree in Sociology, had taken a few courses toward an M.A. in English and American Literature, and had never taught anything before. Despite my complete lack of the usual qualifications, I was given an opportunity to teach English Composition to freshman.

A secretary twenty years my senior handed me a suggested syllabus with a sink-or-swim look on her face and said, "Good luck, Hon." Having tested out of Freshman Composition myself, I had never even *taken* the course I was about to teach. Good luck, as it turned out, had thrown me into the briar patch of a career that suited me perfectly.

Although Auburn was the second largest university in the state system, the tiny Montgomery campus was brand-new and scheduled classes in a shabby downtown office building. On the day my teaching career began, the dean of the Humanities division, who had never seen me before, and the head of the English department, who had hired me, were still nailing up the temporary partitions that designated my classroom.

Most of my students were over twenty-five and more experienced in life than in academics. Many were middle-aged; the oldest was in his seventies. Most had never had a chance to go to college before. All were highly motivated.

Mark Twain's *Huckleberry Finn* was required reading for freshmen, and I had been in graduate school long enough to know that college professors were supposed to be familiar with what literary scholars said about the books they taught. I was juggling babysitters and household responsibilities and commuting one hundred miles three days a week to take my own courses. When one of my children came down with a fever, it became simply impossible for me to make a special trip to the library to find out what the critics thought about *Huckleberry Finn*. So I read a book I hadn't thought about since childhood and winged an open discussion in class the next day.

That day remains so vivid in memory that I can still see the faces of most of the students—though all but one of the names have left me. That class taught me one of the central lessons of my teaching career: given something provocative to read and a bit of guidance, any roomful of readers will, on their own, come up with most of the great interpretations of what they have read.

After many years of teaching—and developing a writing career of my own—I have added another pair of axioms to the one *Huckleberry Finn* taught me: first, writing is a natural means of self-expression; second, with much writing and revising plus a little guidance from a teacher or editor, anyone's writing will improve. I once told this to a student who, with a look of horror on his face, said, "You mean it's like practicing the piano?" That was exactly what I meant, and I have come to think that heavy red penciling limits a writer's opportunity to learn the necessary lessons of a craft that is part practice, part skill, and part gift.

The last of my three pedagogical axioms is the one most relevant to Diane Scharper's wonderful collection of student memoirs: students (and all writers) write best when they write about an experience that is deeply felt and long remembered. In teaching literary journalism and creative nonfiction, I have found that students often experience extraordinary cognitive and psychological growth from immersing themselves for an extended period of time in a writing project with which they feel a substantial personal connection. The work of someone whose writing is generally pedestrian or immature will come unexpectedly alive if the content gets close enough to home. I have come to suspect that intense experiences may actually be processed and logged into memory in language that is qualitatively different from (more accurate and more sensitive than) the words imprinted by everyday events.

This book is a collection of intense experiences.

A few years ago, Professor Barbara Harrell Carson asked Rollins College alumni (1964-1990) to recall their most effective professors and found that teachers were remembered less for what they taught than for teaching in a way that produced "transforming moments" or "developmental turning points."

She surmised that "critical moments where we learn to look at life in a different way may be remembered with the clarity of a conversion experience" and described not with the language of information but with metaphors from "religion—or love: inspiration, revelation, passion, enthusiasm, charisma, transformation." (*Change* magazine, November/December 1996, pp.11-17.) A similar inquiry into the lasting freshman-year memories of Wellesley alumnae who had graduated two, twelve, or twenty-two years earlier also found that emotionally charged and transitional events were the most vividly remembered. (*Journal of Experimental Psychology: Learning Memory and Cognition*, 1988, pp. 709-715.)

Studies like these (not to mention William Wordsworth's emotion recollected in tranquility) suggest some of the reasons why memoir will often produce a writer's best work. In urging undergraduate writers to cast their most vivid memories in the now well-defined genre of memoir, Diane Scharper—like all good teachers—knows these things by instinct. Her wisdom bears fruit in some of the strongest undergraduate writing I have seen.

It is clear from the comments of these writers that many of them see the experience as a "developmental turning point," one that (to quote Carson again) turns "passive students into academic activists." Jessica Graham, for instance, says, "I learned not only to go deeper in my writing, but to ask why things happened.... I learned to write the truth. That, in essence, is what my memoir is—my version of the truth."

Quite a few of these students have become hooked on writing, thus paying their teacher the highest compliment a student of writing can pay. I think especially of Alessandra Vadala who is collecting material toward a biography of the Italian great-grandmother she writes about with such clarity in "Antonia."

As Annie Dillard says in the introduction to her anthology *Modern American Memoirs*, "There is something to be said for writing a memoir early, before life in society makes the writer ordinary by smoothing off character's rough edges and abolishing interior life." In *Songs of Myself*, we see the rough edges and the interior life reflecting the universal concerns of our times—and all times: the closeness and distance of families; the dangers of escapism and abuse; the shouldering or shirking of responsibility; choices of vocation, identity, and spirituality; the acceptance of death and all the losses of life.

These memoirs usher readers into the interior lives of college-aged adults, and might help teachers direct their own students deeper into the writing life.

Judith Paterson
Washington, D.C., January 1998

ACKNOWLEDGMENTS

I wish to thank Towson University, especially the English Department, without whose support this book would not have existed. Thank you especially to Clarinda Harriss, Chairperson of the English Department, and to Dan Jones, Dean of the College of Liberal Arts. Both of you created an atmosphere where this book of memoirs could grow and where students could learn to love language and writing. Thank you to Haig Janian from Towson University's fine art department for help selecting and coordinating most of the artwork. Thank you to Laura Barnhardt and to Estelle Petri who worked diligently to help me edit this book. Thank you to Mia Emerson and Chris Kridler, "my editors." Thank you to the brave and hard-working students whose stories have made this book possible. Thank you to the staff of The Writing Lab, The PC Lab, and The Writing Support Program. You were with us every step of the way. Finally, thank you to my family. This book would not have been here if you had not been there.

Diane Scharper
Baltimore, February 1998

INTRODUCTION

Over the past seven years, I have asked five hundred college students to write about the best or worst thing that ever happened to them. They wrote about everything from finding God to finding out a fiancé had Hodgkin's disease. They explained what it was like to be born with cerebral palsy, or to be born with big ears, or to be born fat. They described the death of a parent and the drug addiction of a sibling. They wrote about bearing a child in or out of wedlock and about having an abortion.

And they wrote well; so well that I wanted to keep their papers forever. I wanted to inspire other students. I wanted to inspire the rest of the world. That is both the method and the madness behind this book.

These thirty-eight memoirs are history, and literature, and poetry. Above all, they are the human heart. In one sense, they answer the question "Who am I?" In another sense, they present a time capsule holding the memories of a generation who came of age at the end of the twentieth century at a large university. Towson University in Baltimore, Maryland, is the second largest institution in the state-supported university system and attracts a diverse group of students—scholars and athletes; young people from rural and urban backgrounds; students with different academic and cultural experiences. Therefore, it represents a microcosm of typical campus life encountered across the country.

The book originated from a required course—Writing for a Liberal Education—in which students must write several critical papers. To these I added a paper that combines critical writing with creative writing: the memoir. Russell Baker's Pulitzer Prize-winning memoir *Growing Up* gave me the idea for the assignment. My students read Baker's memoir and loved it. They also read his interview with William Zinsser, in which Mr. Baker explained that he learned to write by writing about himself and his family. Writing wasn't just reporting, he said; it was telling a story.

The cliché is "write what you know." If this method worked for Mr. Baker, it could work for my college students. Even if they didn't win the Pulitzer Prize, they'd have something concrete to write about. They'd gain confidence in themselves as writers. But these papers blossomed into more than writing exercises. They revealed the hearts and minds of college students who defy characterizations as materialistic "mall-crawlers" or Generation-X "slackers" that the media often portrays. They're not the heartless druggies or the sex-and-booze crazed groupies that we often see on television. They are caring, thoughtful, sensitive individuals. They love deeply.

And they write personally. "Personal" is the thinking behind this book's title. Like Walt Whitman's classic "Song of Myself," these memoirs celebrate the personal self. Yet because the personal, at its most profound, is universal, these memoirs also celebrate the humanity we share. "What I assume you shall assume," writes Whitman with this thought in mind. "For every atom belonging to me as good belongs to you...."

As you read these memoirs, aspects of your own self emerge in the words of these young people. How many times have you looked forward to the biggest occasion of your life only to find it has flopped? How many grudges have you held against the people you love most? How many people have you loved and lost— in one way or another? How many dumb, crazy things have you done? How few smart, noble things have you stumbled into?

As I read and edited their papers for this collection, eight categories emerged even though I hadn't asked my students to choose any particular topics. They wrote about their passions: high school, pregnancy, coping with illness, near-fatal injury, travels, entering adulthood, soul-making, and family. Passion makes for good writing. Perhaps this is why these selections are so moving, transcendent, and well written.

These writers' age also makes for good writing. If there's ever a time to write a memoir, it's freshman year in college. That year is a crossroad, when students are poised to choose a major and thus begin to see the shape of the rest of their lives. At this crossroad, students do not always fit into a neat social category or demographic type. They also do not fit into a neat "feelings" category. Almost all of them are more emotionally mature than high school students, but some are not completely ready to take on the responsibilities of adulthood.

Having emerged from many of the battles of adolescence, college freshmen tend to be somewhat self-assured. They've proven at least that they are individuals, unique personalities, not merely their parents' offspring. They are still growing, however. And they can still learn new things about themselves. Quite a few of my students are excellent writers, but they do not realize how accomplished they are. Perhaps these students were too immature to work at writing in high school. Perhaps they had never been asked to write anything that caught their imaginations. But whatever the reason, I use my course as I would a fish net—scooping up a wonderful catch of talented writers.

Latent talent often shows itself in the memoir. Memoirs are not merely an opportunity for students to see who they were, who they are, and who they will become. Memoirs also present an opportunity to write on a subject students care about. Anyone invited to write a memoir has a vested interest in doing it well. People need to understand themselves and to be understood. Memoirs tap into this need in a way that no other writing does. This need is the power behind these "songs of myself."

A Note to Teachers

If I asked you to write about the latest rock group or the latest teenage fashion, would you want to? Would you want to write a ten-page term paper on that subject, researching current and past teenage magazines? Would you then wish to express yourself in a way that would agree with my opinion—not necessarily your own. Perhaps I wouldn't tell you my opinion. I'd make you guess it. Crazy? Maybe.

Yet how often do many of us inflict that craziness on our students? How often do we ask students to write about a subject which does not even remotely interest them? Of course, sometimes these assignments are unavoidable. Students, after all, are attending college and must learn to write about, think about, and become interested in many subjects. Such writing is the purpose of a liberal education. But writing itself is a subject and a vital part of a liberal education. We teachers owe students an opportunity to see what real writing is. We owe them the chance to unveil the passion, conviction, and power of writing.

Some teachers call it "writing" when students compose a paper, adding up somebody else's ideas in accord with the teacher's opinion. This exercise is less "writing" than it is an exercise in logic, or rote memory, or even mental telepathy. Then we wonder how young people so filled with life can write dry dead prose devoid of imagination and delight.

Students wouldn't write such prose if they were allowed to write something they care about, which is my point in assigning the memoir. Writing memoirs encourages students to write using their own voice. Writers say that "voice" lies at the heart of good writing. Voice establishes authority, readability, and humanity, but it takes years of work for writers to find their voice. Writing memoirs, however, gives students their voice. It's almost impossible to explain your past and how you feel about it without using your voice.

Writing memoirs forces students to choose significant details. They must tell what made this person unique, this place different, this time significant. They must be logical, clear, concise. They must work with verbs, action, and tense. They must work with beginnings, endings, and middles. They must remember and sort through memories. They must find the inner truth of experience—what T.S. Eliot called the "objective correlative" and Gerard Manley Hopkins called "the inscape."

Writers and writing teachers often wonder whether writing can be taught. Teachers can give students the basic information about grammar, punctuation, and syntax. But that information is not writing, just as learning colors and their position on a color wheel is not painting a picture.

If writing is not simply grammar, punctuation, and syntax (as many students believe), what is it? Writing is the ultimate form of communication—and the most intimate. Writing communicates with a reader and with the writer. It communicates with the writer's many selves. It works through conflicting thoughts and arrives at a synthesis. It analyzes feelings. It's a way of talking to the self and of explaining oneself to oneself...and to others.

Toward the end of the semester, I ask students to tell me what they learned about writing *from* writing. Sprinkled throughout these pages are quotes from the students themselves about writing as well as about life itself. They use words and phrases such as "hard but satisfying," "fulfilling," and "personal." They tell me that writing is thinking on paper. Writing shows them things they didn't realize—not just about punctuation or grammar, but things about themselves. One of my students said that her writing was filled with stories—the stories on the paper and the stories of composition, the stories she thought happened and the stories that really happened.

Ultimately, students realize that writing is something they do for themselves more than for an audience. Yes, they must think clearly, spell correctly, and follow the rules of grammar and syntax, but writing is fundamentally a form of self-expression. This realization allows their thoughts to flow. It teaches them how to write. And it brings them joy. This book offers some of the very best student writing on a variety of subjects. These memoirs could serve as a paradigm to enhance your own writing course, or to launch a course in creative nonfiction writing. Read them and share them for their sheer enjoyment, insight, and inspiration.

THE INTERLOPER: High School

The youth

lies awake

in the

cedar-rooted

garret and harks

to the

musical rain.

"Thinking of the idea for the memoir is easy, but to put it on paper is another story. This was my biggest problem."

Jeffrey Sengebusch

ENDEAVORS OF AN INTERLOPER
by Jessica Graham

"Go hard or go home."

Every athlete and scholar who attended Gloucester Catholic High School lived by these words. Coaches and teachers taught us that determination, faith, loyalty, and hard work were the ingredients for success. We were to "give it our all" or we were to pack up our things and give up on our goal.

I set many goals in high school. Some of them I achieved, and some of them were shoved in the back of my locker along with my dirty gym socks. There were moments when I succeeded, and there were times when I fell short.

Along with "going hard," students learned that pain was temporary, and winning was forever. This lesson did not come from a textbook, but from the trials and tribulations of every-day life.

Pain. There were times in my high-school career when that emotion could not be avoided. Looking back on those days now, I think that it helped me grow. It helped us all. Those mistakes we made, be it throwing away a year in the name of Maturity, or succumbing to the peer pressures so heavily exerted on us, were learning experiences. Maybe some of those lessons could have been avoided if I myself could have tried harder. Maybe if my "silly blonde" reputation was never established, I wouldn't have spent so much time proving myself to the rest of the world. Maybe...maybe...maybe.

As a class, a lot of what we experienced had to do with the institution of high school in general. Within every class, there are cliques. They are invisible, private spheres which are ever present: in the hallways, at parties, during pep rallies, even at graduation.

We had our own groups of friends and they represented who we were as individuals. The jocks congregated amongst themselves, and so did the "clones" and the "stones" and the "honorary nerds." Did we set these social boundaries? They weren't discussed in the student handbook. We were not forced to serve detention if we ventured into another social strata. Cliques were the norm, much like the plaid uniforms we wore.

I think that much of the pain and animosity I felt began on the very first days of school. I dared to question why I was supposed to conform to the social norm.

No one wanted to answer that question. Maybe because at fourteen, a bunch of freshmen did not know the answer. Everyone just went along with the flow. Life was a lot easier for them that way. You aren't as vulnerable to the world if you are a part of a "we" as opposed to being an isolated "I."

Jean-Jacques Rousseau, famous French philosopher, once said, "Man is born free and everywhere is in chains." In Catholic school I felt shackled. I just could not conform. The girls in my class looked like clones. Along with wearing the same uniform, they all bought identical shoes, socks, and hair accessories. During homeroom they mirrored each other's hairstyles. At the lunch table, they sang theme songs from Walt Disney movies. When they wrote papers, they all dotted their "i's" with hearts. (That really bothered me.)

My first year at Gloucester Catholic was utter hell because I hated my environment. Much of it had to do with culture shock. In eighth grade, I attended a laid-back public middle school. I starred in the plays, excelled in my classes, and had an ample supply of diverse friends.

During freshman year in Catholic school, I was nothing. I blended in with the masses of knee socks and ugly maroon sweaters. Priests bombarded me with rules. They gave me more detentions than the school nurse gave cough drops during flu season.

My teachers told me that I "had grown in geometric proportions" since the ninth grade. That always made me laugh because I had stayed five feet, five inches tall since the seventh grade. But had I really grown? Had I gone hard enough to graduate a winner?

These questions plague me even now during freshman year at college. College seems so much easier than high school. Maybe because through all my endeavors and conquests, I discovered who I was, or at least who I wanted to be. There were so many things that I had attempted during those years. I tried so hard to compensate for a tumultuous freshman year. Sitting here in my cozy dorm room, looking at the pictures of graduation, prom, and my friends, I realize that there is nothing left to accomplish in Gloucester City. That era of my life has finally ended.

The rules, the prayers, the uniforms, the cliques, the detentions: all these things made my head spin. I wanted to get out of that school and to go back to the eighth grade where I was a success. That was impossible though. I had to grow up sometime.

The only other option I had was to attend Washington Township High School, a place my parents believed was an educational wasteland. I begged my parents to allow me to transfer. Begging didn't help. "Just give it a year," they retorted.

Yeah right. I was determined. If they weren't going to let me leave peacefully, I was just going to be thrown out. At fourteen, that thought seemed brilliant. At first, I opted for Plan A: allowing my grades to go to hell. My first report card consisted of three Cs and four Ds. I even managed to get a D in gym class! Obviously, I was making progress.

Instead of allowing me to transfer, they grounded me. I didn't see the light of day for three months. Common sense would have told anybody that this form of action was futile. But I had to earn that reputation of being a "silly blonde."

Then I decided to try Plan B: becoming a discipline problem. I dumped a milkshake on another freshman's head during lunch. I got into a fist fight with Danielle, one of the toughest girls in school. She beat the crap out of me. For two weeks, I walked around with the letter "D" in my forehead from her initial ring.

All of the aggravation was getting me nowhere. I was grounded, my social life was in shambles, and I had a month's worth of detention with Sister Gertrude Mary. Plans A and B failed miserably. What was I supposed to do?

In the beginning of my second semester, my father took me to dinner. He talked about successes and failures. I began to feel guilty about my immature attitude. He said something that I'll never forget. "You can leave Gloucester Catholic at the end of the year. Just make sure you leave as a winner or you'll regret it for the rest of your life."

"Leave as a winner." At that moment I knew that I was going to be staying in G.C. a little longer. When I finally completed ninth grade, my parents gave me the option to leave. But I declined. I couldn't go until I conquered G.C.

Somewhere between January and July of '93, my father had a change of heart. Originally, he wanted me to improve my situation in Catholic school. Then the tuition bill arrived. "I'm not paying for Gloucester Catholic anymore," he said coldly.

Was that it? After a year of being grounded, confined to uniforms, rules, prayers, and the Ten Commandments, there was nothing left to say? Maybe all those motivational lectures were just bullcrap. Apparently my father didn't want to use his funds to allow me to "leave a winner."

My mother was furious. Before I transferred to G.C., they both had agreed to pay half of my tuition. Now he was bailing out. Mom immediately called her lawyer. Whenever there was a dispute, it was always handled in court. That was the great thing about having divorced parents. I never saw them fight because they paid their lawyers to do it for them.

The judge ruled in my father's favor. He was not obligated to pay a cent. Fortunately, my mother could afford to make tuition payments by herself. She understood that I wasn't going to throw away another year of my life along with her money. I was determined. Despite my father's lack of support, I was going to go hard.

Little did my father know that he taught me the most valuable lesson in high school: Adversity can either drag you down or it can motivate you to become the best. I could have easily given up and gone back to public school. But there was something inside of me, a sense of urgency. I had to show everyone (including myself) that I wasn't a loser.

I decided that if I was going to make my mark in G.C., I had to get involved. I joined an array of extracurricular activities. Forensics was my favorite. Members performed one act plays, and wrote speeches concerning current affairs.

"Forensicizing," as many of my friends called it, became my forte. It gave me confidence. The "silly blonde" label that I had acquired freshman year was non-existent in the world of forensics, and for the first time since eighth grade people took me seriously. At the end of the season I placed second in the Camden Diocese for Duo Interpretation. As a sophomore, I was the youngest student to represent my diocese at Nationals in Oshkosh, Wisconsin.

Slowly I began to make a name for myself. I was involved with the newspaper and the swim team. These activities helped me make good friends, and I discovered that there was more to G.C. than clones, prayers, and Disney lovers. The students who participated in these activities felt the same way I did. We were searching for our niche. We were all trying to succeed. And we were all going hard.

That June my mom once again gave me the option to return to public school. But there was no going back now. I had yet to make the honor roll. Constantly battling geometry and Spanish, my grade point average was a mere 2.6. My goal for junior year was to improve my academic standing. This was not easy due to the fact that I was placed in an accelerated English class.

I hated English. During the first day of class, a member of the National Honor Society arrogantly said, "What are you doing here? This is Honors English. Shouldn't you have class next door?"

"What are you doing here?" Those words went right through me. All I wanted was to raise my GPA so I could get into college. Now I had to take classes with nerds who thought they were God. Once, my teacher asked for the definition of "interloper."

"One who is an intruder and is not wanted," someone answered.

"Graham has intruded on the honors class. She is an interloper," mumbled another almighty honor student.

Needless to say, I despised those people. They were part of a super clique: no one ventured out of it and no one joined without having an SAT score of 1300. The rest of the class was excluded from their prestigious world.

I invaded their territory and wanted to tell them that there was so much more to life than high SAT scores and class rank. They were not smart enough to figure that out for themselves. The honors kids thought they were superior, but they too were susceptible to pain. Some used their grades like blankets in order to cover up their insecurities.

There were many times when they made me feel inferior. Once again I was the "silly blonde." Although they had the social skills of a bunch of introverted second graders, they still had no respect for me because I was not in the top ten percent of the class. I turned the animosity I felt toward the honors kids into constructive energy. There was no reason for them to look down at me. I worked just as hard as they did. Proving people wrong was nothing new to me. Those geeks may have known the definition of "interloper," but they had never experienced true opposition.

Cut throat competition. There are no better words to describe my junior year of high school. Time and time again I found myself going head to head with Claire Albright, the Valedictorian of my class. My English teacher only gave one A for the first semester. It showed up on my report card. When our grades were distributed, Claire actually cried! Everyone was in shock. Claire never ever got Bs, and Graham, well she wasn't even supposed to be in honors English.

My A was just the beginning. I was interloping all over school! My name was repeatedly seen on the Honor Roll. Along with the grades came leadership opportunities. After my English class submitted writing samples to our principal, Father Chiappa, I was selected to be G.C.'s nominee for New Jersey's Governor's School of the Arts.

Governor's School is a very prestigious program. Students are chosen based on their talent in writing. There were over two hundred applicants. A mere twenty-three made it to final selections, and I was of them. Unfortunately, the state could only accept ten students to the school. After months of waiting I was denied admission. The rejection letter was shoved in the back of my locker along with my gym socks. Although I was disappointed, I knew that there were other opportunities to succeed. I just had to continue to be my best.

The week following the Governor's School letdown, Claire Albright, who ranked eighth in our class, and I were nominated for Girls' State. Only one of us would actually attend. I thought that I didn't have a chance because, academically, I ranked eighty-first. But the people from Girls' State were not impressed by numbers. They knew that there was more to a person than just their academic transcript. They didn't want an introverted, snobby, honor student representing Gloucester Catholic.

They wanted me, the interloper.

Forensics all-star, Governor's School Finalist, Girls' State delegate, Honor Roll. Now who was the silly blonde? Neither honors kids nor my father could point a finger at me. There were times when my motives became uncertain. Was I doing these things for myself or was I just trying to disprove the opposition? To this day, I'm still unsure.

I began to grow tired of the high school scene by senior year. I took advanced placement courses (and got As), represented G.C. in the Junior Miss Pageant, worked as Editor-in-Chief of the school paper, managed the swim team, and placed first in the diocese in forensics. When did I have time to breathe? As if those normal everyday endeavors were not enough, the college selection process was added to my agenda. Teachers, parents, and counselors all had an institution in mind. There were college applications out the wazoo!

Even with a mediocre SAT score and a rather odd academic background, I was accepted to Syracuse, Rutgers, American, and Catholic Universities. These schools had stellar reputations, but my gut feeling told me that they were not for me. My friends and I were accepted to Rowan College, located two miles from my house. Many of them had opted to go there because they didn't feel the necessity to leave New Jersey. But there was something inside of me that wanted more. It compelled me to seek another challenge. I had proved myself to the closed-minded opposition. After another tedious court battle, my father had agreed to pay half of my college tuition. As Tom Petty once said, "The future is wide open." It was time that I looked for myself.

My ultimate goal was to be a broadcast journalism major, so naturally I looked for a school with a solid mass communications program. I also needed to be in an area with ample internship opportunities. I had to be near a thriving city. And I had to be in a college that attracted open-minded students who studied, but also knew how to party. After roaming the east coast—from James Madison University in the boonies of Virginia to the snow covered campus of Syracuse to the fast-paced political hysteria of Washington, D.C., and American University—I discovered Baltimore and Towson University.

Towson. Instead of having a statue of a saint in the health office, the nurse supplies free condoms. The word "detention" is used only in the dictionary and the only place you will find the Ten Commandments is in Philosophy 102. Knee socks are a major fashion "no-no." The only time I am harassed by nerds is when I cut in front of them in the lunch line. The only people who sing Disney tunes are those who major in Elementary Education and most professors deduct points from students who dot their "i's" with hearts.

Some say that adversity can either drag you down or motivate you to become the best. As an interloper, I learned that lesson at a young age. In all phases of our lives, during the awkward moments of adolescence and beyond, we all encounter opposition. Some of us face those challenges with an anticipation to succeed. And others go home.

AMNESIA
by Amber Tolley

I once lost a sense of who I was. Or maybe I really didn't know yet who I wanted to be. My mom always told me that experience is the best teacher. Nevertheless, losing my identity was an experience I wish had never happened, but one that made me remember what was really important.

The slow, painful loss of my identity began when I was sixteen. I had goals, dreams, and hopes for my future. Ever since I could remember, I had always wanted to go to college in the city because I had lived in a small town all my life. However, when you are young, dreams seem miles away, and life is often restricted to a thirty mile radius.

Back then, I knew exactly who I was. I knew what made me sad or mad, or what could make me laugh or cry. I thought my friends would always be there and assumed nothing would ever change. Then Brandon Jones walked into my life, forever altering it.

He was tall and slim. Not gorgeous, but had that type of handsome innocence which is so appealing to a teenage girl. His green eyes were lazy with a mischievous sparkle, and his long legs looked like they went on forever. He had such a young face, and his dark blond hair added to his boyish features.

We got to know each other one warm Friday night before the start of our junior year in high school. It was a typical night in Cambridge on Maryland's Eastern Shore. Six people packed into someone's mother's car, the windows rolled down and the stereo blasting whatever was popular. That night I could barely catch my breath from the laughter that caused me to clutch my sides. Brandon could always make me laugh. No matter what the situation, he always had a smile on his face.

We were so sweetly innocent that, when I look back, tears never cease to fill my eyes over how much we've both changed. From the beginning of our relationship, Brandon's mother was a sore spot. I now realize that it wasn't that Miss Mary didn't like me, but she wasn't used to sharing her son. She ruled every aspect of his life, from where he went, to the time we spent together. Miss Mary made me feel like an outsider because I could never measure up to the impossible standards she set. She could be rude, thoughtless, selfish and fake. I felt in constant competition with her for Brandon's time and attention. To this day I still have no idea why her opinion mattered so much to me, yet somehow it did.

As time passed, Brandon and I got more serious. Time would fly like a faceless clock when we were together. I soon began to see less and less of the friends who knew me so well, including my best friend Lana.

Lana and I were inseparable the instant we met in the tenth grade until I began to see Brandon seriously. She knew me better than I knew myself. Lana was a caring and thoughtful person who always wanted the best for me. The same summer before junior year, we took driver's education together, saw movies, went to the beach, and giggled into the early morning hours about absolutely everything and nothing at all. Lana and I would lay by the pool during those hot summer days and picture faraway colleges, careers, and families that were merely dreams. She was the best friend I had ever known.

When I began to date Brandon, Lana didn't really like him, but if he made me happy, then that was all that mattered. Soon, I found myself in situations that forced me to choose between my best friend and the guy whose class ring I now wore. I always assumed Lana would forgive me when I chose Brandon. However, I still had a lot to learn about friendship.

As the leaves began to change colors and fall gently to the ground, my steady world began to shake. Lana and Brandon could not get along, even for my sake. They couldn't be within a foot of each other without making rude, snide comments and dirty looks. The first fight began over something so petty that I barely remember the issue. But that next day in school as Lana refused to look at me, I knew that our friendship had begun to slip.

I began to pull away from the friend I held so dearly. I missed the long talks with her until the wee hours of the morning, the wild times, singing in the rain, but mostly I missed the dreams we shared. Lana left for Australia right after Christmas. Her present sat under my tree, and I hadn't spoken to her in over three weeks. I didn't know what time she left or when she was supposed to return in January.

It was the loneliest month I had ever known. My best friend was half-way around the world and not even acknowledging my existence. The few friends I had left were slowly drifting away from me just as Lana had. To make everything worse, my seven-year-old cousin, Phillip Lee, was going downhill fast. He had been diagnosed with leukemia two years earlier. I watched as his small body had been probed, prodded, tested, and stuck. But despite it all, he was such a brave little man. Lee always had a smile on his lips that shined through all the pain. I watched as his soft blonde hair and big blue eyes began to distort with the toxins of radiation and chemotherapy. The only thing left to do was a bone marrow transplant.

I soon fell into a deep depression. The more Brandon pulled me close, the more I pushed him away. I soon began to cry over everything. My grades started to slip, and all I wanted to do was crawl in my bed and sleep. Brandon was worried and began to smother me with care. As my family grew concerned about me, I only grew vague and indifferent.

Lana and I began speaking again shortly after she returned from her trip. It was hard for me to hear the excitement in her voice as she spoke of her adventure in the "land down under," while I had nothing new to say. The time we spent together soon dwindled to nearly nothing. And if she called me, I rarely called her back. I couldn't take the shell of a human being I had become. Life was just too serious.

Finally, on a spring day in March, I convinced myself that Brandon must be the problem. I began to question my feelings for him. Was he worth losing my best friend? It was obvious his mother didn't like me and never would. I told him we needed to talk. The tone of my voice must have frightened him. We sat down, eye level, at a table together, but I could barely look into his already sad, green eyes. I began to cry and as he reached to hug me, I pushed him away.

"You love me too much," I told him. He looked at me with confusion. I suddenly got angry for the lack of friends and the damage I had done to my own life. I needed someone to blame. "Stop calling me so much, I can't breath; you're smothering me," I said. "I don't know if I love you. You just don't make me happy anymore." He turned his head from me, and I saw his tense profile that seemed a reflection of my own hurt. A sad tear rolled down his cheek to his clenched jaw.

"What are you trying to tell me?" he asked. "Is it over? Do I mean that little to you?" I held my breath with the sobs that were threatening to escape. I slowly exhaled.

"I don't know. I think I love you. But I don't know if I really know what love is," I said.

Everything changed with that one conversation. I now know I had hurt him so deeply that he would never forgive me. He had tried to love me, but because of my own selfish hurt, I wouldn't let him.

We talked, fought, cried, and battled for days until we realized our relationship may have been worth saving. Brandon was cautious of my fragile personality. In the weeks that followed, I wouldn't let him tell me he loved me. I wouldn't allow myself to love him in return. I began to see the damage I had done to our relationship. May approached, and I was convinced if anything could fix my depressed life, it would be the lazy, hazy days of summer.

That summer was very different from the previous one. Lana and I were on better terms, but I kept my problems with Brandon to myself, thinking that she didn't want to hear them. I was indifferent towards Lana, and Brandon and I soon fell into the same old routine. His mother was still a major cause of tension between us. The fights grew more heated; my insecurities grew stronger. The time I spent at his house was just plain torture. But I just swallowed my pride and continued to see him, all for the sake of "love."

Our senior year in high school began on a hot day in September. Finally, it was the last year for me in a town I did not appreciate and with people I didn't like. It would be the first and last year I would have classes with the boyfriend that I had dated for a year. The Brandon I knew was sensitive, caring, funny, and sweet. But to my horrible surprise, Brandon the student was every bit the opposite. He was loud, rude, and obnoxious in the two classes we had together. Brandon was just being himself, but I had never known that side of him. I justified his behavior by telling myself he was a different person with me. I pushed my problems away and began to crack down to improve grades I had let slip during my junior year. Brandon and I began to talk about the future and decided that we wanted to stay together.

In November, we visited a university campus in Baltimore together. It was about two hours from home and I fell in love with it instantly. Brandon was quiet during the tour, and his mood turned almost somber. Several weeks later, Brandon suddenly became rude and mean to me over the phone. I asked him who the other girl was, half jokingly. To my surprise, he began to cry. He had taken out a girl who he knew I didn't like. I sat there in shock and pain and realized that I was losing him.

Once again, we talked, argued, apologized, and I finally forgave him. Suddenly, going to college in the city didn't appeal to me. Brandon had decided that he didn't want to go to any college, least of all one two hours away. What if my weekends home weren't enough for him? Would he begin to forget about me? I was determined not to lose him or the security I felt near him. I thought I was his world and the only one for him, but suddenly my outlook changed. I felt angry and helpless. I was mad at him for losing my trust, and at the friends who didn't understand why I stayed with "the loser."

I looked into Salisbury State University, a college about thirty minutes away from home. I dismissed my dreams of the city and a career in journalism for Brandon. I became obsessed with where Brandon was and mainly who he was with. When he told me that he wanted to spend one night a weekend with his friends, I pleaded with him. I had no friends left besides him. They turned away when I lost myself in Brandon.

At this point, I still didn't know if I loved him or not. I was scared to leave the only life I had ever known. Loving Brandon was a habit. Our relationship was as comfortable as a well-worn t-shirt. I convinced my friends that I wasn't ready for college in the city. Lana looked at me with pity when I tried to justify my reasons for staying nearby. She knew who I used to be and who I could still be. But I had to wake up on my own. I sacrificed who I was and forfeited what was important to me, all for Brandon. As with all habits, you just keep muddling through as time slips by.

Time slipped by for my cousin, too. A spring breeze blew around me at Phillip Lee's funeral. The leukemia had just gotten the best of him. Tears of sadness, pain, and guilt streamed down my face—guilt because I couldn't truly mourn for Lee that gray March day. I was too busy mourning the loss of someone else. If I closed my eyes, I could still see Brandon screaming at me to get out of his house five days before. He had said he was tired of the fighting, late night phone calls, and intense interrogations. That day he had been sitting on his bed crying in anger. I was at his feet groveling for one more chance. I left exhausted, after he pushed me out the door and told me to leave. I can honestly say that weekend was when I hit rock bottom. Everything that was important to me was gone and replaced with numbness. Numbness and tremors.

My mom gave me sleeping pills for the shaking. How was I going to face him? How could I just ignore the person who I had shared so much of my life with? I would just have to go on. I could go to college and leave behind the hurt and the pain. I had been put on a waiting list at both the university in the city and the one closer to home. That weekend was the longest of my life. I cried, screamed, thought, dreamed, slept, vomited, hallucinated, and went through my own personal hell. Sunday evening I finally pulled myself together to face the world. As I was walking to my car, I heard the roar of a truck engine and the sound of tires speeding up the driveway. Brandon's eyes looked tired and swollen with pain. Just when I had started to find myself again, he had come back to me.

I tried to make it work for a while, but my heart was no longer in it. I felt older than seventeen and exhausted beyond what sleep could repair. I finally knew I loved him, but we just weren't good together anymore. I guess I knew it was over when his mother called my house one night looking for him. He was there, but I made up some lie about never knowing anymore where he was. His mother hurt me for the last time that night. She told me her son may think he's in love but that he really didn't know what he wanted or what love was. As I listened in anger and shock, she told me that if I really wanted to do him a favor, I would end it now. I turned to Brandon as I hung up the phone. A look of disbelief must have wracked my face because Brandon begged me to tell him what his mother had said. I told him, and he remained silent.

I began to look back on our turbulent relationship. I just couldn't take the pain and the hurt anymore. The next day I walked into class, but Brandon wouldn't look at me. I think he knew what was going to happen. I put my books down and went slowly over to where he was sitting. I looked into his green eyes for the last time, and I told him that it was over. He stared at me with the same look he had worn a year earlier. I began to cry, and I told him that I loved him but that I really didn't know who I was anymore. We had been "Brandon and Amber" for so long that I had somehow lost the Amber part. We had always wanted different things. He loved Cambridge and his family, and I wanted a future somewhere else with all my dreams intact. When he asked me why I was crying, I said that I was not crying for him but for what we had. A young, first love that had faced too much reality and heartbreak. He wanted one last hug, but I couldn't give it to him. I now know if I had put my arms around him that day, I might have never let go.

From everything that happened I learned many important lessons. That guys can sometimes be total assholes, that your friends are the people you can really count on, and that dreams are very important. But mostly I've learned that life is a one-shot deal. And before you can know and love anyone else, you must know and learn to love the most important person of all...yourself.

SCHOOL DAYS
by Charles S. Ramsburg, Jr.

Today, education is a privilege I treasure. I feel empowered and liberated by everything I learn, and I watch excitedly as every glimmering facet of knowledge opens up yet another exhilarating opportunity. But as a young child, I viewed any form of formal education as a particularly sadistic method of torture. School was thrust mercilessly upon me by the callous world of adults, and I resented it completely. Although I had many close friends in elementary school, I never felt as though I belonged with the other children. When forcibly extracted from the solace of my home and my parents, I felt frightened and abandoned—alone in a heartless world.

It was never the schoolwork itself that caused me discomfort. As a matter of fact, the studying and learning were the only aspects of elementary school that I found gratifying. At a very early age, I found knowledge to be a wondrous and empowering thing. I retained information well and consistently scored good grades. It was the estrangement from home and mothering—life's first taste of independence and responsibility—that caused difficulty.

As my mother's old red Chevrolet roared menacingly to life each weekday morning, exhaust erupting from the tailpipe like black smoke billowing from the top of Mount Doom, my heart began to pound and sweat dampened my furrowed brow. The thunderous din of the old engine turning over was a harbinger of my dark fate: It was time to go to school.

Some days I climbed into the vehicle and closed the door in silence. I was resigned to my destiny, like a death-row inmate walking his last mile to the electric chair. Other days, the anxiety overcame me, and I broke down. The tears ran freely down my face, and I would scream and beg for mercy—pleading to my mother for clemency.

And some days—some extraordinary days—she granted it. My poor mother, haggard and softened by my pitiful beseeching, occasionally submitted to my pleas, at last permitting me a day's absence from school. It was like a last minute reprieve called in by the governor. I was a walking corpse, suddenly and miraculously snatched from the jaws of death.

My father, however, did not display the same compassion. His primary concern was that I acquire a good education, regardless of the detrimental consequences to my prepubescent psyche. He was the enforcer and the disciplinarian, sworn to prevent truancy under any circumstances. Because of the role he played in my life, I feared and loathed my father throughout many of my childhood years.

Each weekday morning, I intentionally tampered with my preparations for school, stalling anxiously until my father left for work. As I watched his Corvette speed down our long driveway, turn right, and disappear up the street, I heaved a sigh of relief and immediately set my plot into action—"Operation: No School."

"Mom," I implored, "I don't feel so good. My stomach hurts. Maybe I should stay home and rest today."

Her first reply was always a refusal, but I knew that with a little effort I could change her mind. My begging and whining continued until either we made the long, unnerving march to the car or until she gave in and granted me permission to stay home from school. But her acquiescence always had one clear contingency: "Don't tell your father." My mother and I both knew how angry and disappointed he became when I missed school. It was best to simply conceal my absences from him, allowing him to believe that I was a well-adjusted student with good attendance.

This omission of the truth was well worth the comfort and joy of remaining at home with my mother. And, oh, what a joy it was! At home I was free to pursue my own interests, detached from the tension of human interaction and unchecked by the teacher's watchful eye. Nestled safely beneath my covers while the other children were confined to the schoolhouse, I read stories for hours on end, immersing myself in the fantastic worlds of J.R.R. Tolkien, Lloyd Alexander, Piers Anthony, and Terry Brooks. I found my sanctuary in the mythical lands of Middle Earth, Xanth, and Prydain. My closest friends and companions were the denizens of these realms: elves, dwarves, dragons, and hobbits. Why did I have to interact with other children when everything I needed could be found in a book?

Every afternoon at one o'clock, I joined my mother in the living room where we watched "Days of Our Lives" together. My mother felt about the soap opera the way I felt about fantasy stories. The drama was her pastime, her escape. I also became engrossed in the daytime stories and eagerly waited to discover the characters' fates—who was the father of Laura's baby or whether or not the heroine, Marlena, would escape the grasp of the evil Stefano Dimera. Soon, "Days of Our Lives" became another building block of my fantasy world. It was a beautiful, safe place, this domain where I dwelled when I stayed home from school. Unfortunately, it was a realm easily shattered by the embodiment of the merciless forces of the dreaded outside world: namely, my father.

I particularly remember one crisp, cool autumn morning. The glaring sunlight brightly illuminated the endless sky and reflected magnificently off the red and gold leaves that blanketed the ground. The soothing aroma of burning wood permeated the outside air as gray smoke curled lazily from our chimney. A flock of geese flew languidly southward, honking and beating the wind in unison, oblivious to the house below and to the tormented lad inside.

I awoke on time and feigned getting ready for school, my plan for escape already taking shape. I sensed an inexplicable tension that felt like pins and needles running up and down my body. I nervously wiped the sweat from my forehead and marched bravely downstairs into a world marred by the agony of school and the deception required to elude it.

My father—my own, personal truant officer—loomed over the kitchen table dressed in his dark-blue robe, absently eating a bowl of bran cereal that looked to me like unpalatable strips of milk-soaked cardboard. The morning edition of *The Baltimore Sun* was spread out in front of him. My mother smiled pleasantly and wished me a good morning as she served my father a mug of fragrant, steaming hot coffee.

"Morning, Charlie," my father said with a sleepy smile. As I took my seat at the breakfast table, he ruffled my hair lovingly. "All ready for school today?"

"Sure, Dad," I replied, forcing a smile. Hide the fear, or he'll know what I'm up to, I thought.

My father chatted over breakfast about throwing the football around with me over the weekend or perhaps the three of us taking a trip to the mountains to watch the leaves change. The more he talked, the more my stomach became sick with guilt over the way I planned to deceive him. But he didn't understand. I knew that he would never understand my passionate fear of school.

After breakfast, I hurriedly returned to my room. There, I planned to stall until my father departed for work. Then, once I was alone with my more lenient and compassionate mother, I would implement my strategy. I knew things had to be timed perfectly for my plan to work. My father typically left for work at eight. I, on the other hand, was not expected to depart for school until approximately ten after eight. This left a ten-minute window of opportunity. The moment the cat's away, the mouse will play, I mused nervously, the stress of the morning nearly pushing me over the edge.

I grew more anxious as the digital alarm clock next to my bed switched to 8:11. Through the floorboards, I could still hear my father chatting with my mother. He hadn't left yet! How could this be? I had synchronized my bedroom clock with my father's wristwatch the night before, just to be certain nothing went wrong. And my father, as tenacious in his punctuality as in his wardenship of potentially truant children, always left on time (8:12...). I sat on my bed and hugged my trembling knees against my chest, my heart feeling like it was about to leap out of my chest (...8:13...8:14...). I could still hear my father's voice echoing menacingly from the kitchen downstairs.

(...8:15) I heard my mother's knock resound through my bedroom door and echo through my brain like the gothic bells in a H.P. Lovecraft story—the harbinger of death. "Time to go to school," she said, but to me it sounded more like "time to die." The terror of the morning transformed my mother's angelic voice into that of a bloodthirsty succubus out to drink the blood of little school-hating children. Time to die. I opened the door and went out to face my grim fate.

There was no point in showing resistance as my mother and I walked the "last mile" down the stairs, through the kitchen, and outside to the waiting car. If my father had gone, my pleading may have earned me a stay of execution, but today there would be no mercy.

"See ya, Charlie," My father said as I passed through the kitchen. He was dressed in his suit now, smelling of Dentyne and English Leather, nearly ready to leave for work. But his departure was too late for me; my plan had been ruined. "Have a good day at school." He might as well have said, "Have a good day of torture in the deepest, hottest pits of hell—ha, ha, ha!"

I forced a weary smile and followed my mother out to the car. I felt as if I was going to vomit. As the old red Chevrolet rumbled to life, a glimmer of hope flashed behind my terrified eyes. I had to force myself to stop feeling like a deer caught in the headlights before I could quickly begin to formulate a new plan. I inhaled the comforting scent of my mother's perfume ("and they call it 'Chaaarlie!'"), which helped me relax and think. Again, my plan hinged upon my father finally leaving for work. When he was out of the picture, anything was possible.

"Mom," I said, my throat dry and raspy with fear, "can we take the back way to school?"

My mother glanced at her wristwatch. "I don't know, honey, we're running a little late this morning."

"But, mom," I pressed, my voice clearing, confidence returning. I was doing what I do best. "It's such a beautiful day. The leaves are changing. It would be a nice drive. We have time."

My mother should have known better. Since when was an eight-year-old boy interested in the changing of seasons or a nice drive? The back way to school was only appealing to me because it was not the way my father took to work.

As our car languidly rounded sharp curves on the old country road, I glanced nervously at my wristwatch. 8:24. My heart pounded in my chest and my temples throbbed powerfully. I felt that I would burst (can young boys have strokes?).

Grasping the door handle in one sweaty palm, I counted to myself (one...two...three!).

Suddenly, I flung the car door open and threw myself out, tumbling over and over, finally landing roughly in the soft grass next to the road. The schoolbooks that had been sitting on my lap flew in every direction, expelling a thousand papers into an autumn breeze. My mother screamed and slammed on the brakes. The old red Chevrolet screeched to a halt twenty feet ahead of me, and my mother—as frantic as I have ever seen her—rushed to my aid.

I sat upright, a bit dizzied by the fall. I had, however, escaped with only a few scratches and bruises. But by the terrified look on my mother's pallid face, one would have thought I had just been run over by a Mack truck.

"Are you all right?" my mother questioned breathlessly. "What in the world did you just do?" (And she did say "world." My mother never said "hell," for fear, no doubt, that if she referred to the netherworld too often she may end up there.)

I gazed up at her defiantly, a long scratch across my forehead just beginning to bleed. "I'm not going to school today," I declared, with a very implied (but unspoken), "you can't make me."

We drove back home in silence, my mother too shocked and flabbergasted to resist my demands. We stayed to the back roads, purposefully avoiding my father's typical route to work. My only concern now was timing. Had I acted too soon? Had my father already left for work? As we turned into our long driveway, I was relieved to see that my father's Corvette was gone. A deep pain in my chest swelled and faded as I released a breath I had been holding for what felt like hours.

"Victory is mine," I flatly declared to my mother, quoting, no doubt, a brave warrior from one of my fantasy novels. She gazed back at me, mouth agape, as if she were looking upon the son of Satan. I saw the pain behind my mother's tired eyes and wondered why her suffering affected me so little. Everything was secondary to escaping from school.

"You better hope your father doesn't hear about this," my mother scolded. "If he does, he'll have both of our hides."

"He won't," I assured her.

My mother and I went inside the house, and I tossed my disheveled schoolbooks onto the kitchen table. I was free; the day was mine to do whatever I wished. I trotted easily into the front hallway to hang up my jacket, casually glancing out the window as I did so.

What a beautiful autumn day it was! Trees were awash in a sea of reds and golds beneath a flawless azure sky. At the end of our long driveway, school-buses rumbled lethargically along, impeding the progress of angry men and women late for their jobs in the city.

Fools, every last one of them, I thought of the workers and students. They're just like sheep to the slaughter.

And then, suddenly, my eyes focused on one particular car as it slowed down to turn into our driveway. I didn't want to believe what I saw.

My heart stopped.

My father's Corvette sped back up the driveway.

"Oh, no!" I exclaimed, hurriedly grabbing my coat and rushing madly back into the kitchen. "Dad's back!"

My mother looked altogether befuddled as I hastened to gather up the chaotic mess of books and papers I had left on the kitchen table. "What are you talking about?" she asked incredulously.

"Just tell him I'm not here," I shouted as I sprinted up the stairs, leaving a trail of crumpled papers behind me. "Tell him that you dropped me off at school."

I ran into my bedroom, frantically throwing open the closet door and tossing my books and coat inside. What am I going to do? My mind raced. No time to think. I leaped into the dark, cluttered closet and shut the door behind me. The impact of the door closing sent the entire rack of clothing tumbling down on top of me, burying me in the darkness somewhere between my Sunday's best suit and my AC/DC "Highway to Hell" t-shirt (the one where Bon Scott has horns). My heart galloped in my chest and I gasped to catch my breath.

My body stiffened as I heard the door open downstairs. My father entered, his heavy footsteps echoing up from the kitchen floor. He mumbled something about how he forgot his briefcase. He and my mother chatted for a few moments, too quietly for me to get the gist of what they were talking about. Just take the damn briefcase and go, I thought.

And then all was quiet except for the sound of my racing heart. Had my father left? I hadn't heard the door close. What was going on? Suddenly, the closet door flung open. I squinted as bright sunlight filled my hiding place. My mother stood, silhouetted—a dark shadow looming above me in the doorway.

"Get up, Chuckie," she said. "Your father's downstairs and he wants to talk to you."

Betrayed! Mom betrayed me! If I couldn't trust her, who could I trust?

I stood up reluctantly and followed my mother down the stairs. I walked slowly, knowing what I was in for when I reached the kitchen, wanting to delay the inevitable. My father stood in the kitchen sipping another cup of coffee. His stern eyes followed me into the room, his hand tensing around the coffee mug, threatening to shatter the glass.

"Hi, Dad," I said meekly, pretending I did nothing wrong. I stared at the floor. I could not face him.

"Your mom tells me she had a little trouble getting you to school this morning," my father replied. He struggled to keep his voice calm.

I shrugged. What could I say?

"Well, get your things together," he continued. "I'm taking you to school."

"No!" I protested, my eyes suddenly filling with tears. "I don't want to go!"

It was quite obvious to me that my personal preference for staying home from school meant very little to my father. This became particularly clear, though, when he grabbed me by the ear and dragged me out the door. On the way, he shouted to my mother: "Grab his books and put them in my car. I'm taking him to school."

I looked back at my mom. Our eyes met. She looked sympathetic. I must have been a sight, crying and trembling as my father hauled me out the door. A lot of good my mother's sympathy did me now. My father tossed me into the passenger seat of his Corvette, accepted the jumbled pile of books and papers from my mother, and plopped them down on my lap. He said a quick goodbye to my mother, started the car, and angrily pressed the accelerator to the floor, spinning wheels as we shot off down the driveway.

"I don't want to go to school!" I cried. By now, my cheeks were stained with tears and my eyes were red and swollen. "Please, just kill me if you have to, but don't make me go there!"

"Get a grip, Charlie," my father said. "It's just school. You'll be fine."

"I won't be fine, damn it!" I retorted, grasping the door handle and trying to leap out. We must have been going sixty miles-per-hour, but I would have rather died than go to school that day. But my father was too quick. He simultaneously hit the power locks and grabbed my wrist, preventing escape. All I could do was sit helplessly and weep as my father lectured me about the evils of using bad language. My heart pounded faster and faster as we neared the schoolhouse.

By the time we pulled into the school's parking lot, it was after nine and classes had already begun. My father turned off the car and looked at me.

"Come on, Charlie," he said sternly. "Let's go. I'll walk you in."

"No, I'm not going," I declared weakly. Tears drenched my pale and clammy face and dripped onto my shirtsleeve.

My father got out of the car, walked around to the passenger side, opened my door, and grasped my arm.

"Come on," he ordered.

"No!" I shrieked, clinging to the seat, struggling against my father's grip. The terror was so great now, I felt as if I might pass out. Everything seemed strange and surreal, as if I was out of my body watching the scene below. Colors and shapes blended together. My world crumbled.

Finally, my father lost his patience and hoisted me up in his arms. I screamed and kicked like a madman. I was, in my mind at least, fighting for my very life. I was frantic, desperate. I would have done anything to escape, but my father's grip was too powerful. I was helpless.

My father carried me into the schoolhouse, down the long, empty hallway and into my classroom. I screamed and fought every inch of the way—biting, clawing, begging any god that would listen to save me from this dark fate. None listened.

The other children stared at me, their mouths agape, as my father lugged me kicking and screaming into my classroom. My fellow students seemed shocked that I could make such a scene. Some of them were frightened; others laughed and pointed. My teacher looked befuddled, not unlike the way my mother appeared when I bailed out of the car. All of their faces blended together, weaving a nightmarish tapestry. My vision faded. Everything spun. No longer could I stand the fear, the pounding in my chest, the grotesque faces.

I closed my eyes, and there was only darkness.

FOOTBALL
by Brian M. Davis

"Down!"

"Twenty!"

"Down!"

"Twenty-one!"

"Down!"

"Twenty-two!"

Oh Lord! When will he stop saying "down?" If I do one more push-up, I'm going to throw up.

I remember seeing people give up but I wasn't a quitter. It seemed we were going to do push-ups until everybody died and I knew that I would be the last one to do so. With Coach Daven yelling "Down!" and the players yelling "Forty-eight!" I collapsed. I could do no more. When I rolled over to see who was left, I was surprised but excited to see that I finished last.

Few things in a young man's life define who he is. In ninth grade, when I made the varsity squad, my personal definition began to evolve. On the field I was a merciless monster—that was my job. Off the field, I was calm and confident. In my school, people admired the football players. I was in an elite crowd. Football put me in control.

Sometimes, I find it hard to believe that I remember the little details as I do, but football was my life. I thrived off the discipline. I learned to react quickly to a situation. I had most of my friends there. And I honestly believe that how I carry myself today can be based on the experiences that I endured while playing football.

It was the last day of football practice and about 100 degrees. With all of the equipment on, it felt like 120 degrees. Looking around, someone else only would have seen a bunch of tired-out boys. But we had just spent one full month together and had grown into a family.

It happens every summer when new players come to the varsity team. At all times, I knew what everyone else was thinking and they had the same power over me. We all knew that every time the Coach would yell "Left!" while we practiced marching towards the field, Ron would step with his right foot. Coach would then make his only attempt at humor by saying, "Your other left Ron," to the beat of an army cadence. Now, with a long hard season approaching, it was time to get serious.

The season turned out to be harder than we expected. We won the first game but lost the next three. Unfortunately, in the fourth game, we also lost our starting quarterback. His name was William, but everyone called him Boobie. I don't really know how he got the nickname and I'm not even sure I want to know.

While shaking hands and congratulating the other team, one of their players said, "Good game, nigger." I looked up to see Boobie's reaction, but it was too late. The fight had started. I broke it up, but the damage was done. For being involved in a fight, Boobie was suspended for five games. With only one game left after his suspension, Boobie, which now was an appropriate nickname, decided not to return.

Of the next five games, we lost three. Again, in the ninth game of the season, we had an altercation. This time the casualty was my best friend, Brendan. In what's called "football fury" (a state of mind in which you don't think—you react), Brendan went crazy.

The tension was like a thick yellow haze hovering over the field. In the last play, a player on the other team maliciously speared his helmet into Brendan's gut. "Spearing" is illegal but not uncommon. It is something you have to deal with when you live the life of a gridiron warrior. Unable to handle it, Brendan grabbed the other gladiator by the face mask and threw him to the ground. This resulted in his ejection and, ultimately, his suspension from the next (and last) game of the season.

Coach gave him the bad news and without any remorse turned and walked away. Leaning against the wall, Brendan slid his enormous frame down to the floor. His normally rigid body was sitting like a lifeless bag of bones. He just kept saying, "Why?" I felt so much pity for him. Never before had I seen a six-foot-two, two-hundred-twenty-pound football player cry. Brendan did. I remember the look he gave me as he sat there on the floor. He tilted his head to the side, looked to the ground and, without saying a word, conveyed a complete feeling of emptiness. Brendan was lost. He always gave one hundred percent and I felt that Coach had betrayed him, as well as the rest of the team, that day.

Unlike our former quarterback, Brendan still felt like part of the team and continued to practice. Seeing Brendan's dedication, I worked harder that week than I think I ever had before. In my mind, not only was I playing the last game of my high school career for myself, but I was playing for Brendan, too. The next day would be my last chance for a win.

As I dressed in the locker room, my concentration was intense. All I could think of was Brendan's tears, my hard work, and victory. Before we marched to the field everyone gathered around me, the only senior left, for a prayer and speech. Looking back, it seemed very odd to want to stay in the locker room any longer than necessary. This was a place where, if you left your white shirt on the bench over night, it would be a dingy shade of yellow and infused with a horrible stench for eternity. This was no place to socialize, let alone pray. We did.

I remember saying, "Everybody remembers the last time they did something with a family member that has since died. After today, I'm leaving the family. This is my last game. Please don't make me remember a loss. Definitely, don't make me remember someone not trying their best. Next year, when practice starts, you guys will probably only remember this game. It will be the one freshest in your memory. You won't remember the fifth game. That game doesn't matter now. So let's go out there and kick some Parkville ass!"

Everyone left the locker room. I stayed a few extra minutes to focus my thoughts. Right before I left for the field, Brendan popped into the locker room. He didn't say anything; he didn't have to. Brendan was the only other senior on the team. He was the only person there who knew what it was like to play in your last game. The stare he gave me was bone chilling. It seemed like he was blaming me for his suspension even though I knew that he wasn't. This was his way of showing me that I was out there for both of us. He left without saying a word.

I was pissed off. After all that we had been through, he could have at least said, "Good luck." I grabbed my helmet and headed toward the field.

The swirl of spectators and the chaos couldn't distract me. As I stepped onto the grass, I saw my family. My mother, father, brother, and sister came to every game. If it was pouring down rain, and the other team didn't show, my family would be there. The thing that really snatched my attention was Brendan's family. He wasn't even playing. They came to see me play—for us.

Earlier in the season I separated my shoulder. With blood curdling screams, I fell in the middle of the field. It sounded like no one else was around. The trainer ran to me, sat down, put one foot on my neck and wedged the other in my armpit. Then, suddenly, he pulled on my arm and with more cracking than Rice Krispies, it was back into its joint. Because of this injury, my shoulder had to be taped for every game. Usually, an assistant coach taped up the players. Today, though, Brendan came over to do it. I immediately forgot that I was mad at him.

He reminded me that the guy on the other team I would be going against weighed three hundred pounds.

"Get off the ball fast," he said, "and push that fat boy down field. When he leaves the field, make him do it on a stretcher."

His words rang in my head. My hands shook from the rush of adrenaline. My eyes watered and my nose ran from the cold weather. Spit dripped down my chin from my mouthpiece. I was just about to enter "football fury" when I heard Coach Daven yell for me.

I walked over to him and he told me that if we won the coin toss, to tell the official we want to receive. He slapped the top of my helmet and told me to go stretch. I walked alone to the end zone and began to warm-up. I exercised for five minutes and then the referee called for the team captains.

Both teams went to the side lines. Coach reminded me what to do and I started to walk toward the center of the field. Parkville's three captains met me there, and we shook hands. The referee said, "I'm going to toss the coin in the air. Franklin, you call it."

The coin floated in the air, and I yelled, "Heads!" When it landed that way, I told the official we wanted to receive the ball. Again, we all shook hands and headed back to our side lines. On the way back, I realized that Parkville's captains were also seniors and their mission was the same as mine—to win.

Unfortunately for Parkville, I wasn't going to leave without winning. My teammates met me on the side line with loud cheers and helmet slaps. We all gathered around Coach for a quick pep talk. He said, "This is it fellas. You know what to do, now go do it."

We all jumped up and down as if Coach had told us that if we won, we would all receive professional contracts. That's not what he said. In fact, if you read into it, he said, "I really don't know what to say."

But that's pretty much what he always said. Coach Daven was a man of action—not words. With that in mind, we ran onto the field.

The referee blew his whistle to start the game. Parkville's kicker drilled the ball and it went sailing down field. Mark caught it, put his head down and started running. Putting your head down is not the correct thing to do. But Mark wasn't the best runner. Honestly, he was one of the worst runners I have ever seen. On the other hand, he got the job done.

Getting the job done was harder than we thought. The game was scoreless after the first quarter. By the second quarter, it was pouring rain. We were soaked, bloody, and covered in mud. Dave, our running back, took the ball on a hand-off. He skated on the mud behind me and I collided with one of Parkville's linebackers. As we fell to the ground, Dave punched his way into the end zone.

Slowly getting up from the swamp that I landed in, I looked for Dave. With the raindrops clinging to the metal bars of my face mask, and the mud and grass embedded between them, I could hardly see. I took my helmet off. The steam coming from my head reminded me how cold it was. And it hurt. But it was just enough time to give Dave a hug and get back into the game.

Jimmy added the extra point by kicking the ball through the goal posts. Parkville threatened to score, but didn't. The first half ended with Franklin in the lead 7-0, and we headed for the locker room.

During halftime, back in the locker room, Coach told us to keep doing what we were doing. Some of the players gave hints to each other on how to be more effective, but most of us told lies about how good we were doing. Then Coach gave us the call and we went back to the field. It was a long cold walk. The rain had turned to sleet and most of our fans had left. I looked around to find my family. When I spotted them huddled under a tree, shielded from the weather, I was ready to play.

The second half was not much different from the first. In the third quarter, both armies held their trenches. Neither team scored. But neither team quit.

In the fourth quarter, Parkville played harder than us. They scored with one minute left in the game. They were ruining my chance to win. The score was tied 7-7, but we still played hard.

By now, it was almost dark. I was exhausted from three hours of playing. We were in triple overtime and had just scored. We attempted the extra point, but failed. The score was 13-7 in our favor. But Parkville had one more chance.

My stomach churned. My heart pounded. I was so nervous, I almost threw up with my helmet on. I could feel some burning chunks of my lunch fill my mouth. I spit them, as well as my mouthpiece, out. Then I heard Parkville's quarterback.

"Down!"

"Set!"

"Hut."

The ball was snapped and bodies went flying. Their quarterback rolled to the right and I chased him. He cocked his arm, turned around, and fired. As he released the ball, we collided chest to chest.

We both looked up through the gray sky and steady rainfall. He was delighted, but I was emotionally crushed. Parkville's receiver caught the ball in the end zone, and the score was 13-13. Parkville wanted a story-book, come-from-behind victory, but I wasn't going to allow it.

We had to stop them from scoring the extra point. Since it was wet, and it would be hard to kick the ball, they decided to try and run it in. Their quarterback started barking signals and the ball was snapped.

Come on. Come on, Brian. Get to him. There he is. Boom.

Thunder clapped in my chest. I had never hit a person this hard before—so hard that the quarterback's helmet popped off his head. I was sure that I had killed him. He was destined to be a permanent part of Franklin High's football field. In a fury, I peeled myself off him. It was like ripping a band-aid off the hairiest part of your body.

I stood over my prey. He spat mud out of his mouth and looked for his helmet. But where was the ball?

I looked around. And again, emotionally crushed, I realized that it was safely snuggled against the breast of Parkville's receiver—in the end zone!

We lost.

We lost? How the hell did that happen? I fell to my knees and searched for answers.

All I saw was a bunch of exhausted guys wearing Franklin football jerseys. It was my last game and I felt like I could die. It would take some time before realizing it was not the last day of my life.

ROAD TO RECOVERY
by Eric Canfield

I suppose one could claim that my whole drug problem started the first time I ever hit off a marijuana pipe. I, however, wouldn't say that. I would say that the problem started about a year later, after I went to my first rave. Raves opened me up to a whole new culture that I never imagined, and I just got much too deeply involved in it. Every weekend I could be found at a party, maybe two. During the week, I always hit at least one club. All the while I absorbed too many amphetamines. My drugs of choice were cocaine and crystal meth. Clubs and raves quickly became the center of my existence. I devoted all my time to having fun and, in the meantime, putting school and responsibilities on the backburner. But, hey, I didn't have a problem. I still kept decent grades in school. I wasn't fighting with my parents that much. No more than usual at least. Having any kind of problem with drugs was the furthest thing from my mind. I suppose that kind of thinking is what ended up putting me into rehab.

Life at my house was more or less normal. I lived with my dad and stepmother at the time—a second stint since my parents' divorce. First I lived with my mother, then with my dad, back to my mom's, and back once again to my dad's. I always had a good relationship with my dad, but lately things around the house had gotten a little bit tense. It seemed that he didn't understand me at all. He thought that my friends were a bad influence on me, and that I was beginning to get out of control. But what did he know? He was my dad. He hardly knew any of my friends and completely overreacted. I couldn't turn to my stepmother either. Our relationship was very unstable. We had virtually nothing in common, and constantly bickered over the smallest things. I never really said it to her face, but I hated her, and there was nothing that anyone could say to change the way I felt.

Okay, so maybe things at home weren't so great. To tell you the truth, I made it a point to avoid home as much as possible. Not because of abuse or anything, just because, at the time, I wasn't too fond of the people I was living with. When I actually was home, they constantly nagged me to do things—clean my room, take out the trash, straighten up the house. Nothing out of the ordinary, but for some reason it just felt like they asked too much of me.

The only people I enjoyed being around were my friends. There was always someone I could call up to hang out with. We would all get together, find some place to go (usually my friend Mike's house), and just smoke weed all afternoon. This was a normal occurrence within my circle of friends. We all loved to smoke and we did it all the time. We also loved to go to clubs and raves.

My friends introduced me to the rave scene and changed me for life. In the beginning, these places were a magical new world: loud music, tons of brand-new faces, and drugs—lots of drugs. At my first party, all I did was smoke weed. But that soon progressed. At my next party, one month later, I tried crystal meth for the first time. With that, on top of a hit of acid and some marijuana, I felt like I was on top of the world. I danced all night, and had one of the best times ever.

The next party—my first large-scale rave—came about a month later. It was unbelievable. Over four thousand people turned up and I was swept up in a sea of people and light. Over the next couple of months I went to three more parties. During that time, I started to experiment with cocaine. At first I would just split a twenty bag (about a quarter of a gram) with some friends. No big deal. Pretty soon, though, one twenty between some friends turned into two or three twenties. But still, there was no problem here I thought. Despite the fact that I was doing more partying than ever before, I still managed to keep up with school. In fact, that semester I fell just one point shy of the honor role.

Then came New Years Eve—the beginning of the end. I believe that something "broke" in my brain that night; something that took a long time to repair. It all began around 6:00 p.m. I arrived at my friend Mike's house to find half a dozen people and a ton of marijuana. We headed into the garage to partake in our almost daily smoking ritual. Afterward, I was motioned into the bathroom by another friend of mine. He shut the door behind me and took out a small vile of the purest cocaine I had ever seen. I proceeded to do what was being offered. A few hours (and a few lines) later, our group piled into two cars and headed to a party.

I don't really remember a whole lot. By the time we reached the place, everyone in my car was completely stoned. We made our way into the huge warehouse. I immediately found some familiar faces, and began smoking the opium they offered. Things started slowly, but by the stroke of midnight the once seemingly abandoned warehouse was filled with over five thousand hardy partyers.

(Memories of what happened later that night have grown somewhat fuzzy.) Half an hour passed since I dropped some liquid acid, and about fifteen minutes or so since I took two ecstasy pills. I soon felt nauseous. I made my way to the water stand, bought some water, and then sat down completely still for a half an hour. Once I regained my composure, I simply wandered aimlessly around the party.

The next thing I knew, I was tripping harder than I ever had. I was having trouble walking, and, according to my friends, I wasn't able to talk correctly. For the rest of the night, I clung to my friends, trying my best without much luck not to step on people crowding the floor. I thought morning would never come.

Finally, though, it did. Everyone made their way to the car and we drove home. How we got there, I can't remember. All I know is that as soon as I walked into my friend's house, and found the bed, I was out cold.

After that night, I decided that raves were everything. I began going to clubs and parties all the time. They soon became a way of life for me. Although I was still going to school, it was like a memory—just some place to go to fill up my days. Friendships slowly began to dissolve now that I was a "party kid" and they were not. I had new friends now, "cooler" friends. I thought because I was hanging out with them that, somehow, I was "cooler," and that made me feel good. Feeling good is basically what all of my actions became based on. Lying was like second nature to me now. I did whatever it took to get by while remaining in the best possible light in people's eyes. It worked for a while. I took advantage of my reputation for being a "good kid" to manipulate others and get away with just about everything. I had nothing to worry about. I had everyone fooled—or so I thought.

My daily routine changed drastically over the months. In the past, drugs were more of a weekend thing; however, now they had become an anytime-I-can-get-my-hands-on-them thing. I started nearly every day by smoking weed before school. Once the day was over, if I didn't have to go to work, I would be at one of any number of peoples' houses getting high again (and again, and again), only now it wasn't just marijuana. My habit had progressed, and now included cocaine and crystal meth use. My downhill descent, although not known to me at the time, was in full swing.

My home life was now worse than ever. I constantly fought with my father and stepmother. I always challenged their authority whether it be over my driving privileges, school work, curfew, or whatever. More often than not, I lost control of my temper and became violent. There were countless occasions when I would either put a hole in the wall, break a piece of furniture, or even use physical force when I didn't get my way. As far as I was concerned, it was all their fault. They just didn't understand.

School also became an issue. I was in danger of failing most of my classes. My charm, I suppose, wore thin. Teachers at my school started to notice my decline, but I ignored their concern. I wasn't in any real disciplinary trouble, so I figured there was nothing they could do anyway. I continued to carry on my lifestyle of reckless abandonment by staying up all night, nearly every night, doing speed. I left home for a couple of days at a time, but still went to school so that my teachers wouldn't get too involved. I thought they were clueless about what was going on in my personal life, and that was fine by me.

In February, on the night of my best friend's birthday party, I decided that it would be a fun idea to eat a hit of acid even though I had to go to work the next day. The next morning, after taking about an hour just to get out of bed, I managed to get myself home and ready for work. Just before walking out the door, I sat down for a final rest—a big mistake. The next thing I knew, it was eight hours later. I had slept through the entire day. I immediately called work to explain (not that I had much of an explanation), only to be fired over the phone. One of my only links to responsibility suddenly vanished. But the funny thing was, after a couple of hours, I didn't care anymore. All I thought was "Hey, I don't have to go to work anymore." Maybe I should take that back. I really did care; unfortunately, in the state that I was in, there was nothing I could do about it. In my mind, I still didn't have a drug problem. I simply figured that I was at the point in my life when all I wanted to do was have fun, and I wasn't going to let anyone stop me— not my parents, not school, no one.

Then one night I couldn't take it any more. I was staying at my mother's house because things at my father's were intolerable. Episodes of fighting and shouting had become commonplace the previous couple of weeks. I thought that I could escape the whole situation by running away from it. But my problems followed me and there was no escape. After a few hours, things heated up with my mother. I don't remember exactly what we fought about, but I felt that I couldn't stay with her any longer either. I blamed everyone but myself. I stopped caring about everything that I did, or the consequences of my actions.

Eventually I decided that I didn't care whether or not I was in school any more. I used school as an excuse to blame all of my stress on. If I didn't have school, there would be no stress, or so I thought. I called a friend of mine to ask for a ride to a local club. My plan was to get kicked out of school. I had already been warned that one more unexcused absence would result in my expulsion, so that would be my way out. At around ten o'clock I left my house and met my friend at a nearby gas station, and from there we went to the club. That night, surprisingly, I didn't really do any drugs. I think I was too full of anger to do anything. The following morning I went back to another friend's house to get a little sleep. The only thing going through my mind was, "Should I go to school?" I convinced myself that I really didn't need to: I had made a decision, and I was going to stick with it. So I ditched school, took a train to D.C., and caught a show at one of the downtown clubs...and shared a gram or two of coke.

"Did they kick me out?" I asked my mother the following morning as I stumbled through the door. To my dismay, I had not been expelled from school. What's worse, my mother was sitting there crying hysterically, telling me that I needed to be hospitalized. I just ran upstairs and went to sleep. That night, I went to yet another party. To make a long story short, I ended up doing a lot of coke, along with two-and-a-half pills of ecstasy and a lot of marijuana. The next morning, back at a friend's house, I did even more coke.

I was completely out of control. I was doing whatever I could to get thrown out of school, slowly destroying myself with narcotics, not to mention losing all connection with my family. However, the Monday morning after that crazy weekend, I was finally given an ultimatum.

To stay in school and graduate, I had to get both a drug test and a psychological evaluation. I went to a hospital for the test, which revealed no surprises—positive for cocaine and other amphetamines, as well as high levels of THC. It was now clear to everyone (except me) that I had a serious problem that needed to be treated. The counselor recommended that I go to an in-patient rehabilitation center for a month. I immediately disagreed. I told the counselor that I didn't have a problem. But what I thought didn't matter any more.

As soon as we returned home, I packed my bags. I had one more plan—one more desperate way out. A couple of months earlier I met some great people from New York who said to give them a call if I was ever in the area and they'd let me crash. With the Big Apple in my sights, I grabbed my clothes and bolted past my parents out the door. I got about a mile or two from home when something hit me like a brick. All of a sudden, I remembered something that my friend, Aaron, told me about dropping out of school. It was the worst mistake he ever made. He had to work his ass off just to survive, and that was how it would be for the rest of his life. I didn't want that, and I finally came to the conclusion that I had to go to rehab—if not for myself, then just for the sake of graduating high school. I walked to the nearest pay phone, called my dad, and told him that I was ready.

As soon as I got to Oakview Treatment Center, I was taken to a check-in room and completely searched to ensure I wasn't sneaking anything in. A counselor asked me a series of questions about the drugs I had done, problems at home, grades at school. Before being assigned to a room, I gave a sample for urinalysis to reveal what exactly was in me at that moment. I said goodbye to my parents and was assigned a room.

Day-to-day life at Oakview was monotonous. Our routine consisted mainly of group meetings. We discussed our prior experiences with substance abuse, along with related topics, such as how drug abuse affected our family and social lives. Once a day we also met in small groups for more individualized therapy. Free time was rare, and when we did have any, we were restricted to our rooms. I honestly don't think I've slept more in my life than I did during the month in rehab.

All of this counseling and therapy meant virtually nothing to me—until one particular day. My parents came for a visit and an evaluation of my progress. I expected to leave Oakview that day and just get on with my life. In my mind, I was cured. I learned my lesson and now it was time to go. I met with my parents and a counselor and told them how I felt about my situation, and that I felt ready to go home. That's when they told me what the situation really was, which altered my entire way of thinking. My parents said I frightened them. They were afraid of me...their son. My violent tendencies had a much greater effect than I ever imagined. I was now more guilt-stricken and confused than ever. I finally come to realize that I did have a serious problem, and, no matter how much I fought the idea, I knew that I had to stay at Oakview. I returned to my room and cried.

From that point on, I put every effort into my treatment. I did what was assigned to me, participated more in group, and endeavored to make myself comfortable with my surroundings. On my twenty-third day of treatment, my counselor decided that I could leave. He felt that I was ready to take on the "real world" again.

Adjusting to school again was tough. Though I had only missed about a month, I really had not been there at all for my entire senior year. Luckily, I had teachers who knew what I had been through, and who made it a point to give me extra help. Two long months later I graduated from high school. I learned a lot at Oakview. Not only did I gain a new understanding of myself, but new appreciation of my parents and how our lives affected one another. I promised myself and my friends and family that I will never again be the way I was. Still, I must be careful. There is no such thing as a recovered addict. My addiction waits for me to return so that it can once again try to destroy my life.

DAYS TO REMEMBER
by Kelly Lynne Nyman

"These are the days to remember."

Those words would eventually become our junior prom theme. Ironically, they were days I'd rather forget. September had marked the beginning of our sophomore year in high school. We were in the midst of "the best years of our lives." So, why did so much go wrong that year? I considered myself an optimist. I generally saw the good in everything. I treated mistakes as opportunities to learn from and problems as challenges rather than obstacles.

My sophomore year was filled with these opportunities and challenges. Still, it wasn't a year from hell. It was the year I grew up—the year I learned one of life's toughest lessons.

I was part of a close group of friends. Some were closer than others, but everyone still cared about each other. The nine of us napped through the same boring classes and scrambled to finish the same tedious term papers. We became known as the "gifted and talented kids." The rest of the school considered us a clique, but we knew that wasn't true. We were not carbon copies of each other. We were individuals. I was best friends with Laura and Iggy. People thought of us as the "goody-two-shoes" of the group because we studied the most and rebelled the least. Kelley, Erin, Nicole, Angie, Jenni, and Jeanine comprised the Funkettes, the wilder part of our group. They seemed to sniff out trouble like hound dogs sniff out rabbits. Then they would pounce. This hunting game was far too dangerous for me. The idea of getting in trouble didn't appeal to me. I let everyone know it, too. And if they seemed to forget, I gently reminded them. The Funkettes respected my choices and appreciated my concern. Unfortunately, that wasn't enough. Problems multiplied like rabbits.

These problems actually started the year before when Jeanine began dating a senior named Rob, who was infamous for his wild behavior. Hurrying past his locker, I would often see well-known drug dealers lounging against the wall conducting business with him. As I bought dance tickets and yearbooks, he bought ounces of pot and hits of acid. I never completely understood why Rob appealed to Jeanine. I finally decided that she desperately craved the attention he lavished on her. I wished she would have realized that there were other ways to get "love" and I wished even more that I would have had the courage to tell her that.

Unfortunately, Jeanine intimidated me. She was so popular. Who was I to contradict her? But with no one to stop them, Jeanine and the other Funkettes were drawn into Rob's world. They began to experiment with drugs. I felt left out, but I was smart enough to realize that it was better that way.

By the time our sophomore year started, my friends' experimentation with drugs had developed into regular use. Their schemes to conceal their true plans from their parents and teachers were more complex than some war maneuvers. They wove complicated webs of lies and became experts at hiding their chemically induced states. They claimed to spend the night at one person's house; instead, they partied at colleges, in dark alleys, and in desolate fields. They cruised the streets of Baltimore with strangers who were in no condition to drive. They explained that their red eyes were the result of late-night studying. The Funkettes checked in with their parents from pay phones when they were supposed to be going to sleep. And their parents never questioned their honesty. They were supposed to be "good kids," but I knew better.

In the beginning, the Funkettes just smoked marijuana and guzzled beer. But, within months, the thrill of these drugs wore off. They needed something new and more powerful. The idea of entering a world where colors had sounds and music could be seen fascinated them. Acid and its world of illusions and hallucinations became popular with the Funkettes. Unlike my friends, I did not find the idea of tripping completely appealing. While the idea of experiencing the impossible intrigued me, the risks involved out-weighed the benefits. If acid were legal and had no permanent effects, I would have tried it. But, since tripping is clearly against the law and flashbacks are always a possibility, I refused to touch acid.

I found it difficult to be friends with the Funkettes and still remain distant from their activities. They never tried to force me to join them, but I often sensed an unspoken pressure. One weekend, I was invited to a surprise birthday party for Erin. Because her parents were hosting it, I felt safe going even though neither Iggy nor Laura would be there. The first few hours were fun, but then everyone decided to go "out." By this time, I was well versed in what "out" meant. It would include "going places" where I did not want to go. I felt childish, but I decided not to go with them and called my parents to come get me. I was glad that I had the courage to stand up for my beliefs, but it was embarrassing when my friends left and I had to sit with Erin's parents until my ride arrived. To my relief, the incident was never mentioned.

Ironically, I was more afraid than the Funkettes were. Not only did their actions scare me, their attitudes horrified me. They saw nothing wrong with doing drugs. It was fun and they'd never get addicted. Besides, they only smoked up and tripped at parties. To them, their images were more important than their safety. The Funkettes weren't even affected by bad trips, such as the time they said rats escaped from the TV and attacked them. They simply laughed. The Funkettes thought that they were invincible; nothing could ever hurt them. I knew better, but still hoped they were right.

This hope was crushed when Jeanine's relationship with Rob ended and her drug use intensified. In the privacy of her bedroom, she would slip a hit of acid under her tongue and enter a world where reality couldn't hurt her. She claimed she was bored and used acid only as entertainment. I knew that she was trying to escape. I didn't know what she was running from. I could only guess that loneliness chased her. I wanted to tell her everything would be fine, but couldn't since I didn't truly know if it would be.

By January, nothing improved. Jeanine wouldn't listen to anyone—especially someone like me who "just didn't understand." But I understood plenty. I understood that she liked to have sex and didn't care with whom she had it. I knew that she had lost the trust of the other Funkettes when she had sex with their boyfriends. Above all else, I understood that Jeanine was just trying to be loved. She lived alone with a mother who was so involved in her own life that she didn't have time for her daughter. I saw that Jeanine needed attention and I tried to give it to her. Regardless, in Jeanine's eyes, I would never understand.

Jeanine was determined to find someone who understood her. She made new friends who shared her lifestyle of promiscuity and drugs. On her birthday, one of these friends gave her a sheet of acid. I was mortified. What kind of friend would give someone something that would hurt them? On that same day, her former so-called "friends" tormented her during class by making lewd sexual comments. Apparently, the other Funkettes were not ready to forgive her. They had too many problems of their own to be concerned with Jeanine.

I, on the other hand, worried about everyone. I wanted to save Jeanine and all of the other Funkettes. I wanted to be a hero. I was capable of helping them, but as the group's newest member, I wasn't sure how much I could do before they would view me as an intruder.

While Jeanine refused help, Kelley quietly begged for it. She, unlike Jeanine, confided in me. We mailed letters to each other and we stayed up late at night talking on the phone. I was thrilled. Maybe I could help her. At first, the most unobtrusive way I found was with school work. Soon, as I had hoped, our conversations turned to more intimate topics. As I had expected, we talked about drugs and sex. However, Kelley began to hint that something was seriously wrong in her relationship with her boyfriend, Troy. She shared her suspicions that Troy wasn't faithful and acknowledged that their relationship had deteriorated. Troy's bad qualities were more evident. He dominated Kelley and controlled every part of her life. And she was scared.

Finally, one day after a lacrosse game, Kelley admitted that Troy beat her. Kelley's hidden rage emerged as she kicked lockers and punched walls. When she calmed down and dried her tears, she showed me places where he bit and punched her. She told me stories of when he pushed her down steps and kicked her in the stomach. I was glad that she trusted me enough to tell me, but I was more upset that my friend had endured so much pain alone.

Despite my advice, she continued to make excuses for Troy. I was frustrated but didn't give up. Kelley needed help. She became a priority on my mental list of people who were in danger. This list was growing fast and I didn't know how to help the people on it. Finally, in March, a premonition forced me to find an answer.

On a cold day in March, I walked with Laura to her house after school. We were delighted to see a package for Laura in the mailbox. We tore it open and found that it was the enlargements of photographs Laura had ordered. One of these was of our group taken a few months before. We plunged into a reflective mood as we gazed at our friends. We were shocked at how time had destroyed our friendships so easily.

We were still reminiscing in Laura's basement when she suddenly got a feeling that Jeanine was in danger. Even though it sounded bizarre, I believed her. Laura felt certain that something bad was going to happen to Jeanine that weekend. We weren't sure what to do, but we figured we should find Jeanine. We called around and when we found her we felt silly telling her the real reason we were looking for her. We just asked her how she was. She seemed suspicious, but assured us she was fine. We hung up relieved, but still worried about what the rest of the weekend would hold. Fortunately, the weekend passed uneventfully. I was very glad to see Jeanine in school on Monday morning. Laura's intuition had been wrong, but it made me realize that we would have to do something to help Jeanine soon.

On Wednesday, Jeanine arrived at school with her part of the group's Social Studies project incomplete. Iggy couldn't stand the thought of the group failing and rushed to do Jeanine's part. Laura was outraged with Jeanine for being irresponsible. I agreed that Jeanine was wrong for not having done her part, but I wasn't sure Laura was approaching the problem the best way. I thought Iggy should be the one to confront Jeanine. I considered saying so but thought it might cause even more problems. Laura and Iggy were closer to Jeanine—they had even been best friends with her—and I didn't want to interfere. I kept my opinions to myself.

In English class, Laura screamed at Jeanine and called her a selfish, rude druggie. Jeanine pretended to be unfazed by Laura's outburst. To Jeanine, Laura "didn't understand" either. By this point, I was convinced Laura's tactics were inappropriate. I like to work out problems in calm, reasonable ways. I only yell when I feel personally threatened. Jeanine wasn't a threat to me; she was a threat to herself. But Laura wanted to scream and continued to yell at Jeanine during lunch. Finally, Jeanine bolted from the table in tears. After a few minutes, she returned. She announced that she needed to talk to Laura alone. Maybe screaming wasn't such a bad idea after all.

Laura and Jeanine left lunch and didn't return for any of their afternoon classes. I was so curious. What could be taking so long? After my last class, I rushed to find Laura. She met me half-way down the hall. As we left school, she told me Jeanine revealed almost everything to Mrs. Kegel, the music teacher. Mrs. Kegel referred Jeanine to the school psychologist, Ms. Mathews. I thought this was great. Maybe Ms. Mathews could help Jeanine. Even if she couldn't, at least an adult knew about the problem. Laura wasn't so satisfied. Apparently, Jeanine had managed to convince Ms. Mathews that everything was being blown out of proportion.

When nothing else had happened by Friday, Laura persuaded me that we needed to talk to Ms. Mathews. We spent our lunch in Ms. Mathews' office, and for the first time I dredged up the courage to express my opinion to someone other than Laura or Iggy. Ms. Mathews, Laura, and I decided that there should be a meeting of Jeanine's friends. Laura and I provided the names of the people to be invited and scheduled it for Monday. I felt guilty talking to Ms. Mathews and planning the meeting behind Jeanine's back. Still, I knew I had done the best thing.

Though the meeting seemed like a good idea on Friday, I was beginning to have doubts on Monday morning. The Funkettes panicked when they received passes to go to Guidance. They demanded to know what was happening. They accused people of turning them in. Before long, Jeanine found out about the meeting and insisted that she be included. With everyone feeling so defensive, the meeting was destined for disaster.

At one o'clock, the eleven people invited to meet tramped down to the Guidance Office. The meeting started in silence but soon erupted into a screaming match. Laura yelled at Kelley and Erin for denying the fact that Jeanine had a problem. They yelled back that Laura was too nosey. Jeanine acted like a trapped dog—she snapped and screamed at everyone, no matter what they said. I didn't speak. All courage drained from me. Between outbursts, we did manage to discuss the intended topics: drugs, drinking, and unprotected sex.

When the end-of-school bell rang at 2:15 p.m., I wasn't sure how productive the meeting had been. Laura and Kelley left in tears. Jeanine was convinced that everyone hated her. And, once again, I felt torn. Laura and Kelley took opposite sides on nearly every issue. I had to admit that some of what Laura said was a little extreme—such as that she would start shopping for black dresses to wear to their funerals—but I knew she meant well. Kelley took everything Laura said as a personal insult. A meeting that intended to bring everyone together really pushed us further apart.

As I sat with the Funkettes during lacrosse practice that afternoon, I discovered the benefits of keeping quiet. The Funkettes were furious with Laura. Although Ms. Mathews never revealed her source of information, they were sure that it was Laura. They never suspected me. I felt guilty for letting Laura bear their anger alone. But I didn't want anyone to be mad at me. Besides, at least one of us still had their trust.

A week later, Laura and I conferred with Ms. Mathews again. Laura was upset that the meeting hadn't resolved anything and we both were frustrated that we couldn't think of any more solutions. As we stood in the hallway of the Guidance Office, Ms. Mathews pointed out that we had done everything we could. It wasn't our problem—it was Jeanine's. If Ms. Mathews had told me this a month before, I wouldn't have believed her. I had thought that all problems had solutions. Everything could be fixed. And, more importantly, I had thought I could fix anything.

It was scary to think that there were things I couldn't control. I had grown to believe that my friends were a part of me and that, in some way, they made me who I was. Losing control of them was like losing control of myself.

As I lay in bed that night, I pondered what Ms. Mathews had said. I realized she was right. While I may have loved Jeanine unconditionally, there was only so much I could do for her. She was an individual free to make her own choices and live her own life. I could not change her, no matter how hard I tried. She had to want to change and, apparently, she didn't. This realization disturbed me. It meant there were limits to love.

With that thought, I jumped out of bed and turned on the lights. I grabbed my fluffy, white teddy bear from his throne on my desk chair. The events of the past year had destroyed my childhood view of the world. This new discovery was threatening to crush the optimism I cherished. I took my bear to bed with me that night, hoping to recapture some of the innocence I felt slipping away. Even then, I knew it was impossible. I had already grown up.

Two-and-a-half years later, I have failed to recapture my innocence. Fortunately, I haven't lost my optimism. Looking back, I realize that perhaps those cold months were indeed "the days to remember." The lesson they taught me is certainly one I will never forget. I've used it many times since. But it still hurts to watch someone destroy his or her life. I suppose it always will. After that March night, I gave up on changing Jeanine. I suppose Laura did, too. We moved on with our lives.

During the summer between our sophomore and junior years, Jeanine and Kelley were arrested for shoplifting. They served probation and paid five-hundred-dollar fines. Ironically, that incident brought Kelley and me closer. She and Troy eventually broke up, and by the end of the summer she had outgrown her fascination with drugs. Except for Jeanine, the Funkettes stopped using drugs altogether.

Unfortunately, Jeanine's story doesn't have such a happy ending. She never did get help. Her grades and attendance dropped dramatically over the next two years. By our senior year, she was in danger of dropping out. She did not graduate with her class, but she did complete summer school and received her high school diploma the following August. She even enrolled in college classes; however, a few weeks later she dropped out.

Jeanine was a girl filled with potential. Many people would say that she ruined her life. Not me. I'm still optimistic—and where there is optimism, there is hope. I only gave up on changing Jeanine; I never gave up on her as a person. I never will.

TO BE NORMAL: Illness

The sickness of

my folks or

of myself...

These come to

me days and

nights and go

from me again.

But they are not

the Me myself.

"I find it kind of difficult, or at least a bit interesting, to write these 'memoirs' at the ripe old age of seventeen."

Hollie Rice

TO BE NORMAL
by Michelle Haynie

I don't remember how old I was when I first realized I was ugly, but it was probably around second grade. It seems incredibly cruel that a six year old could know that she was different than the other kids. But I did. You see, I was blessed with my great-grandfather's ears. Ears that stuck straight out, perpendicular to my head. Apparently, this didn't bother me when I was younger because I have found pictures of myself with my hair pulled straight back and a huge smile on my face. I don't even remember the last time I had my hair that way.

I was in second grade when I realized that my ears were something I should hide. It was never mentioned in my family that I was different or ugly, but it was definitely mentioned at school.

I never fought back when someone made fun of me at school. Instead, I would laugh along and even make fun of myself sometimes. It was only until I got home that I would cry with my face stuck in a pillow. I didn't want my mother to hear. I thought that she didn't know about my ears. If I told her, then maybe she would see me the same way the other kids did and would stop loving me.

So, I kept it to myself, ignoring my mother's pleas to let her braid my hair until I couldn't take it anymore. Soon, though, I realized that Mom would never stop loving me—no matter what. So, each day after school, I went home and cried to her instead of my pillow. She told me the usual motherly advice such as, "If your friends don't like you for who you are, then they're not your friends at all." I tried to believe this, but I wanted acceptance so much that it didn't matter whether they were good friends or not. Looking back, I guess I did have friends. Still, I was also the target of their ridicule. I heard the ugly jokes from even my best friends. I suppose I allowed it, but they never knew the pain I felt because I never let it show. I laughed along with the kids who called me "Dumbo," or who warned me to be careful because I might fly away. It was some-time during this period that I accepted my flaw—and the ridicule that came with it. The teasing was my punishment for being different. I thought that I deserved it.

Realizing early in my life that I didn't fit into the group of pretty girls with bow-ties in their hair, I decided to hang out with the boys. Typical Tomboy. While little boys can be very blunt in how they tease, I found them to be less judgmen-tal about appearances. So, I traded in my Barbie dolls for He-Man figures and my stuffed animals for race cars. But as time went on, my need for female friends grew and so did the realization of boys being more than just playmates. This was when the full impact of being ugly hit me. As I watched boys and girls socialize, I became more and more reclusive. All I wanted to be was normal, and I couldn't understand what I had done to deserve the way I looked.

One night I came home from soccer practice shattered, which was not unusu-al, and cried with my mom. When people hurt me, it hurt her—even more—to listen to my cries. So, on this night, she said something to me that I will never for-get. She and my father had been saving money to get my ears fixed.

"Fixed?" I asked with tears streaming down my face in amazement. She pro-ceeded to talk about something called "plastic surgery." At first, I thought I was going to get brand new plastic ears until she explained to me what it was all about. She made sure not to mention any words like "scalpel," "knife," or "stitches." She would leave that up to the doctor.

I sat there stunned. I didn't know whether to believe it or not. Had my prayers been answered? Had my dreams come true? It was the most emotional and beau-tiful night of my entire life. And I was only eight years old.

The next day at school, I excitedly told everyone the news. "I'm getting my ears fixed!" I said beaming. Suddenly, I was the center of attention. I was being bom-barded with questions all day long. No one really understood what it was all about—myself included—but it was exciting nevertheless. One thing I did know was that my life would never be the same again.

My operation was scheduled for December when I would be on Christmas break. Since it was only October, I had a long time to wait. When my Mom ini-tially told me about it, I was ready to get up and go that night. Yet again, I received more motherly advice, "Good things come to those who wait."

The following months were filled with doctor appointments and second opin-ions. But it was unanimous—no one could deny that I needed the surgery. I remember the doctor saying, "They sure are big ones aren't they?" I just smiled. It's funny how you remember certain details like that. In fact, that's the only thing I do remember about that doctor. My mom said that he was more interested in the art of creating something than helping people. He showed me before and after pictures of other patients. Their ears weren't as bad as mine. I was probably his greatest challenge.

The commotion at school eventually died down, but I was always willing to answer any questions about it. I was so proud of my upcoming surgery. I thought that afterwards I would be utterly perfect. Maybe I would even have a boyfriend. All of my problems would be solved. Sometimes, I'd dream about what I would look like after the operation. In class, I would stare at the other girls, wondering if my ears would soon look the same. There was one girl in particular who I completely admired. Her name was Nicole and she had perfect ears. She would always wear her curly hair tied up in a bow, showing off her perfect ears. I wanted mine to be just like hers. That was my dream. I just knew I would never be the same.

Winter break finally came. My friends eagerly awaited Christmas day when they would get all the toys they had been dreaming about. I, on the other hand, eagerly awaited December 22 when I would be transformed into a new person. A few days before my surgery, the reality of what I was going to do set in. Only then did I begin to ask questions about the procedure. "Is it going to hurt?" "How are they going to do it?" Even though I had been told these things before, I was starting to get nervous. So, my mom, as usual, comforted me and told me it would be okay.

I woke up especially early on the day of my operation. This would be the last time I would wash my hair for three weeks until the bandages were removed. I remember using extra shampoo in my hair so it would last longer. When I finished, I sat on my lacy pink bed and dreamed about what I would look like the next day. Somehow, I was under the impression that I would go into the doctor's office, get it done, and walk out like nothing ever happened. I had no idea of the pain that this would bring.

At 4:30 p.m., my mother and her best friend, Karen, drove me to the doctor's office. My mom was there to comfort me and her friend to comfort her. This operation was an emotional experience for everyone. When we arrived at the office, I said my goodbyes. I could tell my mom was nervous even though she was trying to hide it. After we hugged, a nurse guided me into the back room of the office and sat me in a huge chair. It looked like a dentist's chair, except there was no water fountain beside it. The nurse then proceeded to stick suction cups onto my chest so that they could see my heart beating on a monitor. Why did I need that? Then, another nurse sterilized her hands and my ears with this brown stuff. She told me specifically not to touch it, but I was so nervous that I subconsciously touched my ears for the last time. I remember her getting irritated with me when she had to repeat the entire procedure again. This time I made sure to stay away from my ears.

Finally, the doctor made his grand entrance and sterilized his own hands. He administered a tranquilizer to keep me calm throughout the procedure. Before he let it kick in though, he brought out his tools—all of the things he was going to use to cut me up. They were big, metal, sharp things. He reached for one that looked like a staple gun. He said that this would numb my ears so I wouldn't feel a thing. I held on to the nurse's hand while he gave me four shots of Novocain in each ear. After these injections, they laid me on one side. I was glad because the light over top of me was very bright. When I laid my head down on my ear, I had the strangest sensation. It felt as if I was lying my head on bricks. It was just my ear, but because it was numbed, it felt like something separate from my head.

I don't remember much about the actual surgery—probably because I purposely wasn't clued in on the gory details of it. I know it lasted for about three hours. I saw the bloody clothes, even though the nurses tried to hide them from me. It didn't bother me, though. Being a Tomboy, I was used to blood. I was always comparing my various scrapes and bruises with the boys. Nevertheless, I appreciated the nurses' efforts.

When the operation was finally over, the nurses had to bandage my head. I was still numb and very groggy. The bandage felt enormous. It wrapped all the way around both ears and covered my head. I was put in a wheelchair and brought out to my mother, who nervously awaited my arrival. Through the anesthetic haze, I could still tell she was shocked to see me in a wheelchair with my head wrapped up and my eyes half-way shut. But, as always, she masked these emotions for my sake.

My ears were numb. And I couldn't stand very well. All I wanted to do was go home. My mom pulled the car up. And Karen helped me walk to the car. I was still drugged, so the car ride home was nauseating. Still, I remember being excited despite all this. I couldn't wait to get the bandages off and see my new ears.

That night, my family gave me the royal treatment. They ushered me into my room and propped me up with pillows. My sister, brother, and father came in to entertain me by asking all sorts of questions about the surgery. I relished the attention. My mom gave me a bell shaped like an apple to ring if I needed something. I rang it a few times just to check if she responded, and, of course, she did. I was in good spirits. Little did I realize that in a couple of hours the pain killer would wear off. I was sleeping when it hit. The pain came in waves and washed over me. I woke crying for my parents, who came running. We were surprised at how strong the pain was. The doctor warned us, but I never thought it would be this bad.

My parents carried me into their bedroom that night to comfort me. They gave me my pain pills, put a warm washcloth on my forehead, and tried to keep my mind off my throbbing ears. Nothing worked though. And when I was tired of crying, I just lay there whimpering. I remember them asking me that if I had the chance to do it over again, would I still go through with it. I said yes. The almost unbearable pain was a small sacrifice to pay for a "normal" life.

Eventually, my suffering made my mother sick and she had to leave the room. Now it was up to my dad to direct my thoughts onto something other than my pain. He turned on the TV and together we watched the movie "It." I vaguely remember the movie, but I do remember his efforts to comfort me that awful night. With his help, I managed to get through it.

I awoke around noon the next day. The pain was still present, but it was definitely not as bad as the night before. I stayed in bed the entire day recovering. My mom made my meals and then served them to me in bed. I got cards from friends and family wishing me a speedy recovery. All of this attention made me realize even more the importance of what I had just been through.

The day school started, I had a doctor's appointment to get the bandages and stitches removed. I had dreamed about the day when I would look like a normal girl. This day was not a dream though. It was real. And I was finally going to see my perfect ears. My stomach turned as the doctor removed the bandages. What if they looked the same? What if he made a mistake? I was nervous, excited, and scared all at once. That moment seemed to go in slow motion. When he finished I looked at my mother's face to see her reaction. This time she couldn't hide her emotions, which were clearly shock and horror. My heart thumped while the doctor retrieved a mirror. Hesitantly, I looked at my reflection. My ears were a bright purplish-blue color. I could feel the hard scabs formed around them. This sight scared me at first, but only for a moment. They might have been purple and blue and covered with dried blood, but they were no longer perpendicular to my head. At that moment, they were perfect.

That day changed me forever. It gave me the self-confidence to make friends, meet boys, and really just be myself. I consider my ears—pre-operation—to have been a disability. They kept me away from everything and everyone. They were a constant reminder of all my insecurities.

People like things that are beautiful. Beauty may be subjective, but it wasn't in my case. "Beautiful" was never a word I heard people call me. Instead, grownups would talk about my appearance in an apologetic tone to my mother. It's no wonder I had a self-confidence problem. It scares me to think about what my life would be like if I never had the operation. And even though I am so grateful to have had my ears fixed, I'm also grateful toward the time when they weren't. I am so much stronger now because of it. It taught me the true meaning of sensitivity. I will never look down upon anyone for any reason. I know how that feels. I was six years old once...and I was ugly.

HODGKIN'S
by Diana Lynn Wheeler

It's been ten months since Chuck was diagnosed with Hodgkin's. What do you do when your best friend and lover tells you that he has cancer? According to Kubler-Ross' stages of grief, you "deny." She's right, of course. I laughed. It couldn't be true. So, it must be a joke. But Chuck is not so tactless as to make a joke like that. He was, thank God, quite understanding about why I laughed.

Then came the tears as I realized that he wasn't joking—that Hodgkin's is cancer and that the past year of sitting up all night trying to ease the pain all meant something that just wasn't supposed to be happening. How could someone so young and so close to me have cancer? It was only that previous February that we had considered getting engaged. There were differences, though, and we'd put it off until we'd had more time to consider them. Now, with a big issue to face, the smaller ones of children, a house, and grad school all suddenly meant little. The tears had just begun, and it was only just beginning to sink in when the tears suddenly seemed inappropriate. After all, I wasn't the one who'd been diagnosed; Chuck was.

There he sat, holding me on the front porch. The roles were all wrong. I knew I should be holding him. In order to comfort him, I needed to know how he felt, but I don't think he knew. That must be what "in shock" means. He hadn't developed full blown emotions yet. In telling me about this sickness, he was struggling to grasp it himself. I later did the same thing as I informed others. In time, we both came to understand and, on occasion, to accept what was happening.

My first opportunity to tell someone occurred during a visit with my mother. Over our usual cups of tea, I calmly informed her of this latest development as if it was serious but nothing to be upset about. She responded in the same calm tone. The first thing out of her mouth was, "At least you didn't get married."

She had a valid point: if the illness undermined Chuck financially, at least the hospital couldn't come after me as well. If I married him, I would be held financially liable right from the start and creditors could take everything. As long as we weren't related, I could hang on to my money and use it to help Chuck if he needed it later.

On the outside, I appeared calm and rational. I agreed with my mother that it was more practical for us to be unrelated...unmarried. But inside, I raged. How could she be so cold? I'd just told her that the person I loved had one of the worst diseases in the world.

Looking back, I suppose it was difficult for my mother to know what to say. It would have been impossible for anyone to sooth away the abrasive shock of it all. But the last thing I expected was to hear how relieved she was that we hadn't married. I was disappointed. I'd tortured myself with the thought that perhaps we'd been wrong. Perhaps we should have married. What if he died? Wouldn't it be better to know that we'd had at least a year, a few months, a couple of weeks together? I was sure that if the worst happened, my grief would be acceptable as the grief of his wife. I wasn't sure that friends and relatives would be so tolerant of the same reaction from his "girlfriend."

Our conversation continued sedately. The tender spot that marked my doubt about not marrying Chuck quickly became numb—a defense reaction, I suppose. I repeated the scene many times with co-workers and friends. I'd give the news in an everyday, matter-of-fact tone and feel slightly numb as I smiled and assured people, "No, it isn't really all that hard, you just deal with it. What else can you do?"

And I guess I did deal with it, but not very well. I was still in denial. After all, I acted like it was no big deal—smiled and chatted about it, answered questions and listened to stories about so-and-so's brother-in-law's aunt's god-child who almost died of cancer but got bone marrow just in time.

At first, I tried to deal with the problem by getting information. At work, I checked every medical encyclopedia I could find. I read entries for "Hodgkin's," "Lymphoma," "Chemotherapy," "Radiation," and more. It didn't tell me anything new. Under "Hodgkin's" I found an in-depth description of Chuck's symptoms from the past year. He'd had every warning sign—backaches, chronic fatigue and illness, eye strain—the classic advanced case. But I still didn't know about Chuck's particular case. The doctor needed a biopsy of a lymph node before we would know any details.

The biopsy surgery was done as an out-patient procedure and Chuck immediately returned home for recuperation. I saw him the day after. He didn't look bad (not any worse than the cancer usually made him look), but he was a bit shaken up. He told me how he remained awake through it all and could feel the tugging as the doctor untangled a node from his neck before cutting it out. It took twice as long as Chuck had expected. Just when he was sure they must be finished, the doctor joked, "Okay, we have the target in sight."

The biopsy revealed the stage of the disease's progression. I think we were all afraid they would tell us Chuck would die. I knew for a fact that he was in the advanced stages. The books I read said that chronic fatigue and illness did not appear until the last stages and Chuck had been experiencing that for at least six months. I was sure the news would be bad.

It was—stage 3B, according to the doctors. On a scale running from 1A to 4B, 3B sounded hopeless. The doctors were optimistic, though, and said he had about an eighty percent chance of remission if he went through treatment. Cancer treatment can be either radiation or chemotherapy, but because tests showed that the cancer had spread through Chuck's whole body, the doctors didn't give him a choice. He would have to have to endure chemotherapy. Radiation only combats a small area where the beam is focused and Chuck's "cancer area" was all over. Chemotherapy would affect Chuck's entire body.

The oncologist gave Chuck a few options, detailing the possible side effects (both temporary and permanent) of each one. Chuck chose a combination of three or four drugs that would cause hair loss, mouth ulcers, deterioration of the stomach lining, nerve damage, and more. The one thing it didn't cause was permanent sterility. Although it was highly probable that the cancer had already made him sterile, there was no way to be sure. It was a trade-off—the drugs with the nastiest side effects for the chance to preserve his fertility.

Still, the inevitable side effects scared him. He didn't want to be sick all the time and he was afraid of losing too much weight if food started tasting bad. But his worst fear was that I would find him unattractive if he lost his hair. He constantly asked me if I would still want him, still hold him, still love him. How do you convince someone that you love more than the outer shell? If his hair turned purple and his skin turned green I'd still love him and want to be with him. My words meant nothing; only actions would convince him. His doubt didn't bother me. I was glad that he shared his concern with me. I was even flattered that he was thinking about our relationship. I felt like an important part of his life because, in the midst of all his problems, he was thinking about me.

Chuck worried that the cancer would put a lot of stress on our relationship, but I assured him that it would only bring us closer. In May, when he wanted to have our picture taken together, I knew that he was worried about more than becoming unattractive to me. He said he was anxious to get the picture taken before his hair fell out. But that didn't quite explain why the pictures were so terribly important. After the treatment was over, there would be plenty of time for pictures. What he didn't say was that his hair might never grow back, or I might leave him before the treatment was over, or he could die.

I think I was the only one who knew these things. Chuck rarely talked about emotions or things that troubled him. He grew up in a blue-collar family where men weren't supposed to have feelings. Every once in a while we would talk about what was going on inside him, but he usually stuck to discussions about the treatment.

The treatment's schedule depended on Chuck's white cell counts. Treatments depress white cell production, so they had to be timed carefully or his immune system might become too weak to properly function. They put Chuck on a bi-weekly schedule, and he had to report to the hospital every other Wednesday. Later, when his white cell counts weren't bouncing back after each treatment, the doctor changed his schedule to every three weeks. He had blood drawn in the morning and when the results came back, an IV solution including the anti-cancer drugs and anti-nausea drugs was started. It would drip for a few hours, and Chuck would go home in the late afternoon. Each treatment took a whole day.

The day of the first treatment, I couldn't concentrate during my classes and went to work preoccupied. My mind was at Harbor Hospital with Chuck. When I thought he would be home, I called and spoke with his mother. Chuck didn't feel well and had fallen asleep. He was still in bed when I arrived that evening. According to his mother, he had gotten in bed as soon as she brought him home and hadn't even gotten up to eat.

When I saw him, it was obvious why he hadn't eaten. He was like a child with the flu. He just wanted to lay there and have me near. I had been sick the year before when I broke my collarbone, and I knew he was feeling what I had felt. I had been like a child who wants her mommy—only I wanted Chuck. And now, he wanted me.

I spent the evening laying close to him and reassuring him with the warmth of my skin next to his. That was all he wanted, but I made several trips to the kitchen to refill his glass of water and once to get his evening dose of medication. I wanted to comfort and pamper him and help him get well. The doctor instructed him to drink lots of fluids, so I held him up to drink even when he protested that he wasn't thirsty. I was powerless against the cancer, but I could nurse Chuck through the chemo. I threw myself into it with passion and determination.

The following weekends passed in much the same way. I sat by Chuck and watched television as he slept. He did eat, but finding something tolerable was a challenge. What his stomach could handle, his tastebuds couldn't and vice versa. Often he was cranky and didn't want me to touch him. Those were difficult weekends. He had moved back with his family and, although I got along with them, I have never been comfortable in their house. Watching television was (and still is) the preferred pastime and cutting remarks are the predominant form of affection. I spent countless evenings in a comatose state—watching sitcoms and biting my tongue as I listened to their comments.

The situation frustrated me more and more. I didn't enjoy the time I spent at Chuck's home, but he was too sick to go out. Worse than that, we had no time alone, and I was not allowed to spend the night. After living together for a year, we knew what it was to hold each other every night and wake up together in the morning. Chuck missed it as much as I did. The separation was maddening and one night, when we couldn't stand it any more, we drove to a hotel. I no longer remember who suggested it or how, but I know we both liked the idea. Of course, I almost changed my mind when I had to stand at the check-in desk with no luggage (besides my one change of clothes) and no ring.

We were smarter the second time. We chose a motel with rooms opening onto the parking lot so I wouldn't have to walk through a lobby. That had an added advantage, too, since Chuck saved a few dollars by paying the single room rate. I felt like a mouse that nobody was supposed to know about and I liked it that way.

I knew what people would think if they knew we were going to a hotel. They couldn't have been more wrong. We spent our evenings watching cable news and snuggling. The TV was on for noise, but we never paid attention to it. We were busy talking. Sometimes we ordered Domino's pizza and sat cross-legged on the bed to eat. Other times we were sad, and he would hold me while I cried. In the mornings, Chuck watched cartoons while I got ready for work. Although there was no clock in the room, we figured out that I had half an hour left when "Peter Pan" was over and I had to leave by the time "The Chipmunks" came on. I laugh now, but I know those mornings weren't happy ones. I hated leaving him and going to work—not knowing when we'd be alone again.

Days became months and everything became the same. We fell into a routine. He would have chemo and be sick for a week, and then we'd have two weeks to have fun before he'd be sick again. We constantly raced the clock, trying to fit good times between chemo sessions. In some ways, that was the best summer we had together. We cruised the harbor in his father's fishing boat, spent whole days crabbing around Fort Howard, and rode bikes down every neighborhood trail he could remember.

We spent a few weekends at my father's hunting cabin in Virginia, which had become our special place after a few previous trips. It was beautiful; standing on the side of a mountain, completely hidden in the forest with the Shenandoah River directly downhill. Its crowning jewel, though, was the wood stove. In the cool evenings, we'd turn out the lamp and dance to the radio with the stove's red flames for light. When it rained, you could hear every drop hit the roof, but it was warm and snug inside.

The mornings were just as wonderful. We spent hours just washing. Chuck would get water from a stream behind the house, or if we'd had rain, from the pans we put on the porch the night before. We'd use the wood stove to heat the water and stood dripping into an old fashioned washbasin as we took sponge baths. At the cabin, we never worried. We lived life to the fullest there, enjoying every minute. At the cabin, quantity never mattered. It was the quality of our time that was important. I think that in the end, that's what we both learned. When we were spending time doing things that we had to do—going to work, recuperating from chemo, waiting for medical results—we were tired and unhappy. We worried about what might happen and what we had to do to prevent that. But when we chose what we wanted to do, we simply concentrated on that moment—not on next month, next year, or the future.

We fought the cancer, raced the clock, and got nowhere. When we slowed down and began to live with the disease we discovered that life could still be good, no matter what happened. Chuck's cancer is in remission now, and although we are relieved, we are still wary. No one knows what causes Hodgkin's, and it could come back any time. I pray that it won't, but if it does, at least we'll know what to do. We'll know how to live.

WHAT IS CEREBRAL PALSY?
by Jennifer Shropshire

My parents' hearts sank when the doctor said that I, their beautiful baby girl, suffered from cerebral palsy. What else could be so cruel and damaging to new, excited parents? The doctor, however, managed to give them some hope as he explained, "With some patience and determination, your daughter may overcome her disability someday."

The last word "someday" hung in Mom and Dad's minds as the doctor continued on, "I want to stress that we will not know the extent of her illness until she grows a little older, but it looks as though her case is mild."

Oblivious to their surroundings, my parents stared at the doctor in horror. "Mild," cried my mother, "is that supposed to make us feel any better?"

"Yes," the doctor stated calmly. "Your daughter could be much worse compared to others with CP."

Dad spoke his first words softly after hearing the terrible news, "Is there anything we can do?"

"Unfortunately no," answered the doctor. "The medical field has failed so far in finding a prevention or cure."

Suddenly my mother asked, "What will happen to my baby?"

"Cerebral palsy affects the motor function of young children. As with Jennifer, the disease is not apparent until a later age, rather than at birth. Often parents like you come in worried that their child is not starting to walk at the proper time or is showing signs of retardation. Your daughter suffered a lack of oxygen during birth, causing damage to the part of her brain that controls the body's movement."

"How often does this happen, doctor?" my father asked.

"About six out of every one thousand births. In the fall, after she turns three years old, I would like to have a surgeon operate in order to lengthen her heel cords. She should recover in approximately six weeks, at which time we will remove the casts and place her in occupational therapy. Although she will not be as sturdy as other children, she should be off to kindergarten with all her class-mates just as planned."

The doctor made everything sound so simple and uncomplicated. "Could Jennifer really have such a normal life?" my parents thought.

"If Jennifer has brain damage, won't she be slower and less intelligent than other children her age?"

"Mrs. Shropshire, you are politely trying to ask if she is retarded, right?"

"Yes," admitted my mother, "I could not bear saying that word."

"I am happy to put your mind to rest by saying that your daughter shows no signs of retardation. Unlike most cases, where retardation is a factor, Jennifer has only been affected physically by the disease."

At the age of three, the doctor's theory was finally put to the test. I made it through successful surgery and endured having casts on both legs for six weeks with only one form of transportation—a wheelchair.

I remember those days of recovery vividly—my triumphs as well as my tragedies. My doctor prescribed the usual occupational therapy, which we expected to last about a year. I also attended a school for handicapped kids run by Easter Seals. There I learned how to take care of myself and walk without the aid of a walker. After the very first day at that school, I knew I wanted to stay forever.

"Mommy, we get to swim and paint and play with lots of toys," I said all bright-eyed and bouncy.

"Sounds like fun, dear, but you have to work hard, too, in order to learn to walk."

She was right. Each day proved a little more difficult. My enthusiasm dwindled every day with the long hours of swimming, walking with my walker, and other tiring exercises. As my will faded, Dad jumped to the rescue. "Jennifer, I know you are losing your interest, but if you want to walk, you have to do what Mrs. Gardner says."

Madeline Gardner, my therapist, talked with my parents to devise a plan.

"I don't like it, Daddy," I pleaded.

"Honey, I think I have something that will make you like it," Dad continued. "Look at this!"

He held up a piece of posterboard with a grid sketched on it. Next, from behind his back, appeared star stickers, every color imaginable.

"Each day you'll walk around the house once, and if you accomplish it, I'll put a star on the grid."

He then taped the posterboard to the refrigerator, while I stared at all the stars in wonder. "When you finish each time," Dad added, "we'll see if you can let go of the walker and take a few steps on your own."

The plan continued for several months, until I was four-and-a-half years old. I complained constantly as the days piled up, but receiving a star each day seemed to boost me for the next day. Then, one day in the winter of 1977, the unexpected happened.

"Daddy, I can't make it any farther. Can't we stop? I'm too tired."

"Just keep walking. You'll be done soon. Do it for me."

Dad sat on his knees in the hallway as I walked toward him. A gleam of hope sparkled in his eyes as I walked closer, with Mom following behind.

"Would this be the day?" Mom wondered.

I successfully completed the walk after a lot of grief and frustration. Now came the test. Dad's voice sounded nervous as he said, "Okay, you made it. Let go and try walking up to me."

I took my hands slowly from the walker's handles as my heart started pounding for fear of falling.

"I can walk," I cried as I stood without falling for the first time in months.

Tears streamed from Dad's eyes after I walked a few steps and fell into his arms to give him a hug. All my hard work finally paid off, just as the doctor predicted. I soon traveled off to kindergarten with all my friends—a little unsteady, but there just the same.

The first day of kindergarten arrived faster than expected. Blind to what might happen, I woke that morning ready for school. "Jennifer, it's time to wake up. The school bus will be here soon."

"All right, Mommy."

I looked forward to my first real day of school and the privilege of riding a big yellow bus. Mom helped me get dressed, telling me everything to expect once I walked in the classroom.

"Your teacher, Mrs. Roberts, seems wonderful. She will help you if you need it."

"Mommy, I can take care of myself. I can walk now."

Dad came in to say goodbye before he left for work. He looked scared enough for the both of us.

"Honey, I know you'll be okay. Just take it slow and don't try to do too much."

"Daddy, I will, but I want to do everything everyone else does."

"You will, Jennifer. It's important that you're careful or you might get hurt."

"Fine, I'll go slow."

Once I finally got dressed, it came time to walk over to the bus stop. Mom had to take pictures before leaving for the bus. What would the first day of school be without pictures? In front of the door, Mom called for me to say "cheese."

"Come on, honey. Let's see a big smile."

"I'm smiling. Take the picture so we can go to the bus stop. I don't want to miss school."

The walk to the bus stop was a short one—only across the street. We waited patiently for the bus to pull up. Mom attempted to make small talk with other excited parents nearby. "Good morning. Can you believe they're already off to school?"

"I know what you mean, Sue," our next door neighbor, Mrs. Stahle, said.

It was a cool morning, and neither kid nor parent wanted to wait for a bus. I remember exactly what I wore that day: a jeans skirt with a yellow, red, and blue boat and a red short-sleeve shirt to match.

Mom's small talk continued: "How is Tami doing, Karen? Isn't she in the second grade now?"

"She's just fine. I'm sure you're a little worried about Jennifer."

"Yes, but she's made it a long way. Nothing short of what we expected."

Soon, the bus pulled up alongside the curb. Mom's eyes swelled with tears as she waved goodbye. I was on my own for the first time and my parents could barely handle it. Then the bus drove off.

I stared out the window on the way to school, thinking about how fun it would be, but my heart started to pound as Brookside Elementary School came into view. Maybe this would be hard. The building looked enormous. I stepped off the bus slowly, like Dad said, so I wouldn't fall. Across the way a patio held new faces I'd never seen—some short like me and others who looked huge from far away.

I crept through the crowd just to get inside. That many people frightened me. The halls seemed cold and bare even with lots of people around. I guess it was because it was a new adventure for me. I hurried to my room to see my teacher Mrs. Roberts, the only person I knew I could trust.

As I turned into my room, I realized I had forgotten how much I liked it.

"Good morning, Jennifer."

"Good morning, Mrs. Roberts."

"Let me show you around again."

The room was so friendly and bright. Cute posters decorated the walls. Words above a picture of a teddy bear stated, "Have you given someone a hug, today?" Around the room sat what we called "Letter People"—stuffed letters with special names. Mr. T, my favorite, had big teeth for us to remember him by. Also, to keep us occupied, a colorful jungle gym, big enough for five year olds, stood off in the corner.

Faces started to filter into the classroom. And Mrs. Roberts began class. I will always remember her features. Her hair was long—down to her shoulders—and she had a thin face with green eyes. Her soft-spoken voice barely carried throughout the room.

The day went by quickly because I had so much fun. We started to learn the ABCs. We painted and colored, watched cartoons, and sang songs at the piano. I made lots of new friends who looked beyond my disability. My new best friend, Beth, and I never separated the entire morning. Along with finding a best friend, I found my first true love, Steve. He was a bit taller than me with dark hair and blue eyes. Who would have thought I'd have so much luck that day? I stared at him all day long and almost hated to leave.

The bus arrived home at noon. Mom stood waiting at the corner. I couldn't wait to tell her everything. I started to yell to her before I even got off the bus.

"Mommy, I had so much fun today at school."

"Honey, don't run or you'll fall."

Before she even got to say a word, I blurted out my day. "I met a great new friend. Her name is Beth, and she lives close to school. She invited me to her house next week."

"That sounds wonderful, honey. Did you learn anything?"

"Yeah, A, B, C, D, E. And I learned some new songs," I replied.

My education began that day. And I had accomplished more than the doctors ever imagined.

The year passed, and I kept up as well as anyone else in that class. But, of course, not everything went smoothly. I received my share of bumps and bruises from a fall here and a fall there. Often a teacher would find me sprawled out in the hallway after someone managed to knock me over. I never let my downfalls get the best of me. I came home every day with a smile on my face. My family and friends to this day say I smile too much.

I started elementary school early the next fall, eager to learn new and better things. The first day of school scared me because I would have to do more explaining. Not everyone may understand. That morning I traveled down the hallway to quench my thirst. I noticed that the boy walking towards me watched my feet as I walked.

"Did you get run over by a car?" he said.

"No," I said, "I have cerebral palsy."

"What's cerebral palsy?"

I had no idea how to explain it, so I said, "It makes me walk funny."

"Okay," he said and walked away.

I am glad now that I could help someone understand me a little better. Elementary school made me realize that the whole world was not like kindergarten where everyone overlooked my disability. If parents and children don't understand it, it scares them.

My motto is "Never give up." Mom and Dad would be happy to vouch for that. Just ask them about the times I attempted (the key word here is *attempted* because I failed when I tried) to ice skate, rollerskate, and water ski. I have a lot to be thankful for in my life. And I know now that I should never complain or feel sorry for myself. This is what God has given me. There are people on this earth who have much more to overcome than I ever will. But with endurance and hard work, anyone can defeat what the world has set against them.

MAN OF THE HOUSE
by Karl Malicdem

Not long ago there was a time when I thought I lived the perfect life. I had it all: a roof over my head every night, three square meals a day, friends who cared about me, and a family that I loved and who loved me back.

However, one early spring, a presence I often took for granted was suddenly stripped from my life. My father died.

I was only twelve years old and in the seventh grade when it happened. It was the worst time of my life, but then again, who is to say that the death of their father would be anything but that? It tore me up. Ever since I was a child, I thought my father would always be there for me—every step of the way—like the way the father-son relationships were portrayed in television shows like "Family Ties" and "Growing Pains." But, in my life, things just didn't happen that way.

I can still remember the day—March 30, 1990—just like it was yesterday. My father lay motionless on his bed. His vision and ability to move and talk had already left him, though he could still hear. I recall telling him something about the shirt he wore. Then I saw his jaw move slightly, indicating to me that either he found my comment amusing or really corny. That would be the highest point of the day.

My dad had been in this condition since two o'clock that morning. This deterioration was typical for terminally ill cancer victims. He had been battling this disease for the last three years. He went through chemotherapy and radiation treatments. The treatments were thought to be successful, until a year and a half later when he needed surgery. Doctors discovered that the cancer had already spread over most of his colon. There was nothing they could do. His days were numbered. And so, my mom, my brother, and I tried to make his last days on earth as special and as memorable as they could be. We went to the beach in Ocean City at least once a month. We traveled to New York City for the first time and spent a whole weekend there. On March 18, his birthday, we threw him the biggest party he ever had. It was so big that he had a total of 168 candles from four birthday cakes to blow out. The most important aspect, though, was the quality time I got to spend with my father. Through those experiences, I realized I had taken for granted one of the most valuable things in the world: the love of a father.

Then, twelve days later, his time came. It was just before six o'clock. He struggled to breath. My mom, our relatives, and friends gathered by his bedside, and started to pray the rosary. My mother slipped her arm behind his head. I held his hand really tight. All the memories I held of my father and me together shot out in my mind. I saw my father teaching me how to ride a bike. I saw myself hitting my dad's fastballs into the woods in my backyard. I saw myself handing tools to him as he built our deck. I saw him pelting me with snowballs on a wintry day. And I saw him cry as he asked me how I felt about the situation and about being the man of the house.

These kind of questions made me very uncomfortable at first, but later as we talked more, my feelings of uneasiness began to fade away. When my father realized that I was handling everything well, he started to tell me his wishes for me when he was gone. He told me that I had to help my mother run the family. He emphasized how he wanted me to step up my role with my two-year-old brother, not so much as being another father to him, but just being there for him and guiding him on the right paths. Basically, he told me to leave the life of being an ordinary teenager, and take on a much more mature, responsible, and challenging role in the family. If it wasn't for our constant dialogue, I do not know if I could have ever made it through that day—his last day.

My father's funeral took place four days later. I still remember the scene at the church. The air was full of the scent of flowers relatives and close family friends ordered. The sound of mourners sniffling and crying, especially my aunt sorrowfully moaning my father's name, echoed all over the church. The whole left side of the congregation gleamed white and light blue from button-down dress shirts donned by classmates, while the color black blanketed the rest of us. Father Joe, Father Dave, and Father Shawn—who all grew close to us since we started praying for my father's recovery—stood at the altar. My three best friends Paul, Eric, and Nick served as the altar boys. At the base of the altar rested my father's casket.

I remained calm, kept a straight face, and refrained from crying the whole time. My brother, who was at the time a restless two year old, shed the first tear. Near the end of the mass he wandered up to the side of the altar where my cousin's violin was propped up. When he touched it, the case slammed down on his fingers and he cried in pain. My mother was unaware of the violin and thought he cried for my father, so she started crying as well. I quickly ran to my brother and took him in my arms. Then we went to my mother and all three of us embraced each other. As their crying quieted, I knew they would be okay for the rest of the mass.

After the mass came the procession to the cemetery. The cemetery was less than thirty minutes away, but the speed of the motorcade made the trip seem to last for hours. The size of the motorcade surprised me, and I know it would have surprised my father. I remember him telling me that he only expected two cars to be present at the procession to the cemetery: the hearse carrying his casket and the limousine carrying just my aunt, mother, brother, and me. Instead, a grand procession of cars stretched for what seemed like miles along the Beltway. The cars stood out from the rest of the Beltway traffic with their shinning headlights and purple flags waving from radio antennas. These were all the people—workers, bosses, friends—that let my father come into their lives. At that moment I saw how special my father was and how he was respected and loved by many.

Finally, the procession arrived at the cemetery. The overwhelming crowd of grieving friends and relatives struggled to make their way inside a small tent surrounding my father's final resting place. In a way, this scene reminded me of a Michael Jackson concert. People had to put up a good fight to get in and, because of the emotion of the moment, many were driven to tears. We sat beside my father's casket. My brother squirmed on my mother's lap. As the priest recited the concluding prayers, I could only focus on the casket. Thoughts kept popping up in my mind. I repeated to myself, "I can't believe he is really gone! Why must God take him now? Why? Of all the people in this world, why him? What's going to happen to my family now?"

At the conclusion of the prayers, my aunt broke down into tears. Immediately, I relieved my mother of my brother, allowing her to comfort my aunt. A number of my relatives escorted both of them back to the limousine. Soon, the only people left at the grave sight were me, with my brother in my arms, and two of my closest uncles. They told me to go in the limousine and join my mother and my aunt, but I responded with a firm "No." At the time I did not know why I answered my uncles like that. Looking back, I realized I was fighting with my emotions. I was trying to prevent myself from breaking down like my aunt and my mom. So there we stood for what seemed like forever. Then, my brother started to grow restless. It was time to go. I approached my father's casket for the last time, touched it, and said, "Farewell Father." Then, my brother touched the casket, and said in a tiny voice, "Bye Daddy." A tear ran down my cheek, and my brother and I ran to the limousine.

When the driver started the limousine's engine, everyone slid to the side window for a last look at the grave. Everyone except me. I could not take it anymore.

Throughout the whole day I tried my hardest to keep my composure. I thought I had been doing okay, but everything kept chewing away at me, making me weaker and weaker with each bite. My brother's farewell to our father was the final blow. After that, I finally gave in to my emotions and cried.

Later, my mother came to my side. By then, Niagara Falls poured out of my eyes. I quickly slid to the window and buried my face in my hands to prevent my mother from seeing me cry. She had to accept the death of my father and now she had to see her oldest son in tears for the first time since he lost his favorite toy in kindergarten class. I really did not want to cause more grief for her. Then, I felt her warm hand on my shoulder. I heard her say, "It's all right. It's okay for you to cry. I was going to be very worried if you didn't."

"Why is that?" I asked.

"Losing a father is a very serious ordeal," she said. "Even though you are a strong young man, the pain of it all is going to build up inside of you until you let it out. Crying is a way of letting it all out."

Just then, I experienced a feeling of enormous relief—the kind of feeling that you get after you've gotten through a big test. I took my face out of my hands and looked at my mom. She smiled back at me. I felt better. I don't know if I had added to her grief, but I know that she took away mine.

In the months that followed, life without my father was difficult for my family, especially my mother. She reduced her hours at work in order to take care of me and my brother. She woke up early and drove us to school. She cooked our meals, kept the house in order, paid the bills, and put up with my brother and me. She faced the challenges of being a single parent.

I did everything I could to help my mother. Therefore, I learned to make sacrifices, take responsibility, and prioritize what's important in life. It was tough, but sacrifices had to be made in order for my family to get off the ground. So many times I thought to myself, "Gee, I should be having fun with my friends right now." But I thought about it again and again, and realized I was doing the right thing. Those days began my new life.

LARK LANE: Travels

...I hunt wandering amazed at my own lightness and glee, in the late afternoon choosing a safe spot to pass the night...

"I wrote my memoir for me. I wrote it and re-wrote it. I spent hours changing sentences, cutting whole pages, and chopping lines. I felt like a writer. I learned to be a writer. It was a difficult task, but I am proud of the way that I found this new part of me."

Abby Forbes

424 LARK LANE
by Jeffrey Sengebusch

I've always thought that one of my roommates described it best when he said, "It was the best time and the worst time." And yes, I can say from experience that it was both. After my high school graduation, I was on my way to live and work in Ocean City, Maryland, with four other people. At the time, I was so anxious to get myself to the beach that I didn't even want to go to my graduation. I was ready for the perfect summer. There would be no rules, no parents, and no limits on what I could and could not do. It sounds pretty great doesn't it? Well, I'm here to tell it all. Being eighteen years old and living on your own has its setbacks and its own unique set of problems to go along with all the good times. If anything, that summer was one huge learning experience. It was a time when I learned a lot about how the real world can screw you over. It was a time when I learned how hard it was to work fifty hours a week. And it was also a time when I learned just how insensitive and disrespectful people can really be.

I will never, for the rest of my years, forget the date of June 10, 1996—the day my journey to the beach began. I packed my belongings, with the help of my sister, into her maroon Toyota Corolla. I was a little on edge and a little nervous about going out on my own for the first time. My mom wasn't helping to calm my nerves, asking me if I had everything packed about every twenty seconds. After debating for about a half hour over whether or not I should take my posters with me, we were finally on our way. My sister was driving me to 424 Lark Lane in Ocean City, where I would meet up with my other roommates who were already down there.

As my sister flew across the Chesapeake Bay Bridge and sped down Route 50, my mind began to drift from one extreme to the next. At first, I found myself thinking back on fond memories I had from the beach. It seemed like every street sign, restaurant, and bridge that we would pass brought back some memory of past trips. But as we edged closer and closer to our final destination, I began to think in a more negative light. I was a little worried about some of my roommates and how I would get along with them.

The original living arrangement that I agreed on was to have myself, along with my best friend Frank, and a co-worker, Rhianna, sharing a two-bedroom apartment. However, a few months later, Rhianna called me up and asked me if two of her friends, Jamie and Scott, could join our already cozy apartment. My first reaction, the one I should have stuck with, was "No way!" Jamie and Scott weren't exactly known for being the most responsible people in the world. In fact, various people who had the unpleasant experience of running across them used words such as "liar," "cheat," "phony," "loser," and "burnout" to describe them. Now, if I had decided to use my head, just a little, I would have looked at the basic facts and closed the discussion right then and there. But Rhianna begged and begged and promised that living with them wouldn't be the hell that I was picturing. Finally, I gave in. Yeah, I know, stupid move. I agreed on the promise that they would help pay the bills and pay us rent money. A few days later, it was finalized—they were coming down with us.

So maybe you can understand why I was getting a little worried about how things would go. Overall, however, I was extremely excited and real nervous. Finally, at about 12:30 p.m., we crossed the Route 50 bridge into Ocean City. I felt like a little kid running downstairs on Christmas to open presents. I looked around with wide eyes at all the various attractions and entertainment centers. Every part of that place was special to me. So many great times were spent in Ocean City, but I never lived there for three months before.

After hours of walking up and down the boardwalk looking for work, I finally settled on a job as a stock boy at a beachwear store called SunStations because I figured it wouldn't require a whole lot of thought or effort. There are about twenty SunStations stores throughout Ocean City, each one a big tourist trap with horribly corny merchandise. As I got on the bus to return to the apartment, I kept wondering if this was really the job for me. Something inside kept saying that working six days a week, eight hours a day, and stocking and pricing cheesy beach clothes wasn't what one would consider a dream job. Looking back on it now, I should have taken that as an omen that my "perfect summer" wasn't going to be so perfect.

My first day may not have been the greatest, but I was really pumped for my first night. I figured that when I got back from my job hunt my roommates and I would go hit the streets of O.C., maybe find a party or start one of our own. The problem was, when I got back, no one was home. About three hours later, guess what? No one was home. My first night came to an end at around 1:30 a.m. as I laid down on my bed—the apartment still empty. I felt so lonely and home sick. I remember thinking over and over again that it was only the first night, and I already felt lost. It was a tough night, and I didn't get much sleep. But at least I got the first day over with, and I was still in one piece.

I hate alarms. I hate alarms with a passion, and one reason that I love summer so much is that it's an alarm-free season. But, day number two at Lark Lane started with a 10 a.m. wake-up call, courtesy of my alarm clock, another omen that I refused to recognize at the time. I was due at work for my first day at 11 a.m., and I really wasn't looking forward to it. I'll tell you right now that one of the most depressing and miserable things that I've experienced is walking to the bus stop in Ocean City to get to work on a beautiful day as hundreds of people around you are walking to the beach to lie out in the sun and go swimming. I found out on my first day on the job that working in a resort town is absolute hell. I felt like God was playing with my emotions or punishing me for something horrible I might have done in the past. I spent a good three hours in the back room pricing t-shirts and watching vacationing teenagers walk in and out as they discussed how tan they had gotten out on the beach earlier that day. I, on the other hand, still had another five hours on the job and eight hours for the next five days. Welcome to paradise?

During the next couple of days I started to get into a routine. I was starting to get used to the way things were done in good old Ocean City. I began to realize that my time at the beach was going to be like no other time I've ever had. I had never before lived the way I was living. Two things that were always very important to my everyday routine back home were practically non-existent. Those two things were called "eating" and "sleeping." Let me hit on the food situation first.

Basically, we were all strapped for money. Yeah, we were working six days a week, but we were paying for things like rent, telephone, and electricity—all things we used to take for granted. We all made an agreement at the beginning about the way the food situation was going to work. That agreement stated that we would all pitch in for groceries and have what Rhianna called "an open kitchen." It sounded good at first, but problems arose right away. It became obvious that the sharing of food was going to be equal, but the buying of food wasn't. I seemed to be the one who was constantly buying food; however, I didn't seem to be eating much of it. Jamie and Scott saw no problem in eating everything I bought. It got to the point where I would buy groceries with Rhianna and Frank, and two days later it would all be gone. Meanwhile, Jamie and Scott spent their money on who knows what as they ate our food faster then we could buy it. One day I came home from the store and specifically told everyone that the food I got was for me only. I was sick and tired of the disrespect that the others showed. I wasn't willing to dish out the cash for people who wouldn't dish out the cash for me. Anyway, the day after I bought the food, I came home from work craving a bowl of Frosted Flakes, which I had bought at the store. I walked into the kitchen, opened up the pantry, and what do you know, the cereal was completely gone. I had consumed all of one bowl and the rest mysteriously disappeared. I guess a thief took it or a ghost ate it because no one in the apartment claimed to have eaten any.

As far as the sleeping situation went, it pretty much came down to the fact that I was not going to get more than an average of five hours a night. I was the only person living at 424 Lark Lane who worked during the day. I would wake up every morning at 9 a.m. to go to work. Each night, I'd come home and everyone else would already be gone to their jobs. By the time they came home I was ready for bed, but they were ready to party. There really was nothing I could do about it. And if I wanted to have any fun I would have to sacrifice sleep.

As the first few weeks of summer slipped by, tensions in our little home started to rise. Some things became very clear to Rhianna and me. The first thing was that Jamie and Scott tended to get in trouble. One evening I came back from work only to find out that they were both in jail for stealing from their work—a SunStations store on 9th Street. They stole merchandise and sold it to people on the boardwalk. Finally, they got caught and thrown in jail, where they belonged. I thought it was pretty funny and the news really put me in a good mood. That night was so peaceful with Jamie and Scott in jail and Frank spending the night at a friend's place. It was just me and Rhianna, to relax, drink a little, and complain all night about our roommates...in peace.

On a more serious note, Jamie and Scott, who spent all their income on drugs, got my good friend Frank hooked as well. I was totally appalled by the fact that Frank, who had been my friend for almost ten years, was totally ditching me to go do drugs with the screw-ups of Lark Lane. Day after day, you could see Frank lose it more and more. He smoked so much pot that he was in a constant state of confusion. He ended up getting fired from his job because he was too busy getting high to even care about work. By the beginning of July, Frank had been hired and fired at eight jobs because he was too messed up to go. It was really hard to see someone I really cared about lose it the way Frank did. He had never been into drugs as long as I knew him, but suddenly he was high all the time.

Things took a much more serious turn not too long after Frank's pot smoking began. Before I knew it, the rumors were flying around Lark Lane about Frank and cocaine. When I first heard about this, I just blew it off and denied it. But I heard more and more stories about it, so I finally confronted him. It was true, but he promised me he was going to stop. I didn't believe him for a second. I knew they had gotten to him. I knew that he had caved in, and he was now another lost soul wandering around with no purpose. I could see it in his eyes and hear it in his voice.

From then on, things started to deteriorate real fast. Sure, there were some great nights and some memorable moments, but the negatives started to outweigh the positives. Every time Frank, Jamie, and Scott would have people over for the night, the place would be a complete mess the next day. Some mornings I woke up to an apartment covered with trash and passed-out bodies. Paying bills also became a problem, as Rhianna and I seemed to be the only ones with any money come the end of the month. The others were busy spending it all on drugs. Their priorities were just a little different than mine and Rhianna's. Each day seemed to bring a new problem to our lives. A day seemed like an eternity. Rhianna and I talked about moving out. We worried about cops, who by July had visited our apartment a few times and knew us by name. But, for some reason, we stuck around. Maybe we were addicted to this kind of living. Sometimes it was almost exciting. Other times, it was like being on some kind of dangerous mission. Or maybe we just had fun playing drinking games at night. Something caused us to stay and put up with Frank, Jamie, and Scott, but the desire to continue the Ocean City summer really started to slip away. Something was going to happen. Something was going to go down.

It was the last week of June, and I counted down the days until July 7 when my parents would pick me up and drive me back home so that I could attend college orientation. I couldn't wait to get away from Lark Lane. My mood, at this point, soured with every passing day. I hated the rut I fell into...work, drink, work, drink, work, drink. It really was kind of pathetic. I was just as white as when I first came down because I never got to hit the beach. My roommates may not have minded the feeling that they were accomplishing nothing, but it bothered me every night when I laid down for my three hours of sleep. I also grew sicker and sicker of Jamie and Scott's friends always stopping over and trying to take the run of our place. Their friends had the combined IQ of a goat, no thanks to the extreme amount of drugs they took.

Finally, one night I decided I had had enough and snapped. There were about ten people at our place that night, and we had rented the movie "Heat." As we were watching it, most people began drinking, but I wanted to watch and enjoy the movie completely sober. However, watching the movie proved to be more and more difficult as time went on and as some of our guests became more and more intoxicated. By the end of the movie, I was sitting in my room alone listening to a Marilyn Manson CD on my headphones. My mind was like a combat zone, and it kept screaming at me to just go off at all the people who turned my perfect summer into a course in temper control. Music flooding in from the headphones screamed the same thing, only twice as loud. Adrenaline rushed listening to Manson yell: "You cannot sedate all the things you hate!"

Finally, after all the build up of frustration, I went off on a guy named Chris who was one of Jamie's burnout friends and the one I hated the most. He was a short, beady-eyed high school drop-out who slurred his words together to form semi-sentences and half-phrases. He was known for being two-faced, kissing up to whomever was in the room with him at the time. Seeing him or hearing him talk made me crave blood.

When I stepped out of the apartment to cool off, Chris decided to have a wrestling match with some other burnout friend. The problem was that my room was the wrestling ring. When I came back inside, my lamp was on the floor broken, sheets were torn from my bed, and the window blinds were twisted on the floor. I'm still not totally sure exactly what came out of my mouth in that moment of rage, but I do know that I hit that boy in his face as hard as I could, and his blood stained my pillow case. I also remember yelling out to whoever wanted to listen to me, "I'm moving back home!"

Later that night, a strange calmness filtered throughout the apartment. After my earlier explosion, everyone seemed to be in a state of shock. I think I really caused some people to sit down and think about how horrible things were. I was kind of embarrassed about my actions, but kind of proud of myself for fighting back. Resting in bed, I stared at Chris's blood on my pillow as I tried to decide if moving out after only four weeks was what I really wanted to do.

I debated the matter for the next few days. I changed my mind every other minute. I'm still not totally sure, but I think I finally decided for good on the Fourth of July. As I took that miserably depressing walk to the bus stop to go to work that morning, I wanted nothing more than to be at home or on vacation in Ocean City—not *living* there.

Tourists packed the streets and I knew that work was going to be an absolute mob scene. Three overloaded buses passed me. I had to be at work at ten o'clock. Finally, at 10:15 a.m., a bus absolutely choked with people stopped for me. The bus ride was torture. There were all kinds of parents, with their little, obnoxious kids screaming at the top of their lungs about how they are going to have so much fun on the beach today. A couple of real brats sitting in the seat next to where I stood fought with plastic "Star Wars" light sabers and repeatedly whacked me in the legs. Finally, they got off at 8th Street, but before I could get their seat, two more brats came running from behind me and snagged the vacant spots. I spent the whole ride standing up, tired and sweaty. At last I exited on Talbot Street, but hatred coursed through my body. I slowly made my way up to the boardwalk and into SunStations, which was already packed with vacationers ready to waste their well-earned money on cheesy t-shirts and cheap trinkets.

I clocked in and headed straight to the back room for a day full of pricing clothes, putting together hermit crab cages, and folding beach towels. The back room on this day, however, was completely filled with boxes for me to unpack. By lunch break at 3 p.m. I wasn't even half way through the boxes. I took a short lunch and tried to finish everything before the big fireworks show at 9 p.m., when the holiday hoards would jam the boardwalk. I priced and priced as fast as I could, but as 8 p.m. rolled around, I ran out of steam. I finally finished at about

9:15 p.m. just as the fireworks began, but it was too late. I was trapped by the boardwalk throng for over an hour. Getting back to Lark Lane proved to be almost impossible. It seemed every person in the city crowded downtown. The usually twenty-minute bus ride took a good two hours. As I stumbled into the apartment at 12:30 a.m., my neighbor Jay came by. He couldn't believe how long I'd been gone for work. I took a peek in the kitchen and realized that there was not a thing to eat or drink in the whole place. I decided then and there that O.C. living just wasn't for me.

The next night, after another horribly long day of work, I partied at Lark Lane one last time. I partied a little too hard because, before I knew it, daylight broke and I was due at work in three hours. I asked Rhianna to call my manager and tell her I was in the hospital with alcohol poisoning. My final day at Lark Lane was spent in bed with a massive headache that throbbed for almost twelve hours. I packed that night and left the next morning. I remember walking out through the living room, trying not to step on the sleeping bodies that covered the floor, feeling a sort of relief that it was all over. As I drove out of there with my parents, I knew right away that I had made the right decision.

Others soon followed my lead. Rhianna left a few weeks later after becoming furious over Frank's drug abuse and the abysmally dirty apartment. The place was unceremoniously trashed by Frank and Jamie before they left, leaving just Scott who stuck it out until Labor day. A bill for the damages arrived at my house in September. I had nothing to do with it, but owed one-fifth of the $1700 in damage because my name was on the lease. I refused to pay. However, knowing how things from Lark Lane work, I'll probably get screwed over somehow.

COMING TO AMERICA
by Oleg "Al" Tsygan

First, let me tell you about myself. I was born in 1974 in Kiev, the capital of the Ukraine. I went to school, and I loved it—until fourth grade. That's when I realized I had to study. My teachers also expected me to do homework! At this point, I started to want to graduate from school as soon as possible and either go to college or find myself a decent job. However, I still had six years of accomplishing good grades ahead of me. It became harder at the end—so hard that I stopped doing my homework. I still had to struggle in the classroom with teachers, who tried to fill my more or less empty head with all kinds of more or less useful things. I still can see it now—our old colonel in military training class, vigorously waving with both hands, explaining to us what to do if an atomic bomb explodes a couple kilometers away. We had a joke about that—cover yourself with a white sheet and move to the closest cemetery.

However, most of the fun started after school. When I was born, my father was able to get a new, bigger apartment. In the neighborhood where I lived now, most of the houses were big nine- and twelve-story buildings. We lived in a middle-sized nine-story concrete monoblock—dark gray and quite depressing—with seventy-two domiciles. In my building alone, there were a dozen children of different ages. That is why when kids would get together from a few buildings, the crowd could grow very big. Having a lot of time on our hands and being young, we did not know what to do. Usually we played soccer, ran around holding toy guns, went to the movies, swam in the river, or rode bikes. We were trying to have fun any way we could.

Nothing was really changing in my life. Day after day, it was all the same. With such a routine, you become used to it. Weeks, months, even years pass, and when you look back, it is just like a blur of faces and places—not much to remember.

The story I am about to tell started about five years ago on one of those regular days. I do not even recall what kind of weather we had that day. I remember that it was a weekday because I had to go to school. That evening—when my parents, my older brother, and I gathered for our evening meal—unexpected things started to happen. After we ate, my Dad walked out of the kitchen and soon came back with a big envelope in his hands. He carefully put it down on the table and stood motionless for a few long seconds. We all watched him. Dad looked at us, one by one, took a deep breath, and said something that changed my life forever: "We received a letter from the United States. We may be able to emigrate to America!"

America! It was a dream land for me! America, with its big cities, huge high-rises, roads full of cars, and supermarkets full of food. Sometimes I thought that all of that was make-believe. It simply could not exist in the world I knew and lived in. And everything that I saw on television or read in newspapers was some kind of big joke—or a government lie. Believing in the existence of such a place was hard enough. So, the idea of going there drove me completely nuts. Somehow, every time I thought about this wonderful country, I had a vision of large cars, big houses, and even bigger bank accounts.

On the other hand, I knew we had relatives who lived there. They were people I only heard about but never met. I also read in newspapers and magazines about dissidents—people who believed that life in the United States is better than life in the Soviet Union. They wanted to leave the USSR, but were not allowed to do so (usually they also went to prison). Now, I had a once-in-a-lifetime chance to find out. I could not fall asleep that night, shifting myself around on the bed, trying to imagine how it was going to be—different language, different customs, and, most importantly, different people.

First thing next morning, I went to the kitchen to find out whether it was just a beautiful dream or a wonderful reality. The envelope lay on the table in the same place we left it. So, we *are* going! However, this reality was the start of real troubles and worries for our family. First, we had to go to a government agency and register to leave the Ukraine. It took us a year just to get an application and fill it out. Meanwhile, we started collecting necessary papers. Leaving a communist country requires all sorts of different paperwork. First, we needed a certified letter that invited us into America. We had that. Next, we would need birth certificates, a marriage certificate for my parents, a certified letter from every place where we studied or worked, and all medical records. To top it all, mountains of paperwork needed to be completed. For example, for working more than ten years in USSR, you receive a medal. When you leave the country, you must return it to the state and later present a document that it was done in front of the authorities. At that time, I felt that the bureaucrats in the Ukraine loved papers more than anything else in the world. Luckily, I only worked about six months and it was with the last school I graduated from. However, before that school, I graduated from two others. So I had my share of long walks and waits in dark and dusty offices for some paper-crazy person to issue the required document, which was almost priceless for me and worthless to others.

This mess continued for two-and-a-half years.

Then a different problem began. For a number of years, my father had medical problems with his liver. He had to go to the hospital. The doctor said that without surgery he would not get better and would definitely not be able to fly overseas. We agreed to the operation. What scared us the most was that Mom had to sign a piece of paper that freed the hospital of responsibility in case my father died. On the day of the surgery, we all waited at the hospital. Surgery took half the day, all the while our family sat in the waiting area. Finally, the doctor came out to talk to us. Everything turned out okay. They had to cut out a piece of liver, he said, and it would be a long time before my father would recover completely. They made him stay at the hospital for another four months.

After all the troubles we had, it was hard to believe that it was all over—we could leave. Dad did not look very well, but he told us that he could handle the flight to America. We were to leave on December 4, 1992. We had sold or given away to friends as many belongings as we could, and the plane was leaving early that morning. To make sure that we would be among the passengers, we had to arrive the previous evening and spend a night at the airport. We traded five bottles of vodka for a bus ride to the airport.

It was already dark when I walked out of our apartment building for the last time. A thick layer of sparkling white snow covered the ground around me. Leafless trees stood quietly. It was very calm and peaceful. The air was so fresh that it delicately bit my throat when I inhaled. I looked around me, trying to imprint this moment in my memory forever. Surprisingly, I did not feel any different than usual. I took one last look around and got on the bus. Forty-five minutes later, we arrived at the airport Borispol, which serves Kiev's international flights. The huge main terminal was unusually dark and empty—internal flights do not fly because of the lack of fuel. We rode on to a smaller building that hosts passengers flying overseas. I knew that I should have tried to sleep before we got on board, but I didn't. I walked around the building, going out to the fresh air, trying to remember the land where I was born.

Finally, morning came. At six o'clock, big metal doors to the customs area suddenly opened. People quickly lined up just like they had lined up for things all their lives. The difference here is that nobody is trying to get ahead of you or start some kind of fight. Surprisingly, customs did not take a long time. I guess, since it was the first flight of the day, customs officers were sleepy and did not pay any extra attention to the passengers. After submitting our luggage to the attendants, we walked to the plane. In the Ukraine, there is no direct access to the plane from inside the terminal, so we had to walk a couple hundred yards. The sun stretched slowly above the horizon, and everything around me was covered by the warm, bright shining light. We carefully climbed steep steps one by one and got on board the plane. I chose the window seat so I could see everything going on outside. We were told that there was not enough fuel on board and the plane would land in the Shannon airport, Ireland, for refueling. I did not want to miss the first glance at another world.

At last, everyone was seated. Engines roared and the plane moved. I felt the thrust of jets pushing me into the seat, and turned my head for the last look at the snow-covered fields of my motherland. After take-off, I tried to watch the landscape pass by underneath, but soon we flew into clouds and I lost interest. I picked up Ian Fleming's *James Bond* and started to read. Four hours passed by unnoticed. The pilot announced that we were going to land in Shannon airport in a few minutes. There would be an hour of free time to stretch our legs. It was my first meeting with the West. Looking out of the window before landing, I did not see a lot. But when we landed, I saw it—the biggest parking lot I had ever seen in my life, completely filled with hundreds of cars. Different makes, models, colors. I probably spent a few minutes just sitting in my seat staring at them. After I filled myself with this image, I got up and walked into the airport terminal.

The first thing I noticed was space and emptiness, high ceilings, red carpet, and long rows of soft chairs. Of course, there were people here and there, but they were hardly noticeable given all the room they had to roam. We all stuck out like sore thumbs with our dumbstruck expressions. Shops lined one side of the terminal—shops filled with everything you could ever want. I saw currency exchange booths, bank machines, and phones. What hit me the most was that everything was clean. There were no cigarette butts on the floor, no dirty handprints on windows, no trash flowing out of trash cans. That was my first impression of western civilization—cleanliness.

As all good things in life, an hour passed rather quickly. Everyone went back on board, and we were airborne again, this time heading for our final destination—America. I went back to my book, since it was cloudy again. Somewhere above the ocean we had lunch. I continued to read, sometimes throwing a glance through the window out over the sea of clouds. Then, over the intercom, the co-pilot announced: "We will be arriving at Kennedy airport shortly. Please fasten your seat belts and do not smoke." This was the moment I had waited for. I turned to the window. At first all I could see were clouds, but we descended quickly. Without warning, they evaporated and I saw a long coastline, the black water of the ocean, and a city—a metropolis that at first looked dark and depressed. I did not see any skyscrapers; just long rows of small frowning houses. Here and there smoke puffed out of long stacks. Still, this new world looked beautiful to me. Our long journey of five years and eight thousand miles was over. We had come to America.

DARRTOWN
by Estelle W. Petri

It was one of the hottest summers on record in Baltimore. There was not an inch of room in the car for stretching our feet or shifting our tired bodies, and the ten-hour drive seemed longer with every passing mile. The family dog, Christie, breathed down the back of my neck. Drips of slobber occasionally slid beneath my shirt down my spine and joined the rest of the collected sweat in the small of my back. I stuck my head out the window of the unairconditioned car and watched my mother glance at every passing rest-stop sign as she tried to see how much longer she had to hold it in. She said that she couldn't help it. I will know after I have children—stops every two hours are a necessity. I was only nine years old at the time and didn't believe a word she said.

My parents and I had already gotten into several fights about the choice of radio stations and, consequently, it was turned off all together. I wanted to listen to the "teenager" station, which played alternative rock music. My parents could never tear themselves away from the oldies station. It was flipped back and forth a few times in protest and then my mother came to the conclusion that if she threatened me with country music, I would just submit. I did. So I entertained myself with thoughts of moving to my grandmother's farm.

I was a little confused about why we were moving away for only one year, but there was no way of asking without receiving complicated and long-winded answers. My father had worked for a Maryland university for over twenty years. This particular year he decided to take a leave of absence and teach at a small liberal arts college in Indiana, which was about thirty minutes from my grandmother's place in Darrtown, Ohio.

I knew my parents grew up in this town and had always wanted to see what it would be like to live there again. "But why now?" was all I wanted to know. Why now, while my mother was in the midst of a battle with breast cancer? It seemed like the worst timing to me, yet we packed up our belongings in the middle of August and headed to the Midwest. I found out later that my mother was the reason we moved. My father feared that my mother was going to die, and this would be their last chance to try for their dream. This bit of knowledge was not told to me until my freshman year in college when I read the beginnings of my memoir to my parents. It was then, after my mother had left the room, the truth was told.

Darrtown was normally a ten-hour drive from my home in Maryland. With our dog, it became a very slow twelve-hour drive. When we finally reached our new home we all breathed a sigh of relief that the long haul was finally over. I breathed an extra sigh for the feeling of loss. I felt as if I had lost everything, and was thrown into an experimental lab to see how I would react to the stimuli, or lack thereof, in a country environment.

We arrived a week before I was to start school—just enough time to unpack and settle into the house. After things calmed down, and we had officially become part of the household, my father introduced me to Mr. Wexler. He had been one of my dad's graduate students and good friend. I was sent upstairs to entertain his daughter, Carla, who was my same age. My parents hoped that we would hit it off and that I wouldn't be so lonely anymore. That night was the beginning of our friendship.

The farm that my grandmother lived on for over fifty years was now our home, too. It included 127 acres of pastures and two separate wooded lots, the Small Woods and the Big Woods. Right before the entrance to both lots was a large pond originally built by my grandfather. Herds of cattails choked the pond and refused to die no matter how many times they were pulled out by the roots. My father always claimed that there were huge bass fish in the pond, but the only ones that ever seemed to be caught were tiny and thrown back in.

The house we lived in was over 150 years old. It had its own sewage system and well water; neither of which ever seemed to work right. You knew that one or the other was about to go bad when a rancid odor invaded the house and ate its way into everything you could smell. I slept in a huge nineteenth-century bed with wooden posts at either end. I was small for my age and could not reach the bed, and practically had to throw one leg over the bed and then slowly inch my body into the center. I imagined at night that I was the princess in the fairy tale about the pea. Some nights I was sure there was a shriveled green pea under my mattress.

I ended up in a school that was being financially torn apart by the college that owned it. The school was split up into three different buildings. The gifted and talented kids attended classes in the town's local Methodist church and the honors kids' classrooms surrounded the university's football stadium. Other kids were put into the classrooms around the basketball stadium. About three days prior to the first day of school, a letter arrived addressed to "The Parents of Estelle Petri" regarding the transfer of my records and my placement at the new school. I was assigned to the church. I didn't understand why, but my parents were ecstatic.

The first day of school was like being thrown into a pit of lions. I got up at the crack of dawn expecting to hear a rooster crow. I took a shower and spent hours trying to make myself look just right. I grabbed my backpack and headed down the half-mile gravel lane. The bus arrived as soon as I was at the end of the lane. Curious faces peered out of the bus windows. They knew this was a new route for the bus to take, which meant a new kid was about to step foot on claimed ground. I boarded the bus looking down at my feet and searched with my hands for an empty seat. I let out a big breath and thanked God I didn't have to sit with a stranger. Since this was an extremely small town, everyone knew everyone else, except for me. I sat on the bus by myself and hoped that no one would talk to me. Well, my wish came true, only they stared at me instead. Their whispers to one another about the stranger on the bus echoed through my mind.

The bus pulled up in front of the small brick church with steeples covered in black and white shingles. Inside there were two levels: upstairs was the English, math, and social studies rooms, and the science room was downstairs. Around noon we were bussed over to the basketball stadium for lunch, which was always brown bag since there was no cafeteria. Finally, I saw a familiar face—Carla. I sat on the curb with her at lunch and watched boys play football in the parking lot, which was their makeshift football field for the year. Her friends sat next to her, away from me. They talked to her, asking questions about me and where I was from, as if I wasn't even there.

The day ended at 2:45 p.m. and I had to get back on the bus for the lonely ride home. It stopped at the lane and I slowly began my journey back up the hill toward my grandmother's house. About half way up, I began to cry and cried the rest of the way. I started to run. Then I ran faster, trying to reach my destination, so I could hide from the world, my fears, and the let down of all my expectations. I had tried to make it a good day, but my attempts failed. Maybe I hoped that if I cried long enough it would magically take me back to Baltimore and to friends whom I belonged with. Why did my parents drag me along with them on this little adventure of theirs?

After my first day at school, I spent most of my nights with my grandmother. She was a wizard with cards, and she taught me games that occupied us for hours. I believe one game was called "Rags," but every time we played it my grandmother changed the name. I became quite good at "Rags," but I never conquered Solitaire the way my grandmother could. Grandma was a woman content with simplicity. She sat in her old beaten up brown chair, a matching pillow propped behind her head, with the television remote within reach on her tray. My mother told me that Grandma always needed something in her hands. First it was her elaborate quilts that she constantly worked on. One quilt went to each child and grandchild. Next it was her cards, always playing rounds of Solitaire until she won at least one time. Soon though, her arthritis got so bad in her hands from years of quilting that she could only deal with the remote control and, of course, her cups of coffee.

Three months passed in slow motion, and eventually my mother needed to return to Baltimore for another dose of radiation and chemotherapy. The long-weekend trip provided me with a chance to catch up with friends and find out what I missed since leaving. Time had flown by for them. On Saturday my father and I drove my mother to the hospital and wished her good luck with her treatments. We were never allowed to come into the building and, from what I heard, we wouldn't want to. A sad expression veiled my mother's face as she stepped out of the car and said goodbye. Two days later we were back in Darrtown, and my mother's hair fell out some more due to the chemotherapy. She had no eyebrows, and only spiky tufts patched her head. The treatments made her constantly sick, and she spent a lot of time leaning over the toilet, praying to God to help her, praying that it would all be over soon, and praying she'd be back on her own two feet again.

She continued to work and continued to find some passion in her heart for me, even though I continued complaining about how much I hated Darrtown, Ohio. She would tell me, "It's only for a year, sweetheart. It will be over soon enough."

Christmas came, and it brought along the only thing that I had been wishing for—my sisters who came out to Darrtown from Baltimore for the holidays. Our tree touched the wooden ceiling, forcing the angel on top to bend and bow slightly to the right. On Christmas Eve, my father rang the sleigh bells signaling that Santa had come and it was time to begin the family's celebration. Christmas is the same every year and Christmas in Ohio was no exception. A bookmark placed in my mother's leather-bound Bible fell open to the story of Mary and Joseph, and the birth of the baby Jesus. My older sister read the story while the rest of us sipped homemade eggnog. Next we read "The Littlest Angel"—my father's favorite. His mother read it to him every Christmas, and the tradition passed onto our family. My sister Kath always read it the best and she read it again just as splendidly. I looked up and saw tears welling in my father's eyes. This was the only time that I ever saw him cry, and it tore my heart apart.

On Christmas morning I woke every soul in the house at five o'clock. My mother heated sticky buns and poured out a pitcher of fresh orange juice, and the feast began. We laughed, and talked, and opened our stockings. We were not allowed to look at the tree—packed full of lights and circled by gifts like a huge skirt—until it was time to open presents. The presents were opened, and too soon, the day ended. My memory of the family together that particular Christmas, however, will never fade.

Five months later we were home in Baltimore again for another round of treatment for my mother and to celebrate my tenth birthday. It didn't matter to me what the circumstances were that brought us back to my sisters in Baltimore, I was just happy to be home if only for a short time.

School was drawing to a close back in Darrtown, and the packing started all over again. Boxes piled higher than me were filled to the brim with clothes and electronics, and things that we acquired during the year in Darrtown. More boxes contained family heirlooms that Grandma wanted to pass down to our family: quilts, china, baby clothes, and toys for the grandkids. We packed up our lives, transplanted for this year in Ohio, and headed toward the station wagon. We loaded the last of the suitcases into the car. I turned back to look at my grandmother who stood on the edge of the porch the way she always did when she waved goodbye. I ran up to her, and let her give me a huge wet kiss on my cheek, and then again on my forehead. She told me to be good girl and sent me on my way. I walked slowly with my head hung down. If I had a tail, it would have been tucked between my legs. How could I be sad about leaving this place I hated? Maybe Darrtown wasn't so bad after all.

So many emotions filled me. I was sorry that I was leaving, happy to be going home, and guilty for making life seem more miserable to my parents than it actually was. My heart ached as I curled into the back seat of the car. I set up my pillow against the right door, kicked off my shoes, and pulled the crocheted blanket up over my head. That way no one could see my face and the tears that admitted that I cared and loved this old farm where I had been stranded for a year. Leaving not only brought me pain, it also brought me a lot of peace, and a mind and heart that understood things much better than when I had first arrived. It was in Darrtown that I grew up, and grew aware.

I heard my mother's choked voice as she kissed her palm and blew it to my grandmother. "Ba-bye Momma," she said. My grandmother receded in the distance, growing smaller as the car pulled farther away down the long driveway. We headed home.

LEAVE NO TRACE
by Brendan Curran

Outward Bound is a course in which groups of six to twelve people go on an expedition into the wilderness. Participants must rely on each other and themselves in order to accomplish daily and long-range goals, such as navigating, hiking, finding water, cooking. "Leave no trace" is Outward Bound's ethic toward minimizing human impact on the environment, taking great pains to limit litter, noise, and disturbance of soil, rocks, and plants.

Day 1: Canyonlands National Park, Utah

The van pulled over in a desolate area to pick up an apparent hitchhiker. It was Mark Johnson, our course director. He ushered us over to an area where we had lunch. Then, he gave us a brief introduction to our trip. The last human structure we had seen was nearly an hour's drive away. As Chris Barber, our instructor, distributed the materials, I realized that the course had really started. I met my patrol-mates.

Elisa, a lawyer from Denver, had previously been an accountant. Ever the adventurer, she considered leaving the law profession and doing something completely different. Jen and Adam were the closest to my age—both in their mid-twenties. Jen works at a health maintenance organization in Washington, D.C.; Adam just moved from New Jersey to Colorado. He knew he wanted to take an Outward Bound course and signed up for this adventure just a month beforehand. He was moving to California, but stopped in Boulder on the way out and liked it so much he decided to stay.

Maggie designed displays for a large department store in Minneapolis. We shared many good talks on spirituality and personal philosophy. She knew much from personal experience. Finally, there was Dave. I didn't know what to make of him at first. This trip was a gift for his birthday, as it was for me, too. For Dave, however, it was a surprise. His birthday was a week before the trip and he never even heard of Outward Bound. He was one of the hardest people to get to know, but the effort was well worth it.

We went through our luggage, deciding what to bring and what to leave behind. I intended to bring everything. Dave suggested I leave my jacket. Fair enough, but I was definitely smuggling in my rock climbing shoes. The literature said not to bring them, but this journey to Utah was an opportunity to do some serious rock climbing. We distributed plenty of food and gear, then Chris gathered the patrol to show us how to bundle and arrange our packs.

Going through these basics was a joke. I am certified in Wilderness First Aid as part of my job at an outdoor learning school where I lead groups on week-long hiking trips. Now come on, this guy was insisting that I pay attention to his pack demonstration? Maybe he didn't read my profile. I tried not to be offended and keep my ego in check. He was, after all, the group leader. And I hated it when know-it-alls in my group didn't listen to me.

Granted, the group was a bunch of adventurers—skiers, surfers, mountain-bikers—but I planned for this trip for six months, whereas most of them decided to do it at the last second. Furthermore, I was the only one in school and the whole group chuckled about all the homework I had to do. At long last, packs and people piled into a truck and we drove even further into the park. The sun was setting as we started hiking. After sunset, we stopped for a quick dinner and kept hiking until collapsing exhausted at our camp spot.

Day 2: Upper Druid Arch Quadrant, Canyonlands National Park

I was grateful to have coffee on our trip. I need my coffee. Chris showed us how to clean up our camp area after breakfast. I had a hard time adapting to his camping methods. He showed us how to poop...well, not *how* biologically, of course, but where and what to do. I was familiar with the "leave no trace" method: dig a hole in the ground, do your business, and fill it in again. Any toilet paper used must be packed out. It's a real pain in the ass...literally.

It took us a while to break camp down and pack our bags. I was used to keeping all my clothes in a trash bag so that when I took out my sleeping bag (which is almost always packed at the bottom), I didn't have a clothes explosion. Chris's method, however, involved cramming clothes around other gear, so that weight is more evenly distributed.

Dave didn't make it out of bed until we had finished breakfast. We yelled at him to get up, but he would not move. He just didn't seem to be fitting in with the rest of us. A little way into that day's hike, Adam, Maggie, and Elisa discussed the problem. Adam was worried—we needed to trust each other one hundred percent when hiking on some of the more exposed areas.

Adam had a point. Dave would tromp over and through vegetation, especially the delicate cryptobioptic soil—from which all life in Canyonlands grew. We agreed that we needed to bring him into the group, but didn't know how. We hiked out of the wooded river bed and up onto slick-rock. Slick-rock is a bit of a misnomer because, in dry weather, slick-rock—basically large slabs of sandstone and limestone— provided excellent traction, and was much easier to walk on than sand. We pushed on to about noon.

After lunch, Chris asked if anyone wanted to lead the group to our next spot. I wanted to, but didn't want to seem like an ass-kisser and waited to see if anyone else volunteered. No one spoke up. Chris pointed out a canyon wall about one mile away. I needed to find the shortest route possible that was doable for everyone, which was a major consideration because the day's hike took its toll on the group. Adam's new Vasque heavy-duty boots were not broken in and they slowly turned his feet into hamburger. Elisa's knees gave her problems. And the reason Dave had such a hard time getting out of bed was because of a stomach virus. On top of that, much of the hiking in the canyons involved scrambling over large rocks. Even with steep rock faces, a very effective way of doing this was to "smear." Smearing involves putting your weight (and trust) on the pads of your feet and lowering your heel. Smearing, however, was a skill we were still learning, and few of us trusted our feet that much.

We eventually, and safely, made it to our spot.

Day 4: East Five Fingers area of Druid Arch Quadrant

Sculpted by wind and rain, the Canyons are a place of balance. Ancient majestic cliffs and spires host delicate plants and soils. Plants and animals blossom and wither in a blink of the Canyons' eternal eye. The midday sun scorches the earth. The moon directs the night winds to carry away the day's heat. In the morning, sun and moon meet and plan the day's weather. They have been generous so far to us on this trip.

I perched on a plate of rock forty-five feet in diameter. It rested at a jaunty angle, having once been flipped like a coin in some violent upheaval perhaps thousands of years ago. Miraculously, plants sprout from cracks in the rock. One shrub is a soft network of green capillaries. Its neighbor has gray, spindly fingers—an explosion of thin branches dried and mummified by the sun's relentless rays. Canyon walls, swathed in orange and burgundy stripes, watched the gradually changing drama. It is an ancient, fragile world. The ancient Pueblo, commonly known as the Anasazi, left this place a thousand years ago. The canyon has changed little since.

Day 6: Solo

In mid-afternoon, Chris showed us each a spot to stay alone for the next twenty-four hours. We left behind food and cooking gear, which would have distracted us from our ultimate purpose. This solitude was an opportunity to pay close attention to everything around me, to reflect and contemplate, and to update my sorely neglected journal.

The scratching of my pen was a cacophony, shattering silence. There was nothing but canyon walls, rocks, plants, and my thoughts. Now was my time to put them to paper. They had been whispering in my ear, echoing from inside over the miles I walked. Writing them down helped them make sense.

I went to sleep watching the stars come out. This was the first time I ever actually watched each one appear. I slept on a large stone slab. Eons of wind and rain had smoothed and sculpted it and its neighbors. I saw the path the water took—there were slopes leading to small, white-crested ripples in the rock. Parts of the surface flaked off like a coat of heavy paint. The exposed, fleshy core had the same sandy grit as the surface.

Sand had collected in valleys in the rock. This was where life began in Canyonlands. The surface was rough and clumpy, forming a half-inch high network of canyons. Some of these tiny peaks were black. This was cryptobiotic soil: mold that forms in the sand. Over a period of decades, it fluffs the soil, providing semi-fertile soil for rugged vegetation. The needlely plants and bonsai-like trees had blue-gray trunks, as if the copper soil and milk-chocolate walls leeched the color out of them. Dead plants could be distinguished by absence of leaves. The leaves, however, were more colorful than Mardi Gras in New Orleans. Some had needles the color of ripe bananas. Leaves on one tree were scarlet, jade on the next, and canary after that.

I planned to get a suntan, but it was a little chilly. A high-pressure weather system had been sitting over us for the past week, keeping clouds out of the area. But on this day our protection vanished. The wind hit the canyon walls like tidal waves. Moments after I heard it crashing over the rim, the wind hit me. Then dark clouds passed overhead.

I tried to continue my day's reflections, but fears of a pending down-pour pushed at the back of my mind. I felt a few drops of rain. I decided to put up my solo tarp and pack my gear away. "Please God, don't let it rain," I repeated over and over. But God, looking at the big picture, does what God must...and it rained.

Time came to regroup, but Chris was late in rounding us up from our secluded spots. If we delayed any longer, we'd hike back in the dark and I did not wish to set up camp in the rain. I tried to stay calm and waited. At last, Chris appeared over the hill, signaled me over to where we departed the day before, and led us back to camp. Everyone was hungry. We huddled up and sat in silence with bowls and forks poised. The wind died down, the rain held off, and Chris launched into a story:

The archangel Gabriel visited an old man the day before his death, offering him a wish.

"I would like to see heaven and hell," the old man responded.

So Gabriel took him. They saw a table filled with delicious food. Seated at the table were people without elbows. They tried to feed themselves, but could not.

"This is Hell," said Gabriel.

Then they saw the same scene, but this time the elbowless people happily fed each other.

"Heaven," said the old man.

Chris had cooked cheese bread and soup while we were gone, and now broke the bread and passed pieces to each of us. Before we fed our starving neighbor we had to describe him or her. The sun set. We decided not to hike, but instead made camp and went to bed early. Eyeing the clouds, we set up our tarp for the first time on the trip. After dinner we gazed at the stars.

Day 8: Sometime after midnight

The only part of my body not wrapped by the sleeping bag was my nose. I smelled rain, then felt the drops. Lord, I thought we had a deal on the rain issue. I tried to sleep. More raindrops. Only the faithless would go under that tarp, I thought. Winds picked up. I stretched my arm out of my cocoon and felt the sleeping bag's wet surface. Shit. So much for faith. I grabbed my sleeping bag, ground cloth, and pad, and dived under the tarp. Everyone crowded under the tarp and the exposed part of my bag got soaked.

The wind howled and shook the tarp; a few of the knots unraveled. If it kept flapping, the whole tarp would come undone and we'll all be screwed. I retied two of the knots, freezing rain pelting my body. My body quaked and I chattered, "This s...s...sucks."

Chris joined us after his tarp blew down. "Finish tying that knot and get your butt in here!" he yelled at me. But as soon as I secured the two knots, another one slipped undone. I think I heard either Maggie or Elisa struggle to retie it, but upon failing, Chris—minus his glasses and headlamp—knotted it for them. Someone cried.

The seven of us lay there and listened to the thunder and lightning. The wind sounded like a jet engine. I shivered inside my wet sleeping bag, and wished the trip was over.

Day 8: Sunrise

The sun saved us. It cascaded through the clouds. The winds and lightning subsided. We beat the night. In the interest of time, we skipped breakfast and started hiking. We were scheduled to meet another other group and do something called a "tyrolian traverse": crossing a large crevasse by rope.

We double-timed it through a huge V-shaped passage in a canyon wall, over slick-rock, and across a valley. It grew cold by the time we met up with the other group. They had been waiting for several hours, but seemed in good spirits. They put on a pot of coffee. We broke out some granola and chowed down, enjoying the warmth of coffee and company on a cold and blustery day. The groups' two leaders went off to survey the site of the traverse, while the rest of us hunkered down behind a rock that protected us from the wind.

Chris and the other group's leader decided that it was too cold and windy, as well as too late in the day, to do the traverse. This news sounded just fine to all of us. We packed up, and the two groups formed a column and hiked out. As we were cruising through a cactus-filled valley, pellets of snow bounced off our rain jackets. We quickened the pace to stay warm, but we were very low on water. There were no major sources of water in the area, so we scooped the precious little we could out of small pools puddling here and there in the rock.

Once we reached higher altitude, the pellets of snow became huge, fluffy flakes. Snow whipped sideways and lashed against our skin. The two groups split up to search for adequate camp sites. The euphoria I felt earlier in the day had worn off. I was exhausted, dehydrated, and cold.

Day 8: Cedar Mesa, early afternoon

We stopped to make camp. Even less water was left. Visibility through the blizzard maxed at barely fifteen feet. Maggie and Elisa searched for puddles of water. The rest of us worked on the tarp. With the tarp partially up, Dave and Jen huddled underneath it for warmth. Dangerously close to hypothermia, they shivered inside their bags. My fingers stiffened. My thoughts turned panicky; movements jerky.

I needed to calm down. In order for us to survive, we needed shelter and warm water. Someone started handing out thick crackers made with lard. After gobbling a few, I pulled myself together. Maggie and Elisa, now tucked under the tarp, handled the water with their bare hands. Adam, Chris, and I finished with the main tarp, and erected several solo tents to make the space large enough for all of us and our gear. We congratulated ourselves on making a "bomber" tent, and even managed to take a few pictures.

On my way to take a leak, I found a puddle containing close to six quarts of water, which doubled our supply. Unfortunately, the only way to transport it was to scoop it up with a plastic bag into a water bottle, and then transfer it into a dromedary. This procedure froze our fingers and got lots of dirt into the water. Nevertheless, we boiled two pots of water for hot cocoa, and I finally crawled into my sleeping bag. We ate cheese and crackers for dinner. The wind gusted. The top of the tarp collapsed under the weight of the snow. We pushed on the ceiling to support it, but snow cascaded down around us. This place smelled like a barn; none of us had bathed in ten days.

Chris took our mind off things by reading Dr. Seuss stories. It wasn't enough. Afraid of lying sleepless, with only the wind to listen to, we talked. Conversation carried us deep into the night, but even that comfort ended. So much snow accumulated that the tarp dipped and touched Adam's face. Arms and legs convulsed—fighting the snow and beating the tarp—until plaintive screams ordered people to calm down. We couldn't afford to tear down our own tarp—the only barrier between our exhausted bodies and hypothermia.

Day 9: Cedar Mesa, first light

"Wakey, wakey!" Chris's standard wake-up call met with obscenities. Today offered our final test: finding our way to our rendezvous point with Mark, the course director, and our final camp site.

I moved slower than everyone else, pausing to regain feeling in my hands every few minutes. I wore three pairs of socks (one polypropylene liner and two wool), but my toes still felt numb. I shivered beneath layers of clothes. I took a piss and it was almost orange, a sign of dehydration. After I finally finished packing my pack, Chris pulled out a map and pointed out our route. I hoped someone else paid attention because I could not concentrate.

We hiked.

Dave possessed a great sense of direction, and served as our navigator for most of the trip; only today he lacked the patience to take time and explain our route. Andy seemed to understand, but Jen and Maggie protested. They wanted to be absolutely sure about the route to be taken. Elisa did not complain, and I couldn't care less. I could scarcely think straight with that damn ringing behind my eyes.

Day 9: South Six-Shooter Region, mid-morning

This route was supposed to be easy: we would follow a ridge until hitting a dirt road. Unfortunately, the snow covered landmarks. We were frustrated and lost. Chris lingered about a quarter mile behind and observed us. We found the trail and headed down a hill. Once we reached the bottom, Chris caught up to us and told us to go back up the hill. He sat us down. "This time everyone needs to pay attention; I'm not going to stop you again." He went back over the fundamentals of topographic map navigation. He had us figure out where we were and where we wanted to go.

We figured it out. We travelled on a ridge leading to the foot of a large mesa (what looks like a pyramid with its top lopped off). We followed the dirt road to the foot of the mesa, then veered left around it. We would then enter a canyon by hiking down an indentation made by the flow of water. It would only be about three miles of hiking in the canyon before we reached our campsite. After that we would not have to carry our packs any more.

But that was getting way ahead of ourselves. Aside from a handful of nuts and dried fruit, we had not eaten. Our water supply was almost depleted. We hiked for an hour before we found any water. A few hundred yards off the path, we saw rock pocked with several puddles. We scooped carefully, but still ended up with brown water. Once we bottled some water, we mixed in handfuls of snow. If we had put only snow in our bottles, it would not have melted but sublimated—gone directly from solid to gas in the desert air.

After another mile or so of hiking we arrived at the base of the mesa. We stopped and happily ate the last of our food. Chris joined us and we pulled out the maps. Once everyone was crystal clear on the route we would take, he headed out. The other patrol was at the rim of the canyon, and we paused to give them room to maneuver. As we started the final leg, I knew exactly where we were going. Jen, who usually drifted in the middle or back of the pack when we hiked, led us. She took us down a ridge into the canyon, over a few slick-rock hills, and finally to our campsite. We cooked a great spaghetti dinner and drank hot chocolate. After the tarp was set up and dishes cleaned, both patrols sat around the campfire. We ate S'mores, while thawing socks and shoes that had frozen solid.

Day 10: South Six-Shooter Region, first light

Damn, it was freezing next morning! I ate a banana and started to limber up. I loaded my pack onto a large truck, and we began an eight-mile run. I started out at a quick pace, fearing the embarrassment of being the youngest in the patrol and coming in last, but I slowed to take in the canyons and spires drenched in early morning sunshine against a perfect blue sky.

"Leave no trace." Throughout the trip, we walked in each other's footsteps when passing through the fragile cryptobiotic soil. Chris had told us of native tribes who would run for days, leaving only one set of footprints. We copied them. "Leave no trace" means enjoying a wild place, and preserving it for others to enjoy. We cleaned our gear, and ate the biggest brunch I had ever seen. Then we met for one last talk and departed. It was then, as Mark said, the true Outward Bound journey began.

A MISSING PIECE: Family

My tongue,
every atom
of my blood,
form'd from
this soil,
this air...

"Not one assignment has taught me quite so much about myself as my memoir. It taught me to laugh at myself. I always had many 'hard' feelings about my experiences in Ohio. I was mad at my parents for taking me out there with them, and I held a grudge ever since. Writing my memoir helped me clear my head and my grudges."

Estelle Petri

A MISSING PIECE
by Judith Shaw

"I have cancer."

The words stung me as if I were bathing in scalding water. My life would no longer be as it once was.

Just returning from a Young Life retreat at Daytona Beach, Florida, I could not have been in any higher spirits, but all good things do come to an end. When the words left my mother's lips, I sat motionless against the couch wanting to slap myself. Maybe I would wake up from this horrendous dream and find myself back on the beach. Realizing that would not happen, I felt as if my jaw were wired shut; my throat tightened, but I was too stunned to cry. Words were still being spoken to me, but I could not ask questions or respond to anybody. The same question continuously ran through my head, "How could this be happening to me?" How could my mother have cancer?

I could not have asked for a more loving, caring, and nurturing mother. From the time we were informed, my brother and I grew significantly closer, and in some ways, he became like a second father, watching out for me, and showing concern for the entire family. The role he took on assisted my hard-working father who is dedicated to both his family and job. My father was torn between constant travel and the need for his presence at home. We had such confusing emotions stirring inside, different for each of us, and this did not make for easy discussion.

I felt I should act as though it did not bother me, as I believe most of my family did, and to this day still does. People build walls around themselves in order to act as though things are okay.

They plaster a fake smile across their faces when inside a heart yearns to cry out: "Help me!"

When the doctors notified her with the final diagnosis (one of the longest waiting periods we'd ever experienced), there was a significant amount of unexpected information. First of all, they said this cancer, which started in her colon, had now spread to her liver. It began to grow when she was in her thirties, but she never suspected a thing until she was forty-nine. Being a healthy person, always going to the doctor for check ups, and eating a healthy diet, she felt no need to ever suspect such a problem. When they informed us that the cancer was terminal, we were in shock.

It seemed as if I were in a dream; things were only getting worse. There was nowhere to turn. The only solution that seemed appealing was to hide until I could wake up, and then my life would be back to normal. My life seemed like a wall that was slowly crumbling, and once it picked up speed it would never stop until I was destroyed. These feelings inside of me must have been the same for everyone else, and worse for my mother. There was nothing that could be said or done to make me feel better, until the doctor mentioned remission.

After reaching the final diagnosis, the doctors were hopeful for remission. With chemotherapy, and her hopeful attitude, the future started to look good. Luckily, that was the case for quite some time, and there were absolutely no side effects from the treatments. My mom had a positive attitude that not only helped her, but also us. Since she felt well and still maintained her usual activities, things seemed normal. Not only were we there to offer love and support, two of her sisters also lived in neighboring towns. One of them always managed to take the time to accompany my mother for her weekly treatments. After a while, it was evident that there were some side effects, but these were minimal. She experienced more fatigue, and a slight loss of appetite, but nothing to cause any extreme fears. Most of the time, it was hard to imagine that she was actually a cancer patient.

Good things can come from any situation, no matter how bad. There were times I had to stop and think of some lessons that could be learned. Some positive insights from this situation could help make me a better person. Because few people have gone through this experience, they are not sure what to say or do. For the most part, I believe my family turned to each other for support, and used family and friends as a means of distraction.

When I felt lost and confused, I began to realize what my mother was experiencing was a hundred times worse, and I wanted to reach out to her. This experience was like riding an emotional rollercoaster. At times, things were excellent, and everybody was confident that remission was in the near future. Then there were the times when nothing worked, and hope dwindled. My heart felt like it could stop beating. Stunned and scared, I acted like an optimist. However, these times made us stronger.

It helped to place things in perspective. There are countless issues people get upset about that are way out of perspective when you realize what someone with cancer is living with. Being able to conquer everyday activities can be a struggle for a cancer patient. Slowly, I began to develop a new outlook on life and appreciate many things that I once took for granted. Going through such an experience opens your eyes. No amount of material items could ever make up for the pain and suffering we felt. But at the same time, we also developed into more well-rounded individuals.

The minimal side effects from the chemotherapy lasted for about eight months, and then things became noticeably worse. As her fatigue increased, my mother had to take a leave of absence from her part-time job at the school and concentrate on improving her condition. At this time, she continued to take on some tasks around the house in order to occupy her time. But she could rest if she felt overwhelmed. She also maintained the usual routine by getting up with me in the morning before school in order to keep things as normal as possible. It grew evident that the cancer was beginning to impact her life. It was harder for her to accomplish the things she often enjoyed doing.

As her weekly visits progressed, the doctors grew concerned and wondered about possible next steps. The chemotherapy was not showing such positive results anymore. One option was to visit Sloan Kettering Cancer Hospital in New York City, which was not such a problem since we lived in Connecticut and only had an hour's drive to the hospital. That helped us keep an optimistic outlook, but not for long. My mom and dad returned from a visit to Sloan Kettering with bad news: doctors felt little else could be done. The only next step for her was to enter the hospital to see if there would be any benefits by staying a week. That option ended up being unsuccessful, too.

As hard as it is to imagine, my mom maintained her hopeful spirits and radiated positive energy. Sometimes, that is the best thing; medication is not the only thing that will make you feel better. Many people offered their love and support. It was good to know that there were others out there offering her their prayers and good wishes.

Eventually her options were limited, and the best possible step was to increase all of her other medication and take her off chemotherapy since it no longer helped her. This course of action resulted in a drastic change in her appearance. My mom grew thin; her skin took on a yellowish tone. Her big, beautiful blue eyes now had dark circles. She was placed on such strong doses of medication that it was hard to imagine this woman was actually my mother. Our roles changed quickly. I was soon the one helping her do everything from sitting up to eating. It grew evident that hospice care was a necessity.

Soon lawyers began making visits to our house to complete her will, and she, along with my dad's help, made the decision not to go on life support...and not to enter the hospital. These decisions were rather depressing because it was clear that her final days were approaching. As this news spread, everyone insisted on doing something to assist us. People made dinners for our family, and would come over just to spend time with my mother, even if she did not actually know who they were. She had a hard time recognizing her immediate family, and did so more by voice recognition than by sight. Her condition continued to worsen.

My mother had five sisters living all over the United States—California to Tennessee. They flew to Connecticut to be with her and to help out. One sister, especially, helped. Being a nurse, she was able to take control of some things herself, making the in-home hospice care a weekly, as opposed to daily, necessity. Having family taking care of my mother made us all feel better. This sister organized all of her medication and kept track of when she needed it. All of the others assisted, too. My mom could no longer bathe herself, or do anything on her own, so someone was always needed. Therefore, all her sisters slept at our house, and someone was always awake to keep a twenty-four-hour vigil over her. All of this assistance helped to ease our nerves, especially my father's, who wanted the absolute best for my mom.

This constant attention was necessary for about two weeks. My mom needed to receive injections of an extremely powerful medication that made her rather incoherent. Because the decision was made that she would not be placed on life support, and would remain on as few drugs as possible, it was evident that her time was growing near. My brother made trips home every weekend, obviously aware of the limited time we had left with our mother. These days were the hardest part of the entire ordeal for me. I continued to go to school every day, and there was always the fear that, when I came home, she would no longer be with us. That was such a horrendous feeling, living the rest of my life without my mother.

On Saturday April 1, 1995, we were going about our activities and trying to live with an optimistic attitude. I had just adopted a four-month-old German Shepherd puppy, which my dad allowed as a way of bringing something upbeat into our household. After picking up the puppy, I brought her over to a friend's house where I spent the day. My friends and I were trying to make plans for that night. When I got home to a house full of people preparing dinner, I somehow made the decision not to go out that night, but rather stay home and spend time with my family.

It was not until that night that I let my true emotions show. I followed my brother to my mom's bedside, so we could share some time together with her. When I sat down and tried to talk to her, I lost all control and ran back to the kitchen hysterically crying. As two of my aunts tried to comfort me, they both began to cry. It finally set in that I would not have a mother for much longer.

After calming down and socializing with everybody, I went to bed—the only place I felt safe. Waking up periodically throughout the night, I noticed that downstairs there seemed to be a lot of commotion, but half asleep, I fell right back to sleep again. At six o'clock in the morning, my dad and brother entered my room. Hearing the door open, I realized they had something to tell me.

This was the dreaded moment, but it almost did not seem real until the words were actually said. The instant they sat on my bed my heart raced and I shook uncontrollably. "Mommy passed away this morning." My dad explained that she went peacefully, and tried to convince me that it was the best thing. He also said that she was still downstairs. If I felt comfortable, I could say my final goodbyes. I don't think there was a "right" or "wrong" thing to do, but I did not go down-stairs. I stayed in bed for about two hours thinking and listening to the talk and commotion below my bedroom. Finally proceeding downstairs, I was greeted with tears, hugs, and the support of all. After a while, everybody left, and my dad, brother, and I had some time alone.

My eyes tear-stained and swollen, I went to my favorite spot on the couch in our den, curled up, and drifted off to sleep. When I woke about half an hour later, I realized I had to notify my friends. Making the first telephone call was extraor-dinarily awkward; I was not sure exactly what to say. When my best friend's voice answered on the other end, I instantly broke down and mumbled the words. She began to cry as well, and neither of us could say much. She said she would make the rest of the calls for me, and then come pick me up. Not long after, she showed up with puffy, blood-shot eyes, and attempted to comfort me and the rest of my family. Later, we went for a long drive and talked. Then we went to another friend's house where I was greeted by all of my friends. They were full of support, bringing flowers and sympathy cards, but nothing lifted my spirits.

Later that day when I went home, I saw there had been a tremendous number of visitors bringing food and offering all they could; even the local supermarket had delivered all kinds of food and flowers. We made all of the arrangements for the funeral. Someone had to write the eulogy, and people were asked to do read-ings. My mom, not being too involved in organized religion, had asked not to have a fancy funeral. Instead, she wanted a memorial Mass and to be cremated. I took the entire week off from school because I was too distraught to concentrate. My friends made a tremendous effort to comfort me.

Throughout the week, we had people flying and driving to Connecticut for the funeral, which was on a Tuesday. The church was full of students from my high school, teachers, family, and friends. I will never forget the feeling I had in my stomach. There were so many thoughts running through my head as I walked down the aisle at the beginning of the Mass. I was afraid of bringing the gifts up for Holy Communion. I was so upset and nervous. How could I ever go in front of all of these people? Trying to control myself throughout the Mass was a tremen-dous feat. I was sobbing from the beginning all the way to the end. We stood in the back of the church before Mass. People entering would come and give their condolences. I was able to handle it until one of my friends since kindergarten gave me a hug. I instantly began to cry in his arms. From that point on, I had little control over my emotions. The feeling I had inside when I was bringing up the communion gifts was horrendous. I could feel all of the eyes looking at me, but I could not look up. Instead I gazed down at my feet, trying to convince myself that I was strong enough to make it. Taking quick glances around the church, I saw that there was not one dry eye. The Mass was the saddest time of my life.

My brother, cousins, and I were the first to arrive at our house after the service. It did not take long for everybody else to arrive. Soon our house buzzed with people setting out food and greeting guests. Everywhere you turned there were people. It was a beautiful day, so most people spent the afternoon outside. That part of the day was the easiest; with so many guests, it was like an escape. All of my friends spent the day with me, and helped to distract me by talking about all the happy times we had shared in the past.

As evening came, the crowd of mourners thinned out. There were many people cleaning up. When the house was empty with the exception of most of our family, I went out with one of my cousins and my brother and spent the evening with them to get our minds off things, even if for just a while.

I cried myself to sleep that night. I began thinking about the new life that now lay ahead of me. Even though I love my father with all of my heart, I could not imagine life without my mother. There is such a special bond between a mother and daughter that nothing could ever replace.

The next day, Wednesday, we had to begin making arrangements for the burial of ashes at the cemetery in our town. We also had to decide exactly what we wanted on her gravestone. My dad wanted all of our opinions. I described the kind of stone and decoration we should have. My dad got what I suggested, a pink granite stone with flowers etched in it and the words "Barbara Shaw Beloved Wife and Mother 1945-1995."

The burial took place on the following Saturday. We kept it rather private; just family and close friends. Once again, I found it difficult to control my emotions. This ceremony ended everything. We were now burying my mother. Now we only had our memories, and what she had taught us, to fill the missing piece in our lives.

Going back to school was awkward because everybody knew what happened, but they really did not know what to say. Then, when I would go home, the house would seem empty. I could tell it was going to take a long time to get used to. The new life I now had to take on was difficult. There was so much change so suddenly. There was no possible way to brace for these circumstances because there was no way to judge my feelings. As a way to cope, I joined a group at my high school for students who had lost parents. The five of us met together weekly with a social worker who helped us deal with our emotions, which changed on a daily basis. One thing she stressed was that there is no recipe for how you are supposed to feel. Everyone deals with this sort of loss in different ways. There is nothing anyone can tell you about how you are supposed to feel. What I found best to do was just think that my mom would not want me to be depressed; she would want me to carry on her spirit and what she had taught me.

Often it is not until someone is gone that you realize how much you miss them, and you yearn for them to be back and a part of your life again. I do not think there are enough words to express how much I miss her. It is not something easily described. The only people who can truly understand are those who have gone through it. Now, I can only find comfort in the fact that she is resting peacefully in heaven, and one day our family will be reunited. That time will not come for a long time, but it is something to think about. For the time being, she can look down at us, and see how she has affected our lives. We all miss her very much and think about her constantly.

Although there is a missing piece in my life now, I have changed because of all of these circumstances. In the end, I have become a stronger person. When I am feeling down, I have to think of things that I learned. I try to carry on all that she taught me. She was such a wonderful lady. I will never forget what she made my family. My advice to everybody is to express your love for all your family members, and make it known to them. Life is too short. Don't wait before it's too late to say what you want to say.

LEAVING
by Valerie Gatzke

"Things won't be that different," she said, but I knew she was lying. Things just wouldn't be the same without my dad. My mother's words bounced in and out of my thoughts as I pressed my forehead against the window pane. The glass was foggy from the condensation of my breath, and I used my finger to write my name in the blemished area. I looked out sadly at the driveway below. The moving truck was already here and ready to move my mom, sister, and me to a faraway place. Memories of the great times with my dad would be all that was left behind.

It was shocking to learn the news of my parents' divorce, but even more difficult to learn that I would be moving with my mother. She had chosen to move to a new house about thirty minutes away—thirty minutes from my school, thirty minutes from my friends, thirty minutes from my father.

It was my last day of eighth grade and my last day at the only home I knew. Although my mother assured me that I would like my new house just as well, I didn't want to leave. Sighing, I plopped face-down on my bed and closed my eyes. I thought about the night when I passed my parents' bedroom and heard someone crying from behind the closed door. It was my father. So upset, he had retreated in solitude. My first thought was to push the door open and run and throw my arms around him. I wanted him to know that he still had his little girl. But for some reason, my feet wouldn't move. I felt helpless in a world of confusion and sadness. I didn't know what to do, and the longer I stood in the dark hallway, the more embarrassed I felt. Finally, I ran to my room to hide. That was the only time I had heard a man cry. It was the saddest thing in the world. Despite the pity I felt for my father, my intentions were to move with my mother.

So that day, I was permitted to stay home from school and help with the moving. I awoke to hollering men and a loud rumbling. I jumped out of bed and darted to the window. Below, three men gathered around the back of a large truck. The truck was as long as our driveway, and it advertised the phrase: THE ONLY WAY TO MOVE. The men wore sleeveless t-shirts and jeans, and stood rugged and powerful. I heard my mother's voice from downstairs, but it was too faint to comprehend. I stood by the window and surveyed the action below. The back of the truck was wide open now, and I could see the empty floor inside. One of the guys was sitting there, smoking a cigarette, and talking away to the other two. Is this what my mother was paying them for?

Just then, I heard the front door open, and saw my mother flutter out, smiling and waving her hands at the three strangers. They seemed to respond happily to her cheery disposition, and immediately rose to greet her. After handshakes and brief conversing, the three strangers followed my mother into the house. The man that was smoking casually tossed his burning cigarette onto our lawn before stepping inside. His action irritated me, but I was too worried about other things to let it get to me.

I puzzled over what seemed important at the time. Would I make any friends at my new school? Would I fit in? What if everyone laughed at me because I was new? God, who would I sit with at lunch? Here I was worrying about the setup of a lunch table, while my family was on the verge of breaking apart. I couldn't help but feel angry. It was an inner anger though, and one that I didn't know was there until many years later.

I quickly got dressed and finished packing my things. I had done most of the packing the night before, so it only took a few minutes to finish. I hated to see the contents of my room tucked away in cardboard boxes and trash bags. The walls, which were once covered with posters and paintings, stared back at me now with white, unfriendly eyes. I would be glad when this was all over.

But who was I kidding? The changes I would have to face wouldn't end after moving to a new house and going to a different school. No, my mother was leaving my father forever, and by circumstance, so was I. That presented me with a life-long change. Was I ready to make a decision like that? I thought, no I wasn't, but somehow my mother knew what was best for me (or so she reminded me). I was going to have to make the best of it.

I decided to step outside for some fresh air. Mom probably wouldn't notice that I was gone anyway. She was too busy showing the movers around to each room, telling them what to put in the truck, and what to leave for my dad. I thought she was being a tad greedy because I noticed that almost everything in our house was coming with us. But at this point, I couldn't be bothered with what belonged to whom.

Outside I felt suddenly sick as I looked around at the empty deck. To the right and up three steps was our swimming pool, rippling and dancing with sunlight. I bent down and dipped my foot daintily into the water—still a little cool for a swim. I sat down, dangling my legs over the edge.

The view from our deck was picturesque. Trees of every kind arranged themselves casually across an emerald terrain that spanned an acre and a half. Sunflowers and colorful gardens brightened the yard. To the right of the pool was a pond shaped like a figure eight, full of goldfish and lily pads. The fish pond, as my family called it, was enclosed in a square area made by tall bushes. The squared-in area was mulched, and on one side, there was a long, white bench. Over the center of the pond arched a wooden bridge. Many a day, my younger sister and I had sat on that bridge, leaning over the water, trying to scoop the fish into our small hands. The fish pond was my favorite place, for its beauty brought me peace and comfort throughout my childhood.

I was definitely going to miss this place. I looked out across my backyard, shielding my eyes from the early sun. The trees softly whistled in the breeze, and the sunflowers in the garden swayed. They seemed to smile at me, and I felt a little better. I stood there gazing, allowing the noise from inside the house and the nearby traffic to disappear softly into the humid morning. There's something beautiful about a big backyard. I remembered the summer days when, after a long day of swinging, a gentle voice called me inside, and summoned me to bed. I hated going to bed, but I knew that the next day brought more play time. Childhood is carefree, and a time to enjoy the beauty of a big backyard. I often think of those days as my happiest.

Looking around, I felt great. Already the sky hummed with the chatter of birds, and the warm sun poured out over the soft grass. This would be the last day to see the beauty of my home, and I wanted to remember it happily. For a while, I just lay in the smooth grass and gazed up at the sapphire sky. After living at that house for ten years, I never fully appreciated the beauty of it until it was time to leave—time to grow up and leave my childhood behind.

I got up slowly, pulling two handfuls of grass with me. As I walked around to the front of the house, I casually dropped the grass with every step. From the corner of my eye, I spotted a rock of some sort peeking out from under the overgrown shrubbery. I picked it up and held it up to the bright sun. It was just a piece of white quartz, but I loved the way it shimmered in the sunlight. I stuffed it in my pocket, feeling happy that I would have something to remind me of that beautiful place I called home.

When I opened the front door, I was nearly trampled on by three immense men—the moving men. They were carrying an antique desk as if it weighed only ten pounds. They moved swiftly out the door, and I set out to find my mother. She wasn't far behind the movers, yelling this and that, about this antique and that antique. She ran up to me and told me to pack the dishes away for her.

As I packed the dishes into a large cardboard box, I listened to our furniture being hauled out and crammed into the immense truck. Would Mom leave anything for Dad? It seemed like everything was coming with us. I knew that if my father had been there, there would have been disputes over what was his. But dad was in the dark about the entire move. I knew that when 5:30 p.m. came, he would walk through the door and find an empty house. The thought of him walking into the kitchen, wondering where his family was, broke my heart in a million pieces. He would stray into each room, hoping for the reassurance that his daughters might suddenly run to his side. But that wouldn't happen. He might call a relative or neighbor in search of some answer, but their reply would be silence. He would be all alone, surrounded by barren walls and desolate rooms. The thought of my father's encounter later that evening brought tears to my eyes.

The dishes I was carefully wrapping became white blurs, and one slipped from my hand and shattered to the floor. The tears fell from my eyes, stinging and burning down my face. From behind, I heard the shuffling of the movers' feet as they slid a mattress across the kitchen tiles. I wheeled around to observe their action. My eyes met the taller one, and I looked away before he could comment on my crying. I felt so embarrassed, being fourteen and crying so uncontrollably. I certainly wasn't a baby anymore, and I had to be the strongest now. But I felt so bad for Dad.

Just then, Mom whizzed around the corner carrying some papers. She stopped abruptly at the sight of the smashed plate on the floor. Her mouth opened to say something, but when I glanced up with teary eyes, her expression changed. I explained that the dish had slipped from my hand, and she seemed to understand. Before I could say anything else, she pulled me into her warm embrace. We were both silent for a moment, and then she pulled away and brought her hand up to brush my face. The warmth of her hand made me feel secure.

I wanted so much to tell her my feelings about my father, but I thought that she would take my words to mean that I didn't support her decision to leave. Honestly, I didn't feel she was handling the situation in the best way, but I figured she knew what she was doing. I had to trust her. Mom smiled at me with that "Don't worry, I'm your mother, and everything will be fine" look, and I felt a little better. The movers were back in the kitchen now, and she danced off down the hall with them, uttering a list of orders. I turned and went in search of a broom.

After cleaning up my mess, I went back to the dishes. Jen, my sister, sneaked up behind me and yelled, "Boo!" I jumped and nearly dropped another plate. Jen stood there laughing and slapping my arm, content that her little joke had worked.

I had to laugh, too. She took a place beside me and started boxing the expensive china. Her small hands worked clumsily to organize the dishes. We were silent for a few minutes, content to finish the task together. I glanced at the clock on the stove. It was eleven o'clock.. The sun was beaming through the kitchen and creating patterns on the bare floor. The air was warm except for the occasional breeze that fluttered through the kitchen window and cooled our faces. Jen and I worked fast, and finally the last dish took its place in the box.

By now, everything in the living room, dining room, and kitchen was sitting in boxes awaiting the trip. We stood there gazing at our consolidated possessions being taken from their rightful home. Signs like FRAGILE and HANDLE WITH CARE made the harsh reality of moving clearer.

My sister and I didn't want to start at a new school, or make new friends, or ride a new bus. I glanced over at her and saw a look of anxiety and sadness. We didn't want "new." We didn't want to leave because we were scared to death. Somewhere in our hearts though, that feeling had buried itself under an even bigger fear: the fear of losing our mother and her acceptance. I had always been closer to my mother growing up. She made me laugh, gave me advice, and somehow always made me feel better about any situation. I felt a need to stay by her side no matter what sacrifices I had to make. Even if it meant not having anyone to sit with at lunch. I didn't want my parents to get a divorce. I didn't want to move away from my friends. But I would swallow my worries and make the best of it.

It took us almost an hour to find my cat. She had disappeared the moment the moving truck arrived in our driveway and stubbornly hid herself away. Her name was Shatzi, which means "sweetheart" in German. My mother had proudly named her, after having taken six years of the language in school. My sister and I roamed the backyard carrying bells and cat food, trying to coax Shatzi out of her hiding place.

She finally peeked her head out of an overgrown bush and waddled slowly to our feet. I scooped her into my arms and carefully placed her in a large cardboard box lined with newspaper. We had to tape the top of the box securely, so she couldn't escape, and I felt bad when I heard the continuous high-pitched meowing. Shatzi was just as scared as I was. Neither of us wanted to be taken from our home or our big backyard where we both played many summer days in the dancing sunlight. I felt guilty because I was doing the same thing to her that my mom was doing to my sister and me.

My guilty feelings soon were replaced with a dozen butterflies turning in my stomach. The last box had been moved into the truck, and I watched the movers pull the back door down and climb into the front of the truck. They started the loud engine and gave a signal. It was time to leave. While my sister and I searched for the cat, my mom had double-checked that we had packed everything. She came slowly down the stairs and stopped at the front door where I stood looking down at the ground. Sighing, she laid a caring hand on my shoulder, and my sister and I followed her out of the house. None of us looked back.

As we pulled out of the driveway at 505 Berryman's Lane, I thought of the great times my family had in that house. I thought of playing tag in the tall grass and dancing through the sprinklers in the heat of August. I thought about the four of us, standing outside, taking a family picture on Easter. That was when the tears came.

DIAGNOSING MY DAD'S DISEASE
by Christopher Jones

"I need an endoscopy? Celiac disease? I could die?" These were the words I heard as I wandered from the kitchen to the dining room where my dad was on the telephone talking to his doctor. I sat down at the dining room table, tears welled up in my eyes, and I felt a heaviness in my chest. I realized that my father could actually die. I said very quietly, but just loud enough for my dad to hear, "It was just supposed to be an ulcer. Ulcers are harmless. They're curable. People can't die from ulcers. Can they?"

My dad came over and sat beside me, and I noticed the eyes that once had a sparkle to them were now swollen and overflowing with tears. This man, my dad, who in my eyes was immune to sickness and lived everyday to the fullest, could actually be taken from my life forever. I cried selfishly, "Don't die dad. You can't do this to me. You promised me you would be with me forever. How can you do this to me?"

I heard no apologies, no assurances, and no promises—he just walked out of the room.

"Endoscopy, celiac disease, I need information," I said to the librarian. She pointed me in the direction of medical textbooks. As I read the procedure for an endoscopy, it seemed fairly safe, and I found myself looking for the mortality rate which was only 0.03%. "This seems harmless enough." It didn't dawn on me to think how devastating the results of this simple procedure could be, the results which ultimately became my preoccupation with death.

My life was complicated enough just dealing with my parents' divorce. I never knew where I would be on any given day. I remember being "kidnapped" by my mother from my day care center, the only consistent environment I knew. I was taken the following morning to a new day care center. As I looked at the stark white walls, the newly waxed floors, and the strange, unfamiliar faces, I felt as if I were in a stupor. I hung my head low, closed my weeping eyes, and envisioned my old day care center, wallpapered with pictures of red houses, bright yellow suns, stick-figure parents, and backyards finger-painted in greens and browns. Even though I was bribed with all the sweets I could eat and all the horses I could ride, I didn't want to live with my mother, her new husband, and my two stepbrothers. I wanted things the way they were. I wanted my own parents, a room to myself, and to be number one.

After what seemed like months, but in reality was only four days, my mom and dad agreed to joint custody. I was going to be shared by both my parents and experience what all my friends said to be "the best of both worlds!" At first I was the center of attention in each separate household, but this got old fast. Just as I was getting involved in the daily kick ball game with my friends in the neighborhood, either my father or mother would pick me up and bring me to the house where I was scheduled to be.

One night while resting in bed, I knew this routine had to stop. I had to make a decision on where I was going to live permanently. I chose my dad, justifying it with knowing that my mom had her own family, but my dad only had me.

As the years progressed, I became overprotective of my dad and was the sole companion in his life. His only goal in life was my happiness and my well-being. It got to the point where I became overly dependent on my dad's reaction to my school work, extracurricular activities, and my feelings. I was selfishly agitated when my dad came down with a simple twenty-four-hour virus and was not able to attend my tennis tournament. I needed the encouragement that my dad always gave to me. This reassurance became a necessity to succeed in all my endeavors.

"Christopher, when you get home from school today, I have something very important to discuss with you," my dad said to me as I was leaving the house. I sleepwalked through the entire school day and made myself sick by worrying about what my dad was going to tell me. I knew it was going to be bad news by the tone of his voice. I reluctantly walked in the door and sat on the sofa next to my dad.

He proceeded to tell me that he was in love with Donna, my best friend's mother, and unbeknownst to me, they had been seeing each other for quite a while. He went on to tell me how we were all going to be a "family." I believe the look on my face was enough for my dad to see my disapproval. I felt betrayed, and I wasn't going to be part of his so-called "family." In spite of my demands on my dad, life went on, and I found myself being "forced" into a new family. My self-centered and monstrous thoughts even surprised me.

When I questioned why I fought this relationship so much, I could only come up with one thing—the only true family I knew was my dad, and I wanted it back!

I often wondered why I couldn't let my dad be happy; why I had to be number one; why I felt angry. I knew I had another option to this problem. I could go live with my mom, but I knew that wouldn't work because she too would have to share herself with her husband and my two stepbrothers. I was in a dilemma, and I saw no way out of this situation. Unfortunately, something beyond my imagination occurred. It changed my life.

"Dad, are you okay?" I asked, while knocking on the bathroom door. It was four in the morning, and I heard someone running back and forth from what sounded like my dad's bedroom to the bathroom. This sound lasted all night. I felt as if I were in a twilight sleep, subconsciously aware of my surroundings, but unable to keep my eyes opened.

"I'm sick Chris, really sick, and I feel so weak. This diarrhea just won't stop. Go back to sleep so you can get up for school tomorrow. I'll be okay."

I could faintly hear my dad talking to me through the bathroom door. I went back to bed and became aware of a sick, appalling smell coming from the hallway, a smell that unfortunately I became accustomed to in the months ahead. After a few weeks, I could no longer smell the horribly pungent odor, not because it was gone, but because my senses had adjusted to it.

I stepped into the hospital elevator and was quite frustrated when it stopped on every floor to pick up yet another visitor whose arms were filled with an abundance of long-stem red roses, assorted boxes of candies, and Get Well Soon mylar balloons. I chuckled to myself as a few of them were still putting the finishing touches on their greeting cards, licking the gum flaps on the envelopes. As I got off the elevator, a feeling of exhaustion overwhelmed me. My head was throbbing. My eyes were so tired that I was unable to focus on my surroundings. My arms were barely strong enough to hold the boxes filled with pictures of special moments my dad and I had shared. And my rubbery legs felt as if they had just run five miles.

I walked along the hallway to my dad's room and saw an emaciated man dressed in a bland, standard-issue hospital gown. It took me a moment, but I realized this was my dad. Just as I had lifted my dad's spirits and heard his familiar one-of-a-kind chuckle, one of his many doctors walked in. Worry flickered across my dad's eyes as he was told that he needed to be ruled out for HIV. I instantaneously felt this lump in my throat and a nauseous feeling in my stomach. I started to tremble and thought if my dad was HIV positive, then I most assuredly would be, too. After all, we shared the same toilet seat, at times used the same eating utensils, and lately I had been assisting him with bathing, dressing, and eating. I wished that I had paid closer attention to the lesson in school pertaining to HIV and AIDS, but I was so sure I would never be in that position.

I knew my mom was overprotective and sometimes a little too caring, but she actually went ballistic when I told her my dad was being tested for HIV. Not only did she have my dad dying from full-blown AIDS, but I too was threatened with death. I told her that I had questioned one of my dad's doctors and he assured me I was not at risk to become HIV positive.

He informed me of a study that involved nonsexual household contacts of patients with AIDS or AIDS-related complex (ARC). All the contacts had lived in the same household with a patient for more than three months and had shared facilities and household items. They carried on personal interactions such as assisting the patient with dressing, bathing, and eating. There was only one child out of sixty-eight children and thirty-three adults who was found to have signs of HIV infection. This child was the daughter of two IV drug abusers, and it was felt the child most likely had been affected prenatally.

When the doctor asked me if I understood everything he just explained, I raised my eyebrows and said, "Somewhat. I would like to know the difference between AIDS and ARC." He explained that ARC was a group of chronic signs and symptoms manifested by people belonging to groups with an increased incidence of AIDS, but who do not manifest the typical infections that characterize the full-blown syndrome. He went on to describe some of the signs and symptoms of ARC, which included weight loss, intermittent fever, general body weakness, apathy, and chronic diarrhea, all of which my dad possessed.

I felt disillusioned when he told me a more severe manifestation of ARC was the wasting syndrome characterized by progressive weight loss (my dad went from 162 pounds to 114 pounds), fever, night sweats, or diarrhea, persisting for more than three months. My dad had been suffering from all of these symptoms for more than six months. I watched my mom roll her eyes as I was clarifying the doctor's explanation of AIDS. Even though I was overcome with relief, my mom did not share the same feeling. She told me she was not satisfied with the mere statistics of one study and wanted me tested for HIV. Luckily my rational, calm, and collected stepfather, Mike, intervened and put things in perspective. We were going to await the results of my dad's test and then go on from there.

Several days later, I walked into my dad's empty hospital room, a room that was my second home, a room filled with thermometers, blood pressure cuffs, and IV stands. There were cards painted with sniffling faces, perky flowers, and the Lord's prayer tacked to a bulletin board that needed to be replaced. Above the wall, attached to a dangling nail, was a clock, outlined with bold-faced hands, making a nerve-wracking ticktock. I stretched out on the bed feeling the comfort of the foam-rubber, egg-crate cushion against my back and glanced over to the bedside table. My eyes wandered around the room until they focused on hospital letterhead which was entitled, "HIV RESULTS." I skimmed the paper as I felt an adrenaline rush until I came across the words, "HIV-negative." As I gave a sigh of relief, I no longer felt the loud thumping of my heart. After perusing the rest of the paper, I looked over to the other bed, which was soon to be occupied by yet another sick patient. So many patients came and went, but my dad still remained.

When my dad finally returned from all his testing, he seemed to be in a stupor, not even acknowledging my presence in the room. Over and over again he whispered, "Celiac sprue disease, celiac sprue disease. They now think I have celiac sprue disease. Do you believe this, Chris? First, I'm overwrought with worry about being HIV positive, and now that fiasco is over, they say I have celiac sprue disease—whatever the hell that is! What's next? Cancer? Death?"

The day finally came when my dad was released from the hospital. One would think I would feel overjoyed, but it really was not much different from the lifestyle I had been living for the past few weeks. The hospital room was now my own living room and dining room, overflowing with IV poles, extension cords, electrical adapters, alcohol wipes, syringes, backup pumps, and bandages thrown everywhere. We even had our own "private greenhouse," alive with plants and flowers camouflaging the smell of sickness.

I filled my oversized canvas book bag with pamphlets and books about celiac sprue disease. It seemed strange that this was such an unheard-of disease, yet there was a ton of information. I actually needed an interpreter for all the medical mumbo-jumbo. The information could have been written in another language. I just couldn't comprehend it. I called my mom, a medical transcriptionist, and set up some time to scrutinize all the information I had gathered. After twelve hours of inflating my brain with celiac disease facts and details to the point of explosion, I reluctantly went back to my dad's house to try to educate him on this catastrophic disease that had transformed him into a "walking corpse."

I defined celiac sprue disease as a chronic intestinal malabsorption disorder caused by intolerance to gluten. His next question mirrored my question. "What the heck is gluten? How can I have an intolerance to gluten if I have never heard of it, and I am sure I have never eaten it? Those doctors misdiagnosed me."

I defined gluten by suggesting he pretend that wheat, oats, and rye vanished from the face of the earth. Then I told him that we needed to change our eating habits to a gluten-free diet, and create a gluten-free kitchen. Easier said than done. Gluten is found in almost everything: commercial soups, sauces, ice creams, hot dogs, hamburgers, etc., and also used as a filler in many prepared foods and medications. Patients with celiac sprue disease need detailed lists of food-stuffs to avoid, and they need expert advice from a dietician familiar with the problems of celiac disease. Little did we know how much we would struggle to master new ways of shopping, cooking, and eating. I remember spending three hours in a food store just reading labels, making sure the gluten ingredients did not appear on the label!

I asked why this had to happen to my dad, and then remembered the words of a celiac sufferer who once consoled my dad, "Thank goodness it's celiac sprue. Thank goodness it's not cancer or mental illness or cystic fibrosis."

In spite of following a strict and monotonous gluten-free diet, my dad continued to suffer. Spending eighteen hours a day sitting on a firm toilet seat, and counting tiles on the bathroom wall, became a habitual way of life for him. He would come out only to change a "feeding bag" that was hooked to a tube routing its way into his chest, a tube that administered nutrients beyond minimum normal requirements in an attempt to replace nutritional deficiencies.

Nursing personnel came and went as the weeks progressed. They would check the catheter site, take weekly blood testing, and monitor my dad's vital statistics. Depending on the results of all the tests, he would either get an increase in a vitamin, or a decrease in a medication, or just be left alone. If he became too weak, and his vital statistics deviated from the norm, he would enter the hospital for a day or two for hydration and more monitoring. It was on his third hospital admission that he finally requested a second opinion on his disease. He based his request on the fact that all the material printed on celiac sprue disease and its gluten-free diet asserted that, when gluten is taken from a celiac's diet for a period of time, the patient should either improve, or go into complete remission. My dad did neither.

Before allowing another doctor to perform a multitude of tests only to "guess" at another diagnosis, my dad requested a trial of corticosteroids. He had read about the benefits of steroids and wanted one last try to end his continuous diarrhea. The corticosteroid therapy was initiated, but was ruinous to my dad. He was unable to tolerate even the lowest of doses. He became nervous and jumpy. His face took on the appearance of a chipmunk. His abdomen was swollen with fluid and was covered with purplish patches, seemingly from the injection sites. He became obsessed with the complications of steroid therapy, which included glaucoma, cataracts, softening of the bones, etc. He became preoccupied with cleanliness. His everyday ritual was to have me dust the entire house with a "white glove" inspection. The sound of the vacuum became more familiar to my ears than the sound of the TV. He would pace the diameter of the living room rug, searching for even the tiniest of dirt specks. He even managed to destroy the long-awaited relationship with his girlfriend, Donna. This once serene and levelheaded man became a monster, and I had had enough.

For months I felt as if a volcano were lying dormant in the pit of my stomach, and it was only a matter of time before it erupted. The time finally came. I held nothing back. I was tired of being the victim of my dad's irritability and depression. I let him have it. "Who do you think you are, Dad? Do you think you are the only one suffering from this disease? I am sick and tired of eating your gluten-free diet. I am disgusted with the filthy, repugnant-smelling toilet. I don't want to change any more diarrhea-stained sheets. I want to go to school, and not have to come right home just to wait until you fall asleep, so I can concentrate on my homework. I feel sorry for you Dad, but I want my father back. I need communication. I am tired of being your hostage. Stop diagnosing yourself and stop medicating yourself. It's time for a second opinion."

We found a new doctor at The Johns Hopkins Hospital. His expertise immediately ruled out celiac sprue disease and the "God-awful diet." He gradually decreased the corticosteroids over the course of many weeks. Various tests were administered that seemed to indicate a bacterial overgrowth. Before this could be confirmed, by some miracle, the symptoms began to disappear. The episodes of diarrhea began to decrease, and my dad improved. The day ultimately came when the chest tube that tied him to life could be removed.

It has been two years since the "reincarnation" of my dad and the "resurrection" of my normal teenage life. My dad and I had travelled a rough and rocky road, and had finally arrived at our final destination—living life to the fullest. There were still times when my dad would have to run to the bathroom, but those times were few and far between. It was those times that reminded us that he was only in remission, and not cured from his final diagnosis of "secretory diarrhea secondary to collagenous sprue," a disease that carries the same signs and symptoms of celiac sprue disease, the only difference being one could eat gluten.

It was an uphill battle for my dad to return to normal. He did daily exercises to restore the strength of his muscles. He rode an exercise bike a mile a day, timing the ride on where he was in a book he was reading. He sought the church again, and was accepting of support from friends and relatives. Against all odds, he again became my dad, a dad no longer self-absorbed, closed off, grandiose, or out of touch with his immediate surroundings. I, on the other hand, felt ready to make a much needed change in my life. I was going to live with my mom. She had been there for my dad and me, even though she never pressured me to live with her. This was my way of "paying her back."

Somehow, being number one no longer is of importance. Somehow, sharing myself with others has become a craving. I find myself wondering if my new-found feelings are due to my dad's near death experience, or are just a part of growing up. Somehow I believe I have been affected by both. My nightmare is finally over, and I am more than ready to accept whatever life has in store for me.

GRANDMA
by Dha wool Chung

"Here is your allowance for the month. Don't spend too much money on clothes."

"Don't worry about it. I won't."

"I almost forgot to give your grandmother her allowance."

"I don't understand why she needs one. She doesn't buy anything or go out with the money."

"It's what I want to do, and when your parents turn old, it's the right thing to do in Korea."

"Mother, here is your allowance for this month. I'm sorry it's not much."

"Dong na dong na."

We weren't sure what my grandmother was trying to say, but it sounded as if she was calling out my father's name in Korean. It was the only word she said after the stroke. I remember when my grandmother gave me one hundred won a day when I was in nursery school. With it, I could buy only a lollipop. A chocolate bar cost about three hundred won, so I never got to eat one. One day I really wanted to eat one. Why not just get one without giving the money? I went into the small grocery store by my house.

"How much is the chocolate bar?"

"It's three hundred won."

"Oh."

As soon as he turned away, I put the bar in my pocket and ran out as fast as I could. When I was safe in my room, I reached for the bar with my shaking hands. And they kept on shaking. They shook until I knew I had dropped the candy bar at the store. I felt really dumb, ashamed, and was glad I didn't have to eat it. The next day I had to go to the same store to get something for my grandmother. As soon as I opened the door, I saw the clerk glaring at me with scary eyes.

"Hi, didn't you leave something yesterday?"

I was numb. Numb to the body and the mind. How did he know I tried to steal?

"I said, did you drop something, like a chocolate bar? Or maybe other things."

"No, I don't think I dropped anything. Maybe I'll go home and think about it."

I ran like a rabbit running away from a hungry tiger. I found out it was useless. By dinner time, my grandmother had found out what I had done. The clerk at the store had phoned her about the incident.

"Dha wool, stealing is the worst thing to do. You could go to jail for that."

"JAIL!!" A six-year-old kid can be sent to jail? I was numb. Numb like I was in the store. How can a little kid like me be put behind bars?

"Now I want you to go to the store and apologize. And don't ever even think of doing it again. If you do, then I'll make sure the policeman takes you away."

I walked back to the store and the man with the glaring eyes.

"Uumm hi, I was just gonna uummm..."

"So, I guess you're probably here to say something."

"Yeah, you see I wanted to say I was sorry for what I had done. Sorry."

"So what are you sorry about? What did you do wrong to be sorry about?"

"Well, I didn't know it wasn't good to steal. I will never do it again."

"I hope not."

I never stole after that. But whenever I saw a policeman, I would sneak behind my grandmother's skirt. I thought maybe he knew about the incident I had with the clerk, and he came by to get me.

The stealing incident happened ten years ago. Now I am in college in the United States far away from Hamra, the small town where I spent my years as a teenager in South Korea. During those years, my grandmother had a stroke. After that, our roles were reversed. She didn't teach me about things; I taught her.

I tried to teach her how to pronounce words, brush her teeth, and eat in the proper way. It was too bad she couldn't communicate with others. She understood everything I taught her, but she couldn't express herself in her own words. Her brain was damaged, and she sometimes even acted like a four year old. I guess my worst days started on the day my grandmother had the stroke.

I could smell the sweet fragrance of roses as I lifted myself out of the car on that Saturday afternoon. My dad had a hobby growing flowers and trees. And as in any other spring, the flowers were alive. They had the cool wind and fresh water to drink. In return, they gave us the fragrance only fresh flowers had.

"I'm back, Mom, where are you?"

There was no answer, just a weird smell. It was far from what I had just smelled outside. At first, I thought it was the scent that came from Candy, my one-year-old puppy. She sometimes just doesn't feel like going to the bathroom to do her things. When I opened the door to my grandmother's, I found out it was she who didn't feel like going to the bathroom to do her things. I can still feel the odor run up my nose. She was looking toward the wall, and I could see human droppings mushed all over her pants.

"Oh no! Grandma, how could you do this again? Mom is gonna be real mad when she finds out." As I said these words, I felt ashamed. I was ashamed of my grandmother and the fact that I had shouted at her for such a thing.

As I shouted, she had a look on her face saying, "I didn't mean to. I'm sorry, I couldn't help it." She didn't even murmur as she usually did when she saw me.

The sweet fragrance of the acacia and roses again came to my nose as I ran to my dad, leaving the horrible smell of what was in my grandmother's room.

"Dad! Grandma has done it again in her pants!"

"What? Again, well why didn't you help her?"

"How can you expect me to clean it up?"

"Well why can't you? She is your grandmother, and she cleaned up after you when you were a child!"

"It's not the same thing; she is a grown up, and I wasn't."

"When did this happen again?" My dad was shouting his lungs out at my mom. I think he was really angry at her for not taking care of his mother.

"I was out getting some groceries for your mother. And I asked her if she needed to go to the bathroom before I left. She didn't want to go, so don't shout at me!"

"She probably did want to go, but the way you asked made her not want to go."

"Well, if you are so good at it, you do it. Don't go to work; just sit by her twenty-four hours a day and ask her nicely if she wants to go to the bathroom."

"Mom is right, it is not her fault!"

"Shut up! Everybody just get out of here."

And I did. I wasn't going to help him clean up after her anyway.

My dad bought her a new wheelchair, and we fixed up her room as if it was a suite in a hospital with a new TV and stereo—just for her. She got all the things I wanted and never got. I got three ugly years of tutors, sleepless nights. "A" in math brought me an even uglier thing called "high school." My mother's cheeks were now hanging down on her face with fat. It looked as if she had small apples in her cheeks, all of which she had gotten from the stress over Grandma. Everybody got older the hard way because of Grandma.

Even she did. She didn't do anything at all except eat and sleep. I guess that made her old. She sure looked like it with her cheeks sucked into her face. It looked as if she were trying to imitate gold fish. She had those eyes that had no fat around them. Her eyelids were brown; it was dark under her eyes, too. It was an absolute contrast to her salt-colored hair. To me she looked like an old American lady with undyed hair.

I still didn't love her the way I used to, but I knew she loved me as much as she did when I was born.

"No Grandma, it's okay. I still have some left." Grandma was already coming to me in her new shining wheelchair. She couldn't come fast. She was pushing with her left foot and left hand, which also held her money. She held on to it so hard, I could see the veins popping out and the knuckles turning white.

"Dong na dong na!"

I could see she wanted to give me her money, even though she couldn't speak real Korean. And I was trying to tell her to keep it.

"No. Just keep it with you. I know you don't get to use it, but who knows?"

I wrapped my hands around her bony hand. She now was trying to let go. I tried harder to make her not unfold her hand, but finally she pushed back with the bottom of her left foot and let go of the money and my hands.

"Dong na dong na."

She had a smile on her face saying, "I won, you lost."

She had changed a lot from what she was. She had thrown thirty thousand won to me that day. Funny, especially when I thought of the time when she wouldn't even give me two hundred won a day.

"Grandma, I'm going back to America to study in college. I won't be back until I finish. It will probably take me about ten years, since I'm not coming back until I become a great reporter. To become a great reporter, I need to go to America to get a better education."

"Dong na dong na."

"Yes, I'm really going back to the country I've wanted to go back to. You miss the United States, too, huh? You did like living in the three-room apartment in Queens. I guess I won't be able to see you for a long time, Grandma."

I said these words without looking at her. I could tell she was trying to get herself together. She didn't want to cry in front of me, since she knew this was what I had wanted.

She was worried about the fact I wouldn't be able to see her for several years. She was sixty-seven. I may never again see the old wrinkled face that I had hated and blamed for all the bad things that had happened to our family.

"God, I really can't stand her anymore! Please somebody just take her away! She should be dead by now. She is too old and too hard to take care of. I really hate it when she acts like this." Mom was again complaining about how Grandma acted in front of Dad.

Grandma would act more sick, and she wouldn't even eat as much as she used to do. She always tried to eat a lot of meat, which she shouldn't be eating much of. In front of Dad, she said she didn't feel like eating anything, trying to get attention from my dad.

When he wasn't there, she would eat a lot of kimchi—the hot, spicy vegetable Koreans eat at all meals. When dad ate with her, she would say it's too hot to eat, acting like a child. Mom hated that. Actually she hated Grandma, the person, herself. I think Grandma did this because she was lonely. She just wanted some affection from her son. Grandma was in her own way stressed out, just as my mom was under the stress of taking care of Grandma. I was in the middle. My dad was naturally on my grandmother's side; my sister on my mom's. I was a little more tilted toward my mom, but sometimes I just couldn't understand.

"Mom, why do you have to show me these feelings you have toward Grandma? I'm leaving in a few weeks; I just want to remember good things about our family."

"I'm sorry, but you just don't know what kind of person your grandmother was before she had the stroke. Even when I was pregnant, she would shout at me for not doing the dishes. I could take that, but you or anybody else in the family couldn't have taken her throwing dishes at me." As I heard these words, the sorrow I felt for my grandmother turned into anger. The same woman who always said nothing when my mother shouted had mistreated my mother even worse.

"You should have seen the things she did to your great-grandmother. Your great-grandmother lived until eighty-eight. It was a long time for a person to live, and a long time for an old woman to take all that crap from a son's wife. What I say and do to her is nothing compared to what she did. She would say to your great-grandmother, 'When are you going to die? You've lived long enough.'"

I hated listening to what my mother had said. I didn't want to believe what my grandmother had done to others. She was the same woman who had been there for me, taking care of my sister and me when my parents were in New York. My dad was studying at New York University, so they needed time to get everything set up before we could go and live with them.

In the two years before she took us to Queens, New York, my grandmother, being very healthy and diligent at that time, took care of me better than any other mother. At nights, when I was scared, she was there to put me back to sleep. When I wanted to get a Barbie doll, she bought me one only after I received a good mark in a test. She was always there to rub my tummy when it hurt.

I looked at my grandmother sitting in her shiny wheelchair; she looked like a woman who wanted people to accept her apology for what she had done over the years. The years, the stroke, and the disabilities had made her more mature than she was years ago. It would have been a whole different story if she hadn't had the stroke. She would still have been mean to my mother. Now she wasn't mean; she was just helpless.

"Goodbye, Grandma, I guess this is it."

"Bow to your grandmother now. It's going to be a long time before you can do that again."

In Korea, it is traditional to bow a big bow to the eldest in the family and parents before you leave on a long journey. You also bow when you come back. It's like saying greetings in a traditional way.

125

I slowly bent my knees down with my arms folded in front of my forehead. As my head touched the floor by the front wheel of her wheelchair, I heard the sound of her pushing with one leg.

"Ahhhhhh. Uhhhhha," she moaned.

She tried to hug me, and instead of saying, "Dong na," she had tears streaming down her face. I then slowly tried to get up without showing tears when she grabbed my right arm and pulled me toward her. I landed on her hard bony lap. I cried silently, hot tears flowing down my red cheeks and on to her paralyzed leg. I cried until my dad pulled me away.

"It's not going to be the end of everything. You should be more strong. Show Grandma what a bright and intelligent person you are and show her you are going to succeed. To do that you should be strong in front of her."

"You are right, Dad. Grandma, I'm going back to America to become one of the best Korean woman reporters, and I won't come back until I do. I'll make you and the rest of our family the proudest family in Korea. I'll make the name Dha wool Chung known for the best reporter."

I guess my grandmother wasn't a very strong person herself. She couldn't stop crying. I remember how she laughed at my great-grandmother who cried her eyes out when we left for Queens in 1984. She was in the same shoes that my great-grandmother was in. She thought she would never see me again, but my great-grandmother did see me six years later when we returned to Korea right before her death at the age of eighty-eight.

Dear Grandma,

It's been exactly ninety-eight days since I left you and Mom in that big house. The cherry blossoms by your window must have been beautiful this spring. They always had been beautiful when I was there, and they should be when I get back. And I hope you are doing all right with Mom.

You wouldn't believe the things I've learned to do here. I now even cook for myself and even work part-time for an allowance. You probably couldn't picture me working for money. I couldn't believe it myself. I remember you giving me extra money at times when I really needed it. Now, I even give some to my sister. I haven't done much in keeping my promise to you on being the best reporter. I'm working on it. It is a little bit hard trying to study and work at the same time, but almost all the students do, so it doesn't seem as hard as it is. It makes me make use of my time even better. I know, to you, there was no such thing as wasting time in your whole life. Even after you had the stroke, you tried to fold the laundry by using one hand and your teeth. To tell the truth I hated you for doing that. But now I thank you for teaching me to use the best out of the things you have. And last but not least, I love you, Grandma.

Love,

Dha wool

THE 'WRITE' THING TO DO
by Andrianne Gamble

Death is a mischievous character, and, seeing him in action, I was destined to become a strong-willed young woman who would beat him at the game of life. This, no doubt, came as a result of witnessing my grandfather's determination to fight off Death's messengers, which had invaded his body in the form of Lung Cancer.

Granddaddy Smith was six feet, three inches tall and had a smile that could melt a heart of steel. He was a kind man who kept a firm and steady hold on his family. His body was well proportioned to his height, and his disposition thrived on laughter and fun. One could learn a lesson and laugh simultaneously in his company, as I often did. He kept my brain twirling, and my lips curling into smiles. He was one of the men I idolized; the other was my father, for his know-how.

One day, the chest pains he had been having forced my grandfather to the doctor's office. Tests showed that malignant tumors, sent by Death himself, were present in his lungs. I did not understand this phenomenon exactly, but described it as "internal chickenpox." As the months went by, I watched my grandfather become weaker, paler, and thinner. However, his way of thinking did not change.

It was a cold November day when he died. Rushing in from school, I answered the phone, and across the line came a sobbing female voice. As Mom snatched the receiver, I knew it was over. That same day, I heard Death laugh and say he had won my grandfather. That's when I vowed that I would not give up until I, not Death, was ready.

The worst junior high school in the city of Washington, D.C., was to be my home for the next three years. I was graduating from elementary school, and though I deserved every award imaginable, I received none because my conduct was not up to par. Yes, I had all it took to attend one of the best junior high schools that stood proudly on the other side of town. The waiting lists were too long and time was too short, so I ended up in the gutter.

The curriculum was challenging enough to keep me studying, but easy enough to allow time for other activities. This school's reputation was equivalent to that of a penitentiary. The neighborhood was the pits—drug-infested—and my peers seemed to have no goals. I did not belong there, yet I showed everyone that I could make the best of the worst circumstances. I had a goal, and I let nothing come between it and me.

I proudly and shamelessly turned down every offer for sex or drugs, and simply refused to skip class. Though I remained at this school for only two of the traditional three years, my determination was strengthened. At the end of my second year, eighth grade, I was given the opportunity to attend high school in ninth grade, and I accepted. As a result, I can truthfully say that going to the "wrong school" was a blessing in disguise, because what it produced was not merely an intelligent young lady, but also a woman who is beneficial to society.

I was embarking upon a strange and dangerous adventure, one which would teach coping with peer and family pressure, studying habitually, and decision making. This exciting journey was appropriately named "high school." At the age of fourteen, I had barely begun puberty and was beginning to formulate my own opinions about various topics. I was naive and had no idea of what was in store for me in this bright but miniature world of conflicting ideas.

I entered high school as a white lamb who thought she was a black sheep. I did not know who I was and how I felt on such important issues as equal rights, blacks and voting, teen pregnancy and abortion. Many of these topics I had seen only on the news or in the papers. Consequently, I did not have enough information to construct a true opinion of my own. Since everyone else had formed his view, and I didn't, I became an introvert.

It seemed to me, and many other teens, that those topics had no effect on my life. However, I remained in this state long enough to realize that these topics did affect me. After reading and hearing about current events on a more regular basis, I became well acquainted with the details and arguments. Once I found my view, I was soon back to my original, extroverted self.

This one-year period taught me to be independent enough to search for what I really wanted, and not follow the crowd. This was the lesson that would have the most impact on my life.

As I continued through high school, I thought all was lost. My parents were separating, and I could not stop them. Why did I force them into this situation? I was blinded by confusion and anger, and figured out everyone's problem except my own. While I was a sophomore in high school, my grades reflected my disturbed state due to my parents' separation.

My conduct and behavior appeared to come from anger, though it was actually discontent because I did not know how to accept my parents' decision. I was assured repeatedly that this incident had nothing to do with me, which just didn't seem true. I was positive that I had the entire situation figured out. I had been doing well in school; therefore, I didn't need them to be together.

I was blind to the fact that they were having problems of their own, and I was selfish to think that everything centered around me. I still couldn't handle it, though, and, consequently, I let my grades drop. I loved my parents and loved seeing them together. I didn't think I could cope with their separation.

When everyone had given up, Grandma came along. She explained to me, in vivid detail, that my parents were human and made mistakes. She encouraged me to look at them as individuals and give them the support they needed. She also insisted that I let go of the childish act and pull my grades up. It took a while, but her words sunk in, and I followed her line of logic.

As a result, I was able to understand, though not agree with, their decision, and therefore be more attentive to myself. The writer in me leaked out like water through a small hole in a dam—slowly at first, then faster. It surprised my family, my teachers, and especially my peers. I had found my hidden talent and I would show the entire world that I was good at something.

The latter part of the tenth grade was my personal renaissance. I was told all through elementary school and junior high school that I was gifted, but, for some reason, I could not find my "gift." Yes, I could do things that some children could not, but so many others could do them, too. I searched for my talent until I reached high school. Then I gave up.

In my sophomore English class, I was given an assignment to write my feelings about my family's situation without telling what the situation was. I could use any form of writing, including poetry, which I chose. This poem was not the first I had written, but the first to get me recognition. I was encouraged, then, to write more poems. I could write ten poems a day, and usually did, but the more I wrote poems, the more I knew that there was something else.

I then began to write plays. I never showed anyone my plays because I didn't think they were good. However, I was still being urged to write poems. As a result of finding my "gift," I also found an outlet for my emotions, and a unique way of sharing my feelings with others.

Eleventh grade held an array of events for me. Discovering my writing ability in my sophomore year merely set the stage for opportunity. Consequently, as my work was circulated, I was smothered daily with compliments and suggestions from my peers and administrators. However, this was only the beginning.

Although I had never imagined labeling myself as a writer, I was aware that I could write poetry. My eleventh-grade English teacher assigned a ten-page essay about each book read in class, comparing its meaning with the objectives of the Humanities. These assignments helped me develop my style of writing and provided material that I could use to enter many contests.

Though I'd only placed entries for pleasure, I often found myself winning. In many instances, I'd place second or third, hardly ever first. It was then that I began to think of myself as a writer. I had had the opportunity to show my work to others, and I had the joy of being chosen as one of the best.

However, I was always prepared for Failure, and was glad not to run into him. This was the time when I developed intellectually. I put everything I had into my writing and thought I was getting everything out. I felt I was all I could be, but, little did I know, part of me was missing.

"One's future can never be accurately predicted, only looked upon when it becomes the past." This line, which I wrote, is true. The world's greatest psychic would have never convinced me that I would not become a writer. This was my senior year in high school, and writing was all I cared about. It took all of my time, effort, and attention.

This particular period is stressful for all teenagers. My stresses came from family pressures, the choosing of a college, and working. This was teamed with the peer pressure of finding the "right date" for the prom. Together, they were ideal in making life difficult. I was stressed even more because I was unsure of a college major. Writing poetry was shaky, and writing plays was even worse. Unfortunately, I remained in this baffled state until I engaged in the most heated argument ever.

As usual, this argument was about American Government. I, for the first time, was actually defending "my country... sweet land of liberty." My great performance in this between-class debate had enlightened me about the field in which I'd be most effective. It was then that I decided to be a lawyer. With my eyes set on the ultimate goal of politician, specifically Senator, I set out to gather information on my field of interest.

It had taken me fourteen years of school to decide, and, with everyone behind me, there was no turning back. I had been an empty shell, a hollow intellect with no goal, no aim, and no purpose. As a result of my new-found major, I was filled with the bubbly excitement of living life to its unfortunately rigid boundaries.

When twelfth grade ended and summer began, I finally realized that I had truly reached my goal. I was a high-school graduate and was ready to attend college. I was hired on the Tourmobile, Inc., team as Tourguide's Assistant, and was assigned to answer questions and smile a lot. It required an amount of patience that I'd not yet gained. This job, though not the career breakthrough I was seeking, was very instrumental in helping me find myself. Yes, I knew who I was, but I had to prove that I could stand my ground alone without the help of my parents.

Prior to this "corporate" position, I had had no previous day-to-day contact with people of any race other than black. Since I had already made plans to attend college, I figured the summer would be a great time to get used to other kinds of people.

Working at a very popular tourist attraction, Arlington National Cemetery, I met people from almost every nationality and walk of life. I had no problems dealing with them because I saw them as my equals. However, I was offended several times when I was treated as if I were unintelligent by people who had never either seen or dealt with blacks. Sometimes people simply refused to accept the word of a black person. This was my very first experience with racism.

I feel this experience was necessary to prepare me for the semester that awaited me. I am grateful. The words of the wise are more essential for growing teens than vitamins. My grandmother had a way of saying what I needed to hear, and the decision to accept or reject her wisdom was placed on me. It was to her ears that I had my first chance to voice many of my opinions on racism, relationships, and politics.

Fortunately, I was one of few privileged children in today's society. My grandmother and I could talk about anything, and I refused to withhold information from her. From my aunts' and uncles' description, we were so much alike that we could be twins. Personally, I didn't mind being like her. I thought she was the epitome of excellence.

Although she was kind to everyone and gave of herself in many situations, she let no one mistake this kindness for weakness. "I don't take no junk," she was often heard to say. I was proud to be just like her.

The relationship we shared proved all psychological theories wrong. Anyone who says that there is a generation gap is sadly mistaken. My grandmother and I could go anywhere and conquer anything together. She was more than a grandmother; she was a cook, a peacemaker, a confidante, a best friend, a roommate, and sometimes even a parent. She also played an enormous role in the shaping of my personality and in the decisions I've made for my life. But, most of all, she showed by example how to do the right thing.

I understand the awesome power of writing and vow to keep it alive in all that I do, no matter what I do. Through it, like my grandmother did by example, I hope to share my thoughts about the right things to do.

ALONG THE ROAD: Religion

In the faces

of men and

women,

I see God...

I find letters

from God dropt

in the street,

and every one

is signed by

God's name...

"This is more than a paper or a story about nothing. It's a memoir about love and truth. It's about the one thing we all have to find—ourselves. This memoir hasn't taught me anything that I didn't know before. Instead, it is a reminder of what I can never forget."

Andrianne Gamble

ALONG THE ROAD
by Abby Forbes

We traveled from church to church in a '93 white Ford van with a red trailer attached. We made it our home. We covered the windows with Noah's Ark Colorforms, and marked our territory with pictures and notes of our loved ones who were not with us. It reminded us, on the hardest of days, that there were still people "out there" who loved us.

When we arrived at a church in the late afternoon, we would meet the contact person and set up all of our musical equipment, which included drums, electric guitars, a bass, and keyboards. We would then sound-check, and after that, we would try to slip in some personal time before our usual potluck dinner, for which church members brought homemade dishes. I can still smell the lasagna and the covered dishes that were prepared for us.

The staff told us at training that we would always be in a "bubble." The people were going to be seeing every move we made. We had to be on our best Christian behavior. The people deserved that. We were there to serve them and fill them with the message of God's love and hope. And that we did, every night, in a program full of contemporary music, skits, and puppet shows.

But our job was not finished yet. After our program, we usually went home with host families, where we spent quality time getting to know these people in just a few hours. They were wonderful to us. People told us how hard it must be to sleep in a different bed each night, but that was nothing. We were treated as special guests every night, as if we were such good people because we gave up a year of our lives to do this.

Sometimes, I wondered just how good I was when the last thing I wanted to do was answer the same questions every single night. I found it draining, even though I'm an extrovert, to always have a smile on my face for people I had never met. But the "bubble" remained. Almost every time I'd be almost completely burned out, I would meet some incredible person or a family or an innocent small child who touched me deeply. I'm sure they had no idea how they impacted me with their strong values or faith, but it was those special people who got me through the hard times with their encouragement.

I had one year of college under my belt when I traveled with Pentecost. It was a one-year commitment to Youth Holiness. We were a Christian band of seven people who had never met before.

I flew to Minneapolis a week before training began to visit with some old friends. They had all traveled with different Pentecost teams in the past, and I had met them when they traveled in my region. I had been a "groupie" and a friend to those "learners," as we affectionately referred to them, since I met Lee in the seventh grade. He was the drummer of the Christian band that I befriended in my twelve-year-old way. I knew then that I would one day be a part of this ministry. And after seven years of anticipation, it was my time to go. It was August 16, and I was going to meet my teammates. I don't think anyone or anything could have prepared me for that day, or more importantly, for that year.

Training began that day at First Pentecost church. The church was filled with nervous faces. There were six national teams and four international teams that Youth Encounter sent out on the road for a year in different regions of the country. As I walked in, I realized that it was real. I met some of my teammates, and we talked excitedly. As I look back now, we were naive about what was ahead of us. I only knew one teammate, Mark. We had gone to college together for a year. It was a rare occasion when learners knew each other, but it was comforting for both of us. Everyone was there the first day, except Karen. She would join us in a week because she had just finished touring with Pentecost and had a week off before starting a new year. I didn't feel that we were complete until she arrived. She seemed to fill this hole that I sensed. Finally we were a whole team, and we could begin.

We were seven: Chas, Karen, Rob, Mark, Penny, John, and me. Seven different individuals from seven different walks of life. And we would live, and work, and play together for the next year.

We spent a week in that church listening to Barry, the monotone; he was the slow-speaking president of Youth Holiness. He taught us about theology. It was some symbolism about circles and squares that most of us never really understood. We all knew what we believed and why we were there. And that was enough for us.

Our first long journey was from Minneapolis, Minnesota, to the Black Hills of South Dakota to finish training. After spending a week together at Lee Valley Ranch, all of the teams grew closer. It was a time of joy and fellowship. At night, we sang songs around the campfire under the stars. The harmony among these eighty musicians was amazing. During the days, we spent hours with our teams in sessions trying to get to know one another and exploring our beliefs. I guess they thought that would make living together easier.

It was a frustrating time for me because I was very open to being vulnerable, and Chas refused to open up. Rob, who came from Denmark, was overwhelmed with culture-shock, and did not have much to say either. John tried, but had never talked about anything emotional before. Mark had too much to say. Penny held back. And Karen shed many tears. I knew then how different we were.

We had all experienced tough times and those affected us in seven different ways. We joked the rest of the year about our dysfunctional team, but I learned there comes a time to take responsibility for our behavior, no matter how much pain we've been through. Because if we don't, it can turn into abuse.

Once we got through the serious sessions, we had no problem having fun. We were always good at having fun and pretending nothing was wrong. It was only the beginning of our adventure. We were heading out on the road to be on our own. There was not much turmoil at that point, but with each passing week, our humanness was constantly being revealed. Usually it was revealed through the hard times.

Hard times. It seems I don't know where to begin. As I look back, the intensity has faded. But in the heat of a struggle, I often wondered how I would make it through the year. My hardest struggle was with Chas. Chas was our team leader, with a hurting soul, a loving spirit, and a very hard exterior. And I was the lucky one because I broke through the Tough Guy shell, or so I thought.

At first, it was touching to be the only one in his life who he could trust with his painful past, but as the months passed by, I fell in love with him. I had seen his soul, and that was very attractive to me. It was a rocky road between us, but I wanted to stand strong beside him.

We had an on-and-off again relationship throughout the year. There were times when he gave me what I needed emotionally, but there were more times when he took his anger out on me. It might have been because I was the bearer of his many secrets. But no matter how difficult it became, I couldn't leave. No matter how bitter our words were, I had to get in the van everyday because I was there for a reason. I had to learn self-worth.

We all acted like one big family. We fought like brothers and sisters, and we loved as only a family can. We cast our roles as family members. I was the mother of our family of seven, and they often reminded me of my motherly ways. I was also the health coordinator and the spiritual-life coordinator. Sometimes I felt that I could never fulfill these roles because the harder I tried, the more I became the "nag." They never called me that, but I felt that way. I wanted us to be closer on a spiritual and emotional level, but my expectations were too high for our dysfunctional team. We were all at different levels, and we learned to accept that.

When I think back to our team meetings, a time when we tried to hash out all of our problems, I remember being so full of distress because everyone refused to compromise and change for the others. It was mainly Chas, John, and Mark who refused to change their attitudes because, heaven forbid, we asked them to alter their personalities. Chas and Mark were sarcastic to the point where they often said things that hurt Karen and me. To them, it was always Karen and Abby being "too sensitive." After all these months, I still believe they said things that they knew would bother us, pushing it too far each time. John had a hard time adjusting to living with people in the beginning. Along with his past, he brought an angry and insecure side that would sometimes explode out of him during a discussion of our musical ability. It got so bad in the fall that we thought he would leave, but something held him there. He eventually learned to change for us and for himself.

Penny was usually a facilitator-type person, but other times, I thought she sided with the guys on issues. She had a difficult time understanding my opinions on feminism, and where to draw the line with jokes. Things that the guys said and did just didn't bother her as they bothered me, and that in itself was frustrating.

Karen and I usually agreed, which often put us in a defensive corner together. She had her own struggles with self-acceptance and body image. Many times she was afraid to say something for fear of rejection.

And then there was Rob, who rarely voiced his opinion when it came to conflicts. But when this wise man spoke, everyone listened. There were many times when I knew he agreed with me on certain issues, but he wouldn't say anything, and that was so hard.

As I write this, I wonder what their perspective is or was of me. If my intuition is as strong as I think it is, I think they would say that my strong, idealistic opinions about equality, helping others, and saving the earth got really old. And in my fight for others, I often added my voice when it wasn't wanted. Seven different sets of values trying to work together was one of the most difficult struggles with which we dealt. But we all learned from each other eventually, even if it was after the fact.

Learning about each other was the most fun. We would stay together sometimes, and play our game called Truth. It was a game of questions that we had to answer honestly. We talked about embarrassing moments and old boyfriends and girlfriends. We knew that because there was a special trust we could say anything and still be loved. Our comfortability level was a treasured thing. There were few things that we would be embarrassed to do or say in front of each other. It was nice to be able to relax and be silly, always laughing about private jokes or past experiences.

And we were a wild team, too. Our hard, alternative style of music marked us as the "Jesus Freaks." "Jesus Freak" was the title of our favorite song, one that we played and sang with our whole hearts. We were the first team in Youth Holiness's history to all get tattoos. They were all Christian tattoos of course. It was a time of extreme emotions. Living so closely with six other people made us truly love and hate, and laugh and cry.

We would rehearse when we found the time. It was always a tense experience. For some reason, we were never able to "leave our egos at the door," as Karen would say. John played the drums, but didn't have much natural rhythm. Karen, on the other hand, was talented at playing Latin percussion. She was also our program coordinator, which put her in charge of rehearsals. John was intimidated by Karen's ability and probably felt inadequate. He used to get angry whenever she asked him to play softer or pick up the tempo. Actually, John often got angry when anyone had constructive criticism.

There were other tensions. Mark, the experienced bass player, would volunteer to sing many of the songs. I was supposed to be a lead vocalist, but in trying to be humble, I lost the chance at singing some songs because I didn't volunteer first. Our selfishness was apparent in situations like these. But at the same time, we often held our frustrations in. There was a feeling that seemed to hover in the atmosphere. It was tension that existed because we chose not to discuss and work through our personal problems and our team frustrations. Sometimes outsiders, people outside of the "bubble," would sense this tension, and we would reprimand each other for allowing them to see the truth. Sometimes, the hidden tension would explode, and someone would channel their anger in another teammate's direction unfairly.

This was living in community. We were so close at times, that it felt like we couldn't breathe. There were days when the small quarters in the van seemed to suffocate me, but we drove on. We played on. We prayed on. Together. Always together. One minute we would laugh, the next we would grow silent in defensiveness. The defense mechanisms we learned in our different upbringings clashed severely. Chas and Mark turned to sarcasm that often cut like a knife. John's anger was a beast inside of him that he constantly tried to control. Rob retreated to silence. Penny said it was just that we were different. Karen got angry and cried, then tried to apologize even when she did nothing wrong. And I pointed out all of our visible problems in an attempt to work everything out. So I looked like the judgmental one, condemning everyone else. That is not the way I wanted to come across.

In the midst of the tension and the defensiveness, once in a while there would be a silent time. We would sit in our familiar circle, and after fighting our own egos, we would all become vulnerable. We would share our common pain of living with each other and our own pasts. Then we would encourage one another and pray together. And we all knew that we loved each other because we had become a family. Those are the times I held onto. The few moments that held us together.

The months passed by quickly. September became December, and then April came suddenly and led us to August. We called it the shortest year with the longest days of our lives. During those days, we formed habits in the ways we treated one another. Nothing ever changed. We knew one another as much as each team member would allow. And although we all said that we would work on our downfalls, we just seemed to hang on to them. But at the same time, we became aware of our negative characteristics, and I guess if we gained anything, it was knowledge.

Our relationships with each other also went through many changes. Mark and Penny spent more and more time together. After Easter break, they told us that they were dating. They started to spend every minute together because supposedly no one else understood them. They acted like children. They would buy toys and play games, which seemed cute in the beginning, but then became obsessive. They also picked up each other's mannerisms and sayings. It was strange and sad to see Penny say things that were not like her. They influenced each other subconsciously and became a unit instead of the individuals they were in the beginning. Penny is now living in Maryland with Mark, and they are engaged.

The team learned to deal with Chas, but I never understood where our relationship was headed. Neither did Chas. There was a time when I thought I would move to live near Chas after the year ended. But during the last few months, I found out that he had pursued another girl behind my back: Christie, an Australian knockout. She was tall and beautiful. Her long, shiny, light-brown hair was always perfect. When she walked by, it was easy to feel her extreme confidence.

The night I found out was the lowest point for me. I didn't sleep. I just cried. The next morning, my eyes were swollen, and I felt as though I were going to a funeral. Unfortunately, that was not the end of the cycle. I still went back a few times to be comforted by him. It was unhealthy, and I regret it. I didn't let go until the night before Homecoming, the final concert where all the teams performed for the last time. I got to talk to Christie. We told each other everything he said to us. It was scarily similar. He told us both that he was falling in love with us, wrote poetry, and kept all a secret. I could hardly believe that I lived through this for a whole year. I haven't seen him since the day we sadly said goodbye, but we have spoken. There is no more trust between us.

My relationships with the rest of my teammates went through changes. Penny and I had our special moments of girl-talk when we stayed together in host homes. It was a comfort for me, but it seemed to become a burden for her. So we started to grow apart because I didn't want to overwhelm her. My relationships with Karen and Rob were the most stable. Karen and I were like sisters. We had our moments, but we could tell each other how we felt even in our conflicts. That was a blessing for both of us. The views that we shared were often different than the rest of the team. We both just thought we were standing up for what we believed in. When the rest of the team was sick of how sensitive we were, at least we had each other.

It is almost funny to think about the team's reaction to us. Sometimes, we laughed at how ridiculous some of their comments were, and we would sarcastically say, "Sometimes all you can do is laugh!" Sean liked one of us one week, and then the other the next week. He was like a brother that I fought with constantly, and then we would pretend nothing happened. But there was always Rob. He was everyone's friend. His European accent made it hard to ever get mad at him. And because he was such a patient, humble person, it was easy to love him and laugh at all the funny things he would say incorrectly.

Rob and I were not close until the end. We both regretted that. He was overwhelmed by my affectionate nature, and I was so wrapped up in the ups and downs with Chas, that I didn't try to get close to him. We both realized that we missed out on a lot. I always felt a kindred spirit in him, but I didn't connect with it until the last few months. He and I shared a spiritual understanding that is hard to find in most relationships. It was the hardest to say goodbye to him. I don't know when I will ever see his spirit-filled eyes again.

The spirit that lived in him was like the spirit of God. He reminded me sometimes of Jesus, and that was the reason we were there. I often forgot that because I was so caught up in myself and my own feelings. But then, sometimes, I would stop and look over at Rob, and God would show me that it wasn't about me or even how I felt about my teammates. It was about love. God's love. The spirit of love that lived in Rob and me. And it lived in Chas, Mark, Penny, John, and Karen. It lived in our tears and our pain and our laughter.

I spent a year of my life dedicated to that love, and God changed me in the midst of it. God changed me and loved me; not because it was about me, but because it was about an unconditional love beyond my understanding.

CONFESSIONS OF A LUNATIC
by Hollie Rice

God wanted me to go to Sunday School. First He told my parents, and then they told me, so I went. I learned early on not to argue with someone who could drop a mountain on your head without moving His pinky. Besides, if God liked me, I could do anything—maybe even harness a little of His power for myself. With this, anything was possible. I used to test this theory often, usually scaring the pants off everyone in the process.

After a plethora of bruises and an injured ego, I realized that maybe God didn't want this four year old jumping on furniture or bouncing off glass doors. But when temptation knocked, I usually ignored what God wanted.

My parents had a cuckoo clock that would cheerfully announce each hour with the appearance of a singing, fuzzy, yellow bird. I wanted that bird. I had a place for it in my room, all picked out. I simply had to climb up the clock and wait for one o'clock to roll around. As I stared up at the clock's face, it seemed unreasonably easy. All I had to do was reach the swinging double doors through which the bird would appear. I concentrated all my energy on the tempting little square, breathing in a deep, steady rhythm. There was just a short leap, and a few feet of chain to climb.

I balanced myself on the armchair, waiting for the proper moment...12:54, 12:55... I sprang into the still air, grasping for the dangling line that had been taunting me moments before. As I felt my hands coil around it, I tried to breathe and open my eyes. "Success!" I screamed silently.

How beautiful that yellow bird would look next to my toy dump truck. 12:57. Suddenly, I felt myself jerk. Feeling as if the weight of the world had just crashed onto my shoulders, I looked up dreadfully. The hundred-year-old cuckoo clock was falling, and I was going with it. I landed on my back with a thud that shook the whole neighborhood. I lay silently gasping for breath, listening to the dying noise. "Cuckoo, cuckoo...." I felt as if I had been thrown into the air by a Mack truck. As the oxygen returned to my brain, and my heartbeat steadied, I looked at the debris that had moments before been a family heirloom. I realized that some things weren't meant to be done.

Elementary school teachers love to tell you about things you do wrong. "If you don't learn from your misfortunes, you'll never be happy," was my second-grade teacher's personal philosophy. Her goal in life was to mold me into the perfect child. Unfortunately, her kind heart and good intentions were usually ignored. It was hard to take her seriously about life when she didn't seem to realize that red and orange just don't work together in the clothing department. It was difficult to listen to someone when a suppressed giggle was making you spit. But respect came, in time, and I learned that not all adults were like my parents, interested solely in how many carrots I ate for dinner.

They actually cared about me as a person, and listened to what I had to say. That wasn't easy, since the majority of conversations consisted of childish babble and complaints. Mrs. Barnhart, when she wasn't clashing her outfits, was a master at sorting through gibberish. She was also very good at settling arguments, telling stories (they always had a moral at the end), and giving out candy. She was, in fact, the one who caused my fetish for gummy bears. You could even give her credit for introducing me to my first best friend.

It wasn't until I entered high school that I actually met Audra. Our love of gummy bears (hers especially) brought us together. She went to Sunday School, too. This was important, because she had God-power. Together we developed some very interesting ideas about this inner strength, and, in the process, became inseparable. She gave me her candy, and I gave her a lifetime friendship. It was through this friendship that I began to develop the self-confidence that I had always lacked. I no longer worried about the opinions of others. Audra accepted me as I was.

Her parents may have had some difficulties with my willingness to begin popcorn fights, however. I discovered that microwave popcorn (the really bad kind with lots of butter and salt) sticks to basement ceilings quite nicely. If you time it correctly, you'll have a piece fall into your mouth every thirty seconds. We discussed a lot during these popcorn festivals; we told each other things we had never mentioned to another living soul. Never did we hold a past incident against the other, and this meant more to me than anything ever had.

She was someone that I could talk to. Sure, I had a lot of people that I spent time with, but I was afraid to be myself around them. I believed I had too much to hide about my past, my beliefs, my life. I always hid behind a mask, covering up what was really inside. I was empty, and I wasn't happy. Why couldn't anybody like me for who I was? What did it matter that I was a year younger than all of them?

It had been my parents' brilliant idea to let me skip fifth grade. Didn't they know the kids weren't going to like me? Everyone around me was jealous, and lived to make my life miserable. So I put on a show, and acted tough and mean. Fights at the bus stop were a common occurrence, and my room was littered with stolen items. I lied my way through every situation, just to mess with everyone's mind, just so I could know that I had power over them. They were so weak, so pitiful that even I could fool them. I managed to have two distinct personalities: the sweet little angel that my teachers and relatives saw, and the nasty, sinful brute that the other kids were used to.

As I sat and told this to Audra, I was scared—scared that she was going to condemn me as I imagined everyone always would. But this didn't happen. She merely sat and listened, nodding to let me know, not that she understood, but that it didn't even matter. All was in the past, and forgotten. The letter I had written her explaining all I had done lay on the floor, a simple testimony to her forgiveness. Things I wrote in that letter made me sick, and I was the one who had caused and experienced them. But she was loving, and simply accepted me. Most of the things were never mentioned again, but tucked on a shelf in the back of her mind. Life went on, but we always gave each other a shoulder to cry on, an ear to talk to, and a friend to hug.

Of all this, the discussions were the most important. They changed my life. I knew that the life I had been living was wrong, and that I had to change. It's difficult to change your mind when you've had the same misconceptions since kindergarten. Together, we changed each other's minds about morals, life, and God. Church became more than a Sunday morning ritual. Christianity became more than presents in December. It became a way of life—a difficult, choppy, insane, and wonderful way of life. We defined our beliefs to each other, making promises about drinking and sex that we swore never to break.

God used us to help each other grow in faith. It wasn't easy turning my back on my sinful ways. I went through hell, but even though life got more difficult every day, it got easier to deal with. I was beginning to realize the true power of God. He could do anything for me, as long as I lived for Him. Jesus had died for us on the cross—was it so much to ask that we try to live as He wanted us to? This new life was so fulfilling, so promising. We were excited, and wanted everyone else to feel the some way. Of course, most people were shocked at this sudden change and gave us many confused glances.

Our mothers stopped giving us second looks sooner than most. It may have been a sore neck, or it may have been understanding. Mothers are like that. They are concerned for a while, but soon accept the changes (as long as their furniture isn't threatened). Unless, of course, you impose on them—especially in their kitchen.

During holidays and family gatherings, the kitchen might as well have had yellow strips of plastic around it saying "POLICE LINE! DO NOT CROSS!" It was difficult to obey such orders, however, unless one has no sense of smell. The odors that emanated from there were irresistible. No Christmas was complete without twenty pounds of cookies. We especially liked the flat, sprinkly reindeer for an after-dinner treat during the holidays. The pantry was always stocked with a rainbow assortment of sugars, as well as tiny silver balls and pastel stars. After decorating, this assortment could also be found on the floor. (Our dog put on considerable weight.) There were chocolate and peanut butter cookies in the freezer and, in a clear glass bottle on the door, maraschino cherries in the fridge.

These tempting little red balls of delight are the one thing in the kitchen that I was forbidden to eat, touch, or even look at. We would barely have them out of the grocery bag before Mother began to lecture. "These cherries are off limits. Don't taste them. Do not even open the door and took at them. These are for the cookies, not for you. Do you understand?" I had understood. I also understood that if you sneak one out every couple of days at about one in the morning, no one will notice they are disappearing—until the recipe calls for a full jar, and your mom finds only half the jar left. Then you get grounded.

I spent a lot of time pouting in my room when I was young. I would sit by the window, cursing my parents for being such tyrants. How dare they ground me for eating something out of my own refrigerator? What did they expect me to eat? Carrots? I didn't think so. These little mental arguments wouldn't last long, however, since I soon grew bored talking to myself. I would stop finding reasons to be upset, and would start to think. I thought happy thoughts, sad thoughts, confusing thoughts, and impossible thoughts, like why God would punish me with two horrible brothers or why He let me make so many horrible mistakes. But then I looked out my window at the rolling puffs of white in the blue sky, and realized that life was more wonderful than I could ever comprehend. I watched the squirrels hopping from tree to tree, listened to the larks singing sweetly between the tree-tops, and inhaled the perfume drifting from my neighbor's flowers.

As I grew older, I didn't have time to notice the birds' song, or the flowers' aroma. The hustle and bustle of society smothered the picture of beauty I had once held so dear. Yet, I would find myself wondering about why things seemed different—why, deep inside, I felt empty. I was on the honor roll, surrounded by friends, and captain of the varsity girl's lacrosse team. But I was unhappy. It wasn't until I was forced to slow down that I realized what I had been missing.

One minute I was twelve inches in the air reaching for an incoming pass, and the next I was face first on the field with a sprained knee and a mouthful of dirt. I was not happy. There we were, ready to begin our first in-county game, and I was stuck on the bench, watching somebody else try to fill my shoes. It had a very humbling effect, one which the ice on my knee did nothing but aggravate. But what else could I do? It was either play in the game and risk messing up my knee for the rest of the season, or sit back and wait for it to heal. I chose to wait, but it was hard not to jump out onto the field when the referee blew the starting whistle. It was physically painful to watch the game.

I stared off into the distance, trying to block out the sounds of the game and, in the process, began to notice other things. I studied the trees across the field, and wondered what it would be like to live inside of one. I pretended to be a cloud, drifting high above everyone's head. I felt what it would be like to be a leaf, floating down to the ground. In time, my knee healed, and I was soon back on the field where I belonged. But I didn't (or couldn't) stop thinking about the world around me, and how wonderfully it was made.

I set aside time each day to ponder such things, and this "quiet time" became something I would look forward to. It became a time of peace, and a time to talk to God.

God is an interesting person to have a conversation with. You can't see, hear, feel, taste, or touch Him; and yet, you know He's there. I began to reexamine my faith to determine exactly what I believed in. I was very gung-ho about my Christianity, but I had lost the excitement I once had. Was I living a Christian life, or was I falling back into my old ways? I knew God was real, and that He had a wonderful plan for my life. I had seen too many coincidences to doubt that. I knew there was a heaven—but would I get to go? Jesus had something to do with it. They said He died for us. But how did this death give me eternal life? How could I claim this gift anyhow? There wasn't exactly an 800-number to call for the answers. I had only the Bible, my church, and the world around me.

I was given my first real Bible when I graduated from my third grade Sunday School class. It's leather bound, and very nice to look at. It fits nicely into your hands. Aside from that, however, it was hard to think of its stories as real. It wasn't that I didn't believe what was inscribed in the pages, but it was hard to relate to. I wasn't around to see the Garden of Eden. I didn't walk through the Red Sea. I have never seen a manger, let alone a child lying in one. Granted, all these things happened, but they seemed outdated. So I went to my minister, and he did a simple thing. Placing his hand on my shoulder, he turned me toward the window. "Hollie, this is where you'll find the answers to your questions. Just look at the beauty of creation. There is where you'll find the answers—when you realize that the wonder that surrounds you is a gift from God."

It wasn't until years later, when I stood at what seemed like the edge of eternity, that I fully understood what God was trying to tell me. I was in the Shenandoah mountains, perched on the top of Old Rag mountain. Below me was solid rock; around me, nothing but fog. Thick fog. It covered the rock behind and in front of me. I felt as if I were standing in the middle of an abyss. It appeared to be the middle of the night, for nothing could be seen. Yet, the sun was shining, illuminating the nothingness. There was no way to escape from that rock. In fact, there was no way that rock could have been there in the first place. But it was, and so was the way out. I couldn't see it, but I knew it was there. Never before had I been so exhilarated and terrified. Surrounded by uncertainty and danger, I was standing firm. I couldn't see the foundation, but I knew it was there and trusted it to support me.

God is as solid as a rock. You can depend on Him to carry you through anything that comes your way. That first step of faith, that movement into uncertain ground, is the most important thing a person can do in life. Since I accepted Christ, and seated Him on the throne of my life, I've been at peace. Sure, life was still hectic and stressful, but it wasn't impossible. It hadn't always been that way. I always thought I had "God-power" when I was younger, but I was still suffering. I thought that God was with me, and He was, but I was being hit from all sides. Until I invited Him into my life, and gave Him control, He had to sit back and watch.

So, watch He did. He watched me steal, lie, cheat. I was crushed. The world was falling down around me, and I knew it. There is nothing more depressing than watching the walls of your life crumble down around you. I couldn't take it anymore. I needed out, and I asked the Lord to give me His hand. I laid on my back in the middle of my bedroom rug, sobbing hysterically. "God, I need help," I began, shuddering as another cry racked my body. "I'm messing up on my own Lord. Please help me. Show me what I'm missing. I'm so sorry. Sorry for the wreck I've made of my life. Please forgive me. Please. Forgive me...."

As I lay there shedding tears of sorrow, I felt something begin to happen inside me. Such peace and compassion as I had never known was flowing through my veins, and I knew that I was beginning a new life. There would still be trials to face, but this time I wouldn't be alone. He would never let me fall.

One of the hardest things a person has to face in life is moving away from home. As a kid I had spent weeks away at camp, and weekends with friends, but none of this really prepared me for going away to college. Like most high school seniors, I could hardly wait until I was on my own, out from under my parents' watchful eyes. I had most of my belongings packed almost a month before it was necessary, and thought of nothing else during the summer.

Of course, with all the new ideas about my future life, came reality. I was going to be faced with some of the most difficult decisions I would ever have to make, and my mommy wasn't going to be there telling me what to do. My morals were going to be questioned, my faith tested. Here was a brand new chapter in my life, and it was up to me to fill the pages. In high school, I had managed to avoid situations where I might goof up. I hung around with my Christian friends, and tried to ignore the sin in the world.

I realized, however, that my hiding from sin wasn't helping anyone, not even myself. The purpose of a Christian's life is to change lives, to fulfill the Great

Commission and make disciples of all men. How could I help anyone if I didn't thrust myself into the world?

Having such a radical lifestyle is not easy for a college freshman. When my beliefs got around, I suddenly found some of my friends avoiding me. They were careful in what they said, afraid that if they swore, or spoke about drinking, I would call down the wrath of God upon them. It was hard to convince them that I would not, really could not, do such a thing. I, too, had once been lost and without Christ. Now that He was with me, it was my job to bring others to Him, to help them see the difference He had made in this person's life.

I couldn't do it on my own. I knew that God was with me, and that I could do anything, with His strength. But I needed physical support. I was only a freshman, stuck in a new world, with a bunch of unfocused energy. And, as usual, the Lord provided. This time He wasn't even subtle.

My granny used to have a poster hanging in her kitchen that read "Lord, nothing is going to happen today that You and I can't handle together." Boy, did I ever need that help. I was absolutely petrified. Standing on the curb with all my personal belongings scattered around my feet, I felt like a lost puppy, faced with living in the pound. Up until this point, I had been excited about moving to college, but now it was a nightmare.

Friends that I had met during my trip to the mountains made the transition easier, but there were some things I knew I could never get used to. I had to share the bathroom with three total strangers. There were men living right next door, and wandering around the halls in their robes. Every door was locked, so I had to always carry my keys. Mother wasn't there to fix dinner. I had to walk outside in the cold weather, and up to the dining hall. All this was nothing, however, compared to my biggest apprehension—the R.A.

As residents assistant for the second, third, and fourth floors, Diane was our disciplinarian, as well as our counselor and friend. As far as I was concerned, however, she was to be avoided. She had total power over me—what if she found some reason to hate me? What if she kicked me out of the building? My friend Steve tried to reassure me. "You're so lucky! She was my TRIAD leader," he explained. TRIAD was our orientation program.

If someone had told me then that in a month Diane and I would be best friends, and that we met because I invited her down for pizza, I would have fallen over in hysterics. But, in the end, they would have been right. Once I met her—actually had a conversation with her—I knew our R.A./resident relationship was no coincidence. Someone had His hand in the situation. Perhaps it was the four-hour conversation we had that Friday night that led me to that conclusion, or our six-hour talk on Saturday. Either way, I knew we had been destined to meet.

The reason was simple. We needed each other. I was able to help her face some problems that had been bothering her, simply because I had just gone through them myself. The four-and-a-half years between us in age were almost forgotten, and our friendship developed into something very special. She was always there to give support, and we both figured out that a hug right before bed helps you sleep better. We slept very well. She listened to my problems, gave advice, and quickly became the big sister I never had. A Mass Communications major in her senior year, Diane was one of the busiest people I ever met. Between her sorority meetings, radio station internship, classes, staff meetings, club meetings, desk duty, news broadcasts, and campus radio shift, she barely had time to breathe. Yet, she always made time for me, offering love and encouragement.

With her by my side, and God at the helm, I was ready to take the world by storm. No longer was I going to sit idly by and be average. I joined the Building Council for my dorm, and was elected Chairperson of the Communications Committee. I joined a Christian sorority, and became an active member of Campus Crusade for Christ. I saw six of my friends become Christians in the first semester at school. It blew me away. Even doing all these things, however, I felt as if I were missing something. When I realized what it was, I kicked myself for not thinking of it sooner.

I have always had a passion for words. All through middle school, I wrote silly stories and poems about princesses living happily ever after. My room was a virtual library—I read anything I could get my hands on. I flew to Never-Never Land with Peter Pan, followed Edmund into Narnia, and flew around the galaxy with Captain Kirk. When I hit high school, and began writing for our paper, "The Bear Press," I began to realize what I wanted to do with the rest of my life. I wanted not only to create new worlds, and meet new people, but I also wanted to help people as well. I wanted to reach them through my writing, and let them know what was really going on in the world. I would be honest, sometimes painfully so. I would be an editor at *The Washington Post*.

Unfortunately, my parents had other plans for me. I was going to be a brain surgeon, or a scientist, or a lawyer, or an engineer. But definitely not a writer. Little did they know that I had already made up my mind. There was no turning back. I wrote about myself, my friends, and God. I wanted to show everyone else the beauty in the world, the magnificence of creation. How better to do this than writing? To show the beauty of a winter sunset, when the rays flicker along the snow. To present the music as the wind rustles through the leaves. To explain the perfection of a teardrop, sliding slowly down a little boy's cheek. But most of all, to create in people a yearning to know God better, to hunger for Him. After all, it was He who gave me my gift—should I not use it to serve Him?

So write I did. Life went on around me, flowing continuously, neither stopping nor noticing the changes in my life. It simply blew by like the wind on a blustery day, carrying with it faces and voices that exist now only in memories. As I stood by, watching life go on and on, I was reminded of a time when a silly little bird caused me to falter. Life had seemed impossible in that brief moment, but now I realized what real God-power was. It was not the physical strength and intelligence I had thought as a naive child, but a reassurance that with God, all things were possible. My problems were all so unimportant compared to the magnificence that is God. I pondered these thoughts, watching life flow by.

Off in the distance, piercing my meditation, I thought I heard a faint noise. A memory, perhaps, of a day gone by. I strained my ear to catch it before it flew away and, in that moment, I heard it. "Cuckoo, Cuckoo...."

And I laughed.

IT DOESN'T LAST FOREVER
by Nina Lattimore

I was a tall, skinny, flat-chested eighth grader. He was a tall, lean seventh grader. For all I knew, we had nothing in common. I wondered what boy would want to have an "ironing board" as a girlfriend, and, because of my feelings, I never opened my mouth to speak to him. Instead I walked the halls head down, holding my books to my chest, praying that the tissues in my bra wouldn't fall out, and hoping that I wouldn't run into him. If I did, I knew my plan was to run, and to continue to run. I can remember telling my best friend, Michelle, about how I thought a seventh grader was so cute. His name was Reno, and boy did I like him, but I just didn't have the courage to speak because I was too shy.

Thanks to Michelle, Reno and I became close in the ninth grade. I now considered myself as part of the cool crowd because Reno was my boyfriend. I didn't hold my head down any longer, but walked down the hall with Reno. However, I still held my books to my chest, praying the tissues in my bra wouldn't fall out. I was fourteen and still never had a group of guys and girls come over to my house. I prayed for the day when my mom would allow me to have "company." When Reno and his friends were finally allowed over, it took me an hour to get dressed. I spent so much time looking for the right outfit, even though all the clothes in my closet were the same: baggy jeans and shirts. I worried about him liking my family, and my family liking him. I also wondered if his family would like me.

The first time I met Reno's mom was on an unpleasant occasion. Reno had sneaked me and some friends into his house, and to our surprise his mother walked in. I thought, "Oh no, now you have really done it, Nina." I was so scared, and I didn't think of going to his house ever again. But I did. Each Sunday, after church, Reno would come to my house, or I would go over to his house.

One Sunday, it was Reno's parents' time to pick me up. I sat in my living room, waiting nervously for the sound of his dad's "Big Green Machine," as all our friends called it. This was my first meeting with Reno's dad because he was usually at work while Reno's mom was home. When the horn blew, I ran to the vehicle, and seated myself in the back. My first impression of Reno's dad was "Reno looks just like his father." Mr. Owens didn't say much on the way to Reno's house, and I thought he didn't like me. I sensed him staring at me through his rear-view mirror. Did he think I wasn't good enough for his son? Was my head too big? Was I too skinny? I didn't know what to do, so I sat in the back seat quietly, hoping that the butterflies in my stomach wouldn't make a sound.

Through the years I got to know all of Reno's family. I became close with his parents and siblings. I enjoyed going over to their house on Sunday, and eating his mother's fried chicken and his dad's homemade rolls. I became addicted to Mr. Owens's Stylistics songs. Reno and I had grown up together, and I felt our friendship would last forever.

Things were going well for me. Reno and I were still together and my family life was great, but suddenly on one hot July day my McDonald's-happyland life was smashed. Around 10:00 p.m., my dad's car zoomed into my grandmother's driveway like a race car in the Indy 500. He stopped in front of her kitchen door, where my aunts, mother, grandmother, and I were eating. Out of breath, he told us unbelievable news. It was something I didn't want to hear. My boyfriend's father had been shot.

Why? When? I just couldn't believe it. I screamed, cried. I just couldn't control my anger. I had no idea what to do, but I began to calm down as my mom comforted me. I thought maybe his dad was only wounded. In other words, I thought everything would be okay. I had no idea what I was supposed to do. Was I supposed to comfort Reno, knowing that I didn't have much strength myself. Flashbacks of Mr. Owens washing the "Big Green Machine" popped in my head. I felt as if my body were lifted from my grandmother's kitchen chair and taken to another planet. By 11:00 p.m., Reno was at my house. Shocked, we decided to call Reno's grandmother to see if everything was okay.

"He's dead," Reno cried.

I yelled, "Oh God, please, this can't be true!"

Reno told me how he and Michelle had just left Westport (a community in Baltimore City) and had seen his father. Reno had no idea that would be the last time he would see or talk to his father. So that's how it is, I thought. It was done. Mr. Owens was gone. I thought about his body leaving earth and going to heaven. I wanted to know what he was feeling. I wanted to ask him, but I couldn't. I didn't have the chance to say goodbye.

We didn't even have the chance to see Mr. Owens in the hospital. He never made it. He died instantly. My cries couldn't help; there was nothing I or anyone could do to bring him back. My brother and friend went to find Reno's brother, Dyandre, to tell him the horrible news, while I sat in my basement sipping Tang and moaning like a zombie. A father is the foundation of a family; how in the hell could they make it without him? I thought about my father dying, and I became tense thinking about everybody dying one day.

Later that night I drove to Reno's aunt's house. On the way, I wondered what I could possibly say. I couldn't tell Reno that my dad would be there to help him. He didn't want to hear that, because he wanted his own father. Would Reno be mad because I had a dad? I felt awkward. Arriving at his aunt's apartment, we saw his mother and other family members standing outside. At this point, I was ready to turn my car around and go home. I felt it was a time for family members, and I was an oddball who should have stayed home.

It was 2:00 a.m. when I arrived home. Reno decided to stay the night with me, while his brother stayed with their mother. We slept in the living room, staying up half the night crying. I couldn't sleep. I tossed and turned until I couldn't turn any more. I was wide awake at five o'clock in the morning. For the first time in my life I watched the sun rise. I sat there thinking about the day I met Reno's dad, and I wished I could have had that Sunday afternoon over again. Nothing like this had ever happened to me. No one in my extended family had ever died, at least no one who I was close to.

Reno and I were both awake, sitting motionless, wondering how could a summer that was so right go so wrong. Around 7:00 a.m. Reno decided to go to his house to shower and change clothes. I sat alone in his house. I was scared; I thought I would hear footsteps or even sounds. While Reno took a shower, I rested in his bed, hiding under the covers, closing my eyes tightly, hoping not to see Reno's dad's spirit. My heart thumped. I stayed still. I kept imagining Reno's dad in the doorway.

During the week, I remember going to the mall and buying unnecessary items. I bought a black skirt that was too big, an ugly jean shirt, and Payless generic Converse. I never was into black, and had no idea why I was buying black at all. I hated the fact that I had to wear black to the funeral. I didn't want to wear a black dress. I didn't want to sit there and hear the minister speak. I just wanted to cry.

July 30 was Reno's dad's funeral. Reno ate breakfast at my house that morning, but I couldn't eat a thing. My stomach hurt so badly. I just wanted to go to the funeral, and return home. While driving to his grandmother's house to meet his family, Reno and I had a chance to talk. I told Reno that he was now the leader for his siblings. He was the one who now had to walk with his head held high, and help his brother and sister along the way. When I said that to him, I thought, "Nina, who do you think you are?" How could I tell him to do something that I might not be strong enough to do myself? I never told Reno that I had second thoughts about going to his dad's funeral. I was scared, and the feelings I had were unbelievable. I couldn't sleep at night, and would lay on my bed looking into the dark.

My heart beat like a drum on the way to the funeral. I didn't want to see Mr. Owens's body, and I didn't like the black dress my mother made me wear. Approaching the church, we saw many people standing outside: Reno's friends, our church pastor, my family, and others I can't even name. I held Aneisha's hand as we walked into the church. Tears rolled down my face. I was terrified. I could not believe I was attending a funeral for someone to whom I was so close. I just couldn't believe that the next time I went to Reno's, Mr. Owens wouldn't be there. I would no longer come over on Sundays and taste his buttery rolls with fried chicken. I shook terribly at the sight of Mr. Owens's body. I glanced at him and hurried to my seat. I sat there looking at Mr. Owens, crying and saying why, why him. This scene was more like something seen on the evening news. It was unreal. I had no idea that this would be something I would have to face one day. Reno's Uncle Sean, wearing sunshades, sat between the two of us. He kept telling us that everything would be okay, but no matter what he said, I couldn't stop crying.

I couldn't stand seeing Mr. Owens there. I prayed, asking God for a miracle. Jesus had raised Lazarus from the dead. Couldn't He come down from Heaven and into our church? Couldn't He let Mr. Owens rise out of his casket and breathe again? But no, He couldn't—for a reason I didn't know or understand.

When we left the church to go to the cemetery, there were at least sixty cars in the procession. Arriving at the burial ground, I began to feel a little better. Mr. Owens's friend sang, "It's so hard to say goodbye," as everyone laid flowers on the casket. While all this went on I stood there looking at everyone. It was so hard for me to believe. Then it was over. Mr. Owens was buried six feet deep, and we wouldn't see him again.

That September I went off to college. Reno was in his last year of high school, and this was our first time being away from each other. After Reno's dad's death, I wanted to commute to school. After talking with my parents, I decided to stay on campus for the first semester, and if I didn't like it, I could then commute. My room was decorated with pictures of Reno's family. Each night I stayed on the phone talking to Reno. I was so concerned about how he was doing. At times he would act as if everything were okay, but it wasn't. At other times, I would get so frustrated with Reno because he was in a daze. It was like I was talking to a stuffed animal. Or at times he would lash out at me for no reason. My feelings toward Reno began to change. I wasn't going to be his punching bag. I was so frustrated with Reno taking his anger out on me. Then, Reno's family moved to a new home, and Reno and I drifted apart.

In Reno's last year of high school, he was crowned Homecoming King. Although it was supposed to be a special moment, it was also sad. Everyone had their father walk them onto the field, but there was Reno with someone else's father. Sitting in the stands I cried. I knew in my heart that Reno's dad was looking down on him, but I wished he could be there to witness such a happy moment for his son.

Time progressed, and Reno's mom met someone else. This made all of us mad. How could she go and meet someone else? Mr. Owens had only been dead for six months. I couldn't believe that the man would even come into a home, knowing what had just taken place. I began to show my anger toward the "new face" by being rude. I wouldn't speak. I missed going to Reno's house and hearing the tunes of Marvin Gaye and the Stylistics. This guy didn't play music. He couldn't even make homemade rolls like Mr. Owens could.

Christmas trudged on by like the rest of the holidays. No one had the good "ole" holiday spirit. I tried my best to make Aneisha's Christmas one of the best she had ever had. I played Mrs. Claus, buying all her Christmas gifts, helping her decorate the tree, trying to get her into that jolly mood everyone except her family seemed to have. Holidays were different that year. Someone was missing and wouldn't be there ever again. I knew how Reno felt and tried to ignore it. I wanted him to be happy, but he wasn't. I had to understand that his mourning would last forever.

When the next spring came Reno prepared for high school graduation and set his sights on Wesley College in Dover, Delaware. I was so happy for him. I knew his father would be proud of him. As Reno walked across the stage, everyone screamed, cheered, and hollered. I thought of Mr. Owens at that moment, and I knew he had to be smiling down on Reno, saying "Good job, son." After the ceremony, Reno was given many balloons, cards, flowers, and gifts. I was happy to see how far he had come.

The summer after Reno graduated, we visited Mr. Owens's grave. Reno, Aneisha, Dyandre, their grandparents, and I cried. This was our first time back. We were so nervous that we couldn't find the plot. Standing in front of the plot I wondered what Reno's dad was doing. Was he looking down on us standing in a circle, crying, holding hands? I imagined Mr. Owens yelling, trying to get our attention, but we couldn't hear him. I didn't like visiting the cemetery. What was the purpose, besides looking at the plot and laying flowers? I couldn't see Mr. Owens again.

During the last year, Reno and I have become closer. In fact, we're best friends. There's nothing that he can't tell me or I can't tell him. There are times when Reno's sadness gets to me, but I understand that it's normal. A couple of weeks ago, I visited Reno's room at college. He had pictures of his dad on his wall. I was glad to know that he keeps his father close to his heart. Times have changed for the better.

Although I still have flashbacks of that horrible July day and Mr. Owens's funeral, I understand that such flashes are normal. This tragedy was one of the worst events of my life, but God taught me a lesson from it: life doesn't last forever, so we should live each day to its fullest.

ANTONIA
by Alessandra Vadala

The day that Nonna Antonia died, I brought her flowers, which did not make it any different from any other day. My mother and I always brought my great-grandmother lilies and lilacs and other springtime flowers. But when a Sicilian woman dies, the way that you give her flowers changes. The flowers no longer bring joy; they remind you of sadness. You no longer place them in front of her, and expect a smile to grow across her face; instead, you place them in "the dead room," alongside her picture, and you light candles all around.

The dead room doesn't let the sun in, except in stubborn, random beams that sneak in under the door. The only movement is the flickering of candles and the falling chips of chalky blue paint that the walls sweat off in summer. I never wanted to "visit" Nonna in that room; it didn't suit her at all.

I wanted the morning of Nonna's last day to be like any other, but it couldn't be. I wanted to see her smile when she saw the flowers I brought, but I had to settle for sitting the vase down on the night table next to her bed. In it, she lay so still that I was afraid she was already gone. I didn't even know if she saw the flowers. If it had been any other day, they would have been just a simple gift. These flowers were supposed to mean more. I wanted them to be seen differently from those sent by others, flowers that looked ready to be placed next to her picture in the candle-lit room.

My flowers were for the Nonna that was still alive. I waited for the other visitors to leave the room to say goodbye. Most of my family would be there that evening, and I probably wouldn't get the chance to feel alone with her. It was supposed to be a time to let go, but I didn't want to. All day, my mother had been telling me that I was lucky even to have known my great-grandmother. Most people don't get the chance to feel close to even their grandparents.

I tried to be thankful, as my mother encouraged, but it was nearly impossible while holding Nonna's almost lifeless hand. Her knuckles were so worn, and her veins rose well above her flesh. I thought of the way those hands stroked aside my bangs from my sweaty forehead when I was sick. I wished that a prayer and loving strokes of a caring hand were all that she needed that day, but I knew that Nonna had led a full life, and that she was ready to go.

My great-grandmother was born Antonia Longo on February 10, 1903, in Torre Faro, Messina, in Sicily. At seventeen, she married my great-grandfather, Nicola Ruello. Together, they had four children. Their third child was my grandmother, Angelina. After Angelina was born, my Nonno Nicola went to the United States to find work and eventually send for his family. Sixteen years passed before his wife and children were able to join him. Nonna Antonia was left alone in Sicily to raise her children, and to survive the frequent bombing during World War II.

Nonna must have been very brave and strong to have lived through such a horrible time. On many nights, she and her children had to run into the mountains to escape the bombings, unsure if their house or town would be left standing when they returned. Eventually, they had to move with many other families into caves in the same mountains. But surviving the war without her husband was not the hardest thing that Nonna had to survive. The death of her oldest daughter, Rosie, was a much more horrible thing to bear.

I first met Rosie in the dead room, when I was six, the age that she was when she died. Her picture didn't fit in with the others. She was just a little girl, with little brown bangs like mine. I wondered what she was doing in there with all of the grown-ups. My grandmother was only three when her big sister, Rosie, died, but she said she remembered Nonna Antonia cursing at the doctors who failed to save her. Tragically, Rosie died of a curable disease that the doctors misdiagnosed.

When she died, they wanted to perform an autopsy, but Nonna couldn't bear to allow anything more to happen to her child. At night, she stole Rosie's body from the hospital and carried her baby home to be buried. The image of Nonna running down the street with Rosie in her arms leaves me in awe. All alone, she buried one child and cared for her others for sixteen years.

When I was old enough to understand the stories of Nonna's past, I realized that she had lived a life that I knew almost nothing about. She was once young, and her skin was smooth. She was full of passion and energy. I knew the facts and saw the pictures, but I really never recognized that Nonna had lived a life in which she was just Antonia.

When I looked at Nonna's pale, almost lifeless hands, I tried to see past the elderly, white haired great-grandmother I knew. I thought back to the times we spent together, and I realized that Antonia had always been there; I just never looked for her. The sturdy arms that carried Rosie home on that terrible day were the same that hugged me every day as a child.

Until I was six or seven, my image of Nonna had always been the same. She had always been the old woman sitting on the right side of the living room sofa, crocheting little flowers to be sewn together into a baby blanket or wedding afghan. She was forever wearing knee-high hose that rolled down to her ankles and felt slippers on her feet. She also wore dark, flower covered dresses that would have been painfully unattractive on anyone else. But even in such garb, she still managed to look elegant.

It always made me smile that even with sagging nylons she remained self-conscious enough to make sure that every curl was in place. She also loved her pearl-diamond earrings. I remember how low her earlobes hung with them on. I think she felt that such jewelry was the key to her beauty. But Nonna's beauty came through in the things she did, not in what she wore.

My childhood perception of Nonna can be explained in the telling of our evening ritual. Every night, like clockwork, she would say her prayers on the living room sofa. I would curl up next to her and rest my head on her lap. The soft whispers of an Italian rosary were my lullaby. I felt very safe in that lap, knowing that one of her prayers was said for me. Nonna provided me with a sense of security and unconditional love. I remember thinking that a woman so old, who prays so much, must be very close to God. I thought that when she prayed, she told God what He needed to do. I felt blessed just to rest my head on her lap.

The very first time that I saw past my childhood image of Nonna, and got a glimpse of Antonia, was around Christmas time when I was eleven. Our whole family sat watching "the good old days" in action. An uncle of mine had put all of our home movies on video tape for the holiday. After a while, most of my family filtered into the kitchen for coffee. I stayed in the living room with Nonna Antonia. While gazing at the screen, we saw my father grow up before our eyes. One second he was an infant, then a toddler, and then he was graduating from high school. Then the scene changed again.

The next movie took place at a big party or a wedding a long time ago. There was a couple dancing together. The black and white film made it look more like a quiet memory than a silent home movie. The dazzling images weren't spoiled by the sounds of voices. The dancing couple said things to each other and laughed. The woman was lovely. The man held her tightly as they whirled across the floor. His huge hands made hers look like a china doll's: smooth and fragile. I didn't realize who the two people were until the woman looked right into the lens of the camera. She wore Nonna's pearl-diamond earrings. I turned to Nonna to find her crying, but smiling through it all.

It was hard for me to visualize Nonna's life without all of us in it. Despite what I could or couldn't comprehend, Nonna did have a life that didn't include me. When I went to Sicily though, I got to see what was left of Antonia, the way she used to be as a young woman. In Sicily, Nonna was in her own element. She was in her own house, in her own town.

Sicily was where she was in charge. Italy transformed Nonna into an able-bodied, rather bossy and powerful woman. A person whom I had grown so accustomed to, had stepped out of the dim, gray light that I had always seen her in. Though she was in her late-seventies, she somehow reclaimed her role as the almighty superior the moment she stepped onto Italian soil. She suddenly had power over the people who usually made decisions. To me, Italy then seemed like the land where the wishes of the old people magically became all important.

Even when I returned to Sicily with Nonna when she was in her eighties, her position of authority still stood; however, it had become slightly false. The adults responded to her requests like a mother would to the demands of an impatient child. When Nonna wanted to do the dishes in her own home, she was refused the right "for her own good." I could see her frustration building. In fact, while we were still in Italy, I had to cook for Nonna on some afternoons while everyone else was out visiting other family members.

On one afternoon, in particular, I was reminded several times to return early from the beach to cook for Nonna. As usual, though, I was late. I ran through the streets as fast as I could, and flew into the house and into the kitchen. There stood Nonna Antonia, at eighty-seven, behind a table covered with a hot lunch prepared especially for us. She had made pasta with red sauce and a big salad. On her face was a look of incredible pride. I then realized that Nonna still needed to know that we needed her. And we did too, desperately.

Nonna was a figure of permanence in my life. She was the oldest person in our family, and no one ever had to do without her. Before she had gotten sick for the last time, we were used to seeing her bounce back from illnesses. But one summer, Nonna got very sick and was hospitalized. Immediately, my whole family swarmed around the hospital.

The effect of my family on hospital staff is pretty significant. Because of our large numbers and overbearing attitudes, the more inconvenient hospital rules are sometimes overlooked. In addition, Nonna received certain perks as a result of incidents during her previous stays in the hospital. For example, Nonna never had to deal with the inconvenience of a roommate, or perhaps a roommate didn't have to deal with the inconvenience of our family. Either way, we managed to ignore the "two visitors at a time" rule also. But the best thing that we were able to do for Nonna was to get her the best food possible: my grandmother's.

I like to think that my family got special privileges because it was so apparent that Nonna was the most important member of our family, but in reality, it was probably because Nonna didn't speak much English, and by supplying food and constant attention, the need for a translator was usually eliminated. Our family had a lot of fun tending to Nonna when she was in the hospital because we were all together, and we could finally do something for her for a change; however, it was impossible to shake our sadness completely. We all knew that, though we were able to sometimes lift Nonna's spirits, she would never get completely better.

My last happy memory of Nonna Antonia is also my favorite Christmas memory. It all started when my grandparents found out that I had sung a song in Italian for a school concert. They eventually badgered me into singing it for Christmas grace. When they insisted so strongly that I sing the song, I realized that it would be Nonna's last Christmas.

On Christmas day, we ate dinner at my aunt's house. All of us gathered around the table and we waited for Nonna to come. My aunt wheeled her up to the head of the table, oxygen tubes attached to her nose and all. I realized that, once again, my grandmother had blabbed the news about my singing when all heads immediately turned to me. I was a little less than thrilled at first, but when I began to sing, my embarrassment turned to pride. Nonna began to sing the song "Tu Scendi dalle Stelle" with me. We sang together, and then she sung a verse I didn't know. It made her so happy that I had learned it. I was so excited, but when I got home that day, I cried for a long time. I wished that I could have done more than sing a little song in order to let her know how important she was to me.

Nonna died that spring. I stood next to her and held her hand moments before she died. Her hand was cold and colorless, but I tried to convince myself that the warmth of her soul still lived. I still feel as though she is on a long trip, that maybe she is waiting for me in Sicily, with dinner on the table. Though she is gone, I know that, in many ways, she is right here with us.

On the night Nonna died, I saw things I never thought I'd see. Our family came closer together than it ever had before. Moments after she passed, we all cried together. Some of us told about things that she had done for us. Some of the cousins told us that Nonna had delivered them, and therefore held them before anyone else in the world. Nonna had gone, but she left us with a bond that could never be broken. Her love was something we all had in common, no matter what the future might bring.

Nonna Antonia's funeral was surprisingly filled with both joy and sadness. It is hard to imagine that any part of a funeral could be funny, but then our family is quite unique. Everything was very solemn for the beginning of the service, but then my grandfather got up to read. First things first: my grandfather has quite an accent. He began to read an eloquent passage that included a beautiful metaphor for life's passing when the accent took over completely. The metaphor was about a ship leaving one port and entering another. Unfortunately, the word "ship" came out "sheep," and the once very touching and appropriate passage was pretty much ruined. Somehow the image of a big sheep leaving the docks of life just didn't do the trick. It took a few minutes, but the church eventually filled with laughter and mocking "Baaah" sounds, to the confusion of a few non-English-speaking family members.

Aside from a few light moments, the funeral was otherwise very sad. A week before Nonna died, I had agreed to sing the "Ave Maria" for the meditation hymn, after the Eucharist, which is the worst time to sing because everyone just sits and stares at you. I wanted to give this gift to Nonna, but I knew it would be very difficult. I cried throughout the Mass, up until it was time to sing. I stood, shaking, in front of my whole family. By doing nothing but staring at the sheet music during the whole song, I thought I could get through it. I concentrated so hard on every little vowel sound that I forgot for a moment where I was. Unfortunately, on the very last syllable, I looked up to see a sea of faces that wouldn't have existed without Nonna. We all owed everything to her. My voice began to quiver, and then the singing stopped. I froze. A woman helped me to sit down in my seat, and the Mass continued.

The next thing I knew, my five-year-old cousin, Joanna, asked me why I was crying. I wanted to put her on my lap and tell her everything I knew about the young Antonia and the Nonna she became, but instead I ran my hand over her little brown bangs and said, "Shhh, I'll tell you all about it later."

STEEL WILL: Second Chances

I pass death
with the dying
and birth with
the new-wash'd
babe, and am
not contained
between my hat
and boots…

"Writing the memoir is like breathing, but revising it is like having a heart attack. The revisions are difficult because I become involved in the piece. Changes feel like they are untrue to who I am and what I was feeling when I wrote the piece. I eventually gave up, resolving to write a new memoir, but I faced the same problem: I couldn't polish it.

"So I returned to the first memoir and discovered that I had gained some distance. With a fresh perspective, I saw things I wanted to change. I worked on the writing without being worried about the content, and learned to make changes without losing something important."

Diana Lynn Wheeler

STEEL WILL
by Emily Hegner

I remember loving my first grade class and my new teacher. I was six, a tiny thing enjoying the privileges of childhood. School was like an adventure. Every day there was something new, something fun. When weekends came, I enjoyed playing with Mom. We would melt crayons to make collages or make stamps out of potatoes. Then on Sunday it was church, no exceptions. Back then I even liked Sunday Mass. Maybe it was because we always went to the grocery store afterwards. My allowance and I would head straight for the candy aisle and carefully calculate. This particular Sunday, September 26, 1982, was horrifically different.

My father, my older sister, and I left for church. My mother stayed behind with my brother, Nana, and my little sister, who had wet her diaper. I wore my patent leather shoes, the yellow Bambi dress my Mom had made, and my purse, which held my weekly allowance. After church we hopped in the Volkswagen Bus and headed for Foodrite. After arguing for shotgun (the front seat), my sister and I both sat in the passenger seat, unbuckled. Ten minutes down Route 144, Dad was driving forty-five miles per hour approaching a road off to the left. A red sports car sped towards the intersection, not seeing the stop sign. Later we learned that the car had been involved in a road rally.

A nearby hill prevented our car from seeing the other car. No one would have thought that at that moment we should be saying our last blessings. Then it happened—impact! As the sports car ran the stop sign, we slammed into it broadside, throwing the car into an embankment. The force from the collision caused the van to swerve left, then forward, and finally, as my body was projected through the front windshield, the van fell to its right side. My father and sister were still in the van. A man who lived nearby called for a helicopter, but, no matter how soon help could have arrived, it was too late for the passenger of the sports car.

I was told my father was in shock at the time. He was walking around the scene not aware he had slipped a disc in his spine or that he was in danger of being completely paralyzed. My sister was hysterical as the helicopter and paramedics arrived. A kind lady had scooped me up in her arms; she cradled my limp body. I was completely silent, my eyes shut. I was looked over by the paramedics as they loaded my sister into the helicopter.

The lady who held me asked the paramedics, "Can't you take her along with her sister? She's so small." And so they did.

Unknowingly, I was in serious condition. My injuries were mostly internal, and I remained quiet, so it appeared my sister was far worse than I. Her face was painted with blood and gravel; her bottom teeth had pierced the flesh under her lips. She had injuries on her knee and wrist. The only visible injury was my torn-up forehead. We were flown to Johns Hopkins Hospital. My father went to Howard County General Hospital. Upon arriving at the hospital, I was immediately taken to pediatric shock trauma; my sister went to surgery. The doctors said I was showing no vital signs. I was dead.

Back at home, my mother was oblivious to what had happened, but was worried because we were late. She remembers vividly when the phone rang. She steeled herself and answered. The doctors said they were calling from Johns Hopkins and asked her to "come right away because your youngest daughter isn't responding to treatment."

I remained without vital signs for eight minutes as the doctors tried to revive me. Thanks to the head doctor and God, life was returned to me. I learned later that the only reason that the doctor tried so hard was because she had a daughter my age at home. Once my vital signs stabilized, the doctors started asking me questions. They watched and listened in amazement as I muttered willfully my name first, then my telephone number. This meant, miraculously, there was no brain damage.

My mother waited with me as I lay in my hospital bed. IVs speared my veins and pumped fluids into my body. Every hour a kind-faced lady dressed in white visited me. She'd prick my fingers, forearms, or toes—whichever looked less used and bruised. I'd watch as my blood filled a little vial. At the same time, I remember the lady gently brushing my hair aside with her fingers and asking me not to cry.

When I was told what had happened, I immediately wanted to know about my sister, Jen. "Where is she?" I asked my mother. "She's over there, in that bed. But they're taking her to her own room now," she told me. I didn't want to be separated from her, not now. I was so lost. I strained to look up at her as they were wheeling her out of the room.

"Jen, is that you, Jen?" I muttered.

"Emily?" she asked.

"I love you, Jen," I said as she was leaving.

Later that week, the doctors took one IV out of my left arm because it hurt so badly. They started me on lemon swabs—those Q-tips with a weak lemon-flavored solution at the ends. They kept my lips moist and got me used to tasting again. I couldn't understand why I couldn't eat real food. Real people eat real food. I was alive, although I wasn't quite sure why, and I should've been able to eat. I didn't understand much at the time. I didn't know why the sheets were so stiff, but I knew they made me uncomfortable. The gifts from my first grade class and the tape of everyone saying "hello" and "I hope you get better" couldn't drown out the dreariness of the place or the smell of rubbing alcohol or the fear I felt when I saw the nurses' tools.

I was becoming restless and wanted to know how bad my injuries were. I wanted a mirror to look at my mangled, stitched-up forehead. After several days, I got a mirror. Black pieces of wire poked through red and purple flesh. I was horrified. I didn't realize I wouldn't look like that forever. Everyone seemed so happy that I was alive and doing so well, but the sight of my forehead scared me. It made me wonder just what I had experienced and why, if God wanted me to live, He had made me so ugly now. Inside I felt something traumatic had happened, yet I couldn't remember anything before the day I awoke in the hospital.

My mom explained the scenario of the accident to me—church, the accident, the red sports car, the lady who held me, my lack of vital signs, and my strong will to survive. I strained to remember, but I couldn't. I still felt like the same person. Maybe my memory repressed this incident. Maybe the synapses of life taken from me held my memory of the event. If so, eight minutes of my life were gone forever along with my emotions about the accident, my visions of the scene, and the pain of the gravel and glass in my forehead. However the cards were dealt, I got life. Someone wanted me here, maybe God, maybe some other force. I was lucky, chosen, hallowed.

I admit I liked all the loving attention from friends and family. It diverted my confusion and made me strong. As I regained my strength, doctors started me on solid foods. That helped me to feel more alive, which, in turn, helped me to recover that much faster. The food itself was horrible, so I stuck mainly to a popsicle diet. By this time, both IVs were out of my arms. I felt emancipated.

After eating solid foods for three days—tasteless, yellow-green peas, small portions of instant mashed potatoes, and Jell-O—I was ready for a greasy McDonald's cheeseburger. I was taken to the activities room once a day to keep me from complete boredom. The first time I went, there were kids that appeared aged because they were bald except for a few sparse hairs. The nurse told me they were cancer patients, and the chemotherapy treatment for their illness caused hair loss. They looked so sad; their head and eyes appeared so big because they had no hair to mask their scalps.

I couldn't talk to them; it was too uncomfortable for me. I sat and made my pot holder and thought how lucky I was to be alive and have only a scarred forehead to remind me of the incident. I might have to be ugly for the rest of my life, but these kids had no hair and most likely no hope of living a long life. I also thought that the kids in school wouldn't know how well off I was. They wouldn't see these kids to compare me with. I would just be the girl who was in the accident and is ugly now. I knew they would talk about me and the thought of that hurt.

Two weeks had passed since the accident, and my doctors told me I would be leaving the following day. I would miss the oversized paintings of Smurfs and my other cartoon favorites hanging on the wall. At home, I wouldn't get all the red popsicles I wanted, gifts from my friends, or my own remote control to my own television. At the same time, I wondered what had changed at home. I also wanted to see my baby sister. By order of my doctors, I was to stay at home for three weeks before starting school again. During that time, I was going to be taken back to the hospital for check-ups and X-rays.

My father and sister were home when I got there. My father wore a big, white, stiff neck brace that stopped him from turning his head in either direction. This contraption forced his chin up and out—it always looked as if he was sticking his nose in the air. He told me this would help his spine stay straight, so it would heal properly. My older sister looked and acted fine except for the scars left on her chin, wrist, and knee. I used to tell her the scar on her knee looked like a caterpillar or a worm when she put her leg out straight.

Then I visited school for a half-day. I couldn't believe how much attention I got from almost everyone at school. I guess the kids who showed me no attention were too uncomfortable, maybe afraid they'd say the wrong thing. Several of my friends told me how lucky I was for being able to leave after half the day. I didn't think so.

I just wanted everything to be back to normal and to be treated like everyone else. Why couldn't I be in school all day if I was well enough to leave the hospital? I didn't go home and sleep afterwards. I wondered why someone or something wanted me alive, but at the same time wanted to keep reminding me I was different. I guess that's the price one pays for being part of a miracle.

After telling about a thousand of my friends about my experience, I was wishing it had been on the news because I was tired of having to remember. I was growing my bangs out, so no one could see my scar. But that only took care of the physical aspects. Every time I got into a car, I was bombarded by the thought of what could happen if I didn't put on my seatbelt. Although I was safer than before, I had to realize this miraculous event would follow me around for the rest of my life.

For the three weeks I was home, Mom and I resumed with the crafts, and my teacher started bringing me homework after the first week. I remember the first time my teacher, Ms. Compton, came to the house. I missed fire prevention week at school, so she brought me a bright red, plastic fireman's hat. The first thing she did when my Mom opened the door was put the hat on my head. Although it was oversized and drooped to my eyes, I felt like a hero.

At the end of the three weeks, I was ready to face the kids in school. It was no use telling my mom how I felt they were going to react; she would just tell me I was beautiful, and the scar could barely be seen. Kids have radar vision when it comes to something grotesque.

Years after the accident, when I was about thirteen, my mother asked me if I thought I was ready to see the pictures she took when my father and I were in the hospital. Of course, I said yes. Up until then, I didn't know any pictures existed, and everyone likes to look at pictures of themselves. However, I didn't especially like looking at these pictures. First, I looked at the scene of the accident—both cars bore many dents and scrapes; both had broken windshields. The red sports car's front end was compacted; it looked like a pug-nose dog. Next, I saw my father when he was in the hospital. Weights hanging from screws were coming from his head. His body lay motionless on a flat stretcher so his spine wouldn't move.

Then my pictures—I started to cry with my mother as she showed me one after another. A picture that sticks out in my mind is the one where I was lying in my hospital bed a few days after the accident. My eyes were closed tightly, my eyelashes were wet, and purple and blue bruises shaded the sunken-in skin around my eye sockets. Tubes ran from my nostrils to somewhere inside me. Worst of all, my stomach was bloated like a starving child's.

I began to see that the money I would be getting from this accident wasn't just lucky or "fair." It was the best the courts could do to compensate for death and a struggle for life. Although the money was compensation, it couldn't give back the childhood glow in my eyes that my mother said was mysteriously gone after the accident.

I-95
by Stacy Spring Knight

One moment I was driving down I-95 listening to music, talking to my friends, and feeling the wind blow through my hair. The next moment I was headed straight for a retaining wall with hardly any way of avoiding a collision. My life flashed before my eyes as I skidded into the wall with a thundering crash. All I kept thinking to myself after hitting the wall was "thank you." That afternoon was the most frightening day of my life.

It was the last day of my junior year of high school. What a wonderful feeling to have gotten through another challenging year at Oakland Mills High School. I experienced a great sense of accomplishment the minute the last bell rang. It was as if I had finished another stage in my life and was ready to enter that ever so important "senior year." I had the whole summer ahead of me. What was I going to do first? Where was I going to go? There were so many plans building up in my head, and I could not wait to get started fulfilling them.

My friends and I decided to throw a barbecue bash at my house to celebrate the upcoming summer. Then we would head off to the annual Columbia fair, which my friends and I have attended almost religiously since middle school. There were so many things to do to get ready for the barbecue. But before I could set up the party, I had to run an errand for my dad. I didn't want to drive down to the Inner Harbor to deliver paychecks, but I was obligated to do so. I estimated that this task would take me only about an hour to complete, and then I would be back home in time for our barbecue. Little did I know that I would not be returning that afternoon.

My friends Teddy, Matt, and Kinyon elected to come with me for the ride. We were all pepped up because my mom let me use her brand new Celica convertible for the afternoon. She had never let anyone drive her car. This was considered a treat because it was the last day of school, and I enjoyed driving her car because it was a sporty change from my Toyota Tercel. It seemed as if people turned their heads as we cruised by blasting the radio. We had not a care in the world during those few minutes; we were loving life and looking forward to the long summer ahead of us.

No one in the car was thinking that it might be our last day to live. We were not worried about the last things we had said to our parents, or whether we had told all the people we care about how much we love them; the only things on our minds were sun and relaxation. We thought that, in a few more days, all of us would be lounging at the beach taking in the rays, walking on the boardwalk, and playing with our friends. Most of the seniors in our school took a trip to Ocean City at the end of the school year. Although we were not seniors yet, my friends and I had many mutual friends graduating, and we were going to visit them for the weekend. Instead of calling it "Senior Week," as the seniors call it, we decided to call it "Junior Week," to suit our purpose.

That day in June the sun was shining, there were hardly any clouds, and it was perfect weather to be driving on the highway. The guys were concentrating on holding their hands over the side of the car to catch air between their fingers. Even after all the advice that I had heard about the importance of seat belts and all the dangers of not wearing one, it didn't occur to me to tell my three friends to buckle up, as I had. It seemed as if they didn't have a care in the world.

Suddenly, a car coming onto the highway hit the right rear side of my car. This collision shocked us all out of our daydreams and into reality. Stunned, I attempted to swerve out of the way to avoid any further collision with the other car. Then, realizing that I was headed in the direction of a retaining wall and earnestly wishing that I make a correct decision, I turned back to the right in order to avoid contact.

Unfortunately, this move pointed us directly toward the right cement wall. I remember thinking, what am I going to do next? I had never been in a car crash before. In fact, I received my driver's license just a scant six months earlier. The lessons I learned in driver's education flashed before me as I tried to find a solution to my problem—to no avail. The only thing left to do was slam on the brakes and pray.

As I skidded dangerously close to the wall, I kept thinking, is this a dream, could this be the end? It almost didn't seem real. It wasn't happening to me. It was just like watching a movie in slow motion: I saw my accident occur frame by frame, not continuously. Just as I closed my eyes, I felt my whole body being launched towards the steering wheel. Suddenly, the air bag blew up in my face, and the seat belt tightened on my shoulder. The air bag looked like a big, soft white pillow just waiting to envelop me.

Silence.

"Matt, are you all right?" Kinyon asked.

"Yeah, I'm okay," he said, "What about you, Teddy?"

"I'm all right," he responded in a shaky voice. "Stacy... Stacy?" I didn't answer. Kinyon repeated, "Oh shit, Stacy, are you all right?"

As I sat back in the seat to answer him, a stream of blood poured down my face. My head was pounding, I was shaking all over, and I could barely talk. I was in shock. I didn't hurt anywhere, but I was bleeding a lot. What had happened? I thought. After seeing the blood that had dripped all over my clothes, everyone started to panic. "I'm okay," I dreamily responded to reassure them. The blood— I distinctly remember the odor of blood—smelled so crisp and fresh that I could almost taste it. Matt threw me the t-shirt that he was wearing, and I used it to help control the bleeding. Kinyon gently wiped the blood from my face and body. He tied my hair back out of my face and calmly tried to ease my mind. I then realized that I was only bleeding from my nose. This has been fairly common for me, so I wasn't too worried. I leaned my head forward and pinched the pressure points on my nose as hard as I could.

Unexpectedly, a man appeared at the side of my car. He told me that he was a doctor, but he didn't look like one. He was plainly dressed and driving a red car. I was very grateful for his help. He gave me an ice pack for my face, which was by then badly swollen. I tried to follow his finger as he waved it in front of my face, but again it was like watching a movie. Then I saw the flashing red lights of the ambulance, some paramedics, and a police car.

A man from the ambulance got out to help me. "Do you want to go to the hospital?" he asked, concerned. I shook my head repeating that it was only a nosebleed, only a nosebleed. He must have left me to help the others because it seemed as if I were all alone.

Two policemen approached me next. One of them started asking me questions that I couldn't answer. It seemed as if he were talking at me, but not *to* me. I was in a daze. He then asked us to get out of the car and stand against the wall for safety. Once I stood up, I felt a sharp pain shoot through my shins, almost like the kind you get from running. I looked down, and my legs were all banged up. I must have hit them against the car, and I knew I would get massive bruises. The cars on I-95 were rushing by at such a speed that it seemed as if they were running through my head. By this time, the police had called my parents, and they were on their way to get me.

The ambulance drove away, and we were left to wait on the side of the road. After it left, I started to think that maybe I should have gone to the hospital, but it was too late. No matter which way I turned, the smell of the burnt rubber followed me. The policemen had by now moved on to question the lady who hit me in the rear. She was parked about a hundred feet away on the side of the road.

As I leaned against the retaining wall, I sat staring, with one eye open because of the ice pack, at the car that I had demolished, my mom's car. I couldn't believe that we had survived. The whole front end of the car was smashed; the right front tire was flat; the hood had folded like an accordion. The air bag had blood splattered all over it. This was my mom's new car! What was she going to say? Was she going to be mad? I didn't want her to get that nerve-wrenching call from the police reporting that I had been in an accident. I didn't want my family to worry.

The ice bag I was holding burned the scratches on my face, and I had a huge headache. The expressions on Teddy's and Kinyon's faces were blank. We were all physically and mentally a mess. Then we started to laugh. It was the only thing we could think of doing to keep our minds off what had happened, which was impossible. Then we all decided to take a piece of the car for memorabilia. We were taking glass from the ground, pieces of the headlights, and parts from the body of the car. Even at this point, my adrenaline was still flowing at full speed. I had the feeling that I had just gotten off a rollercoaster ride at Six Flags.

The guys were reminiscing about what had just happened, the astonishment they were feeling, and the shock they had endured. Matt told me that while the doctor was treating me, an eighteen-wheel tractor-trailer pulled over on the median on the other side of the road. The driver had run across the highway to see if we were all right. Confused, I wondered why the man pulled over. Matt said that the driver had told him that he was driving behind us during the accident and was only able to avoid hitting us because he had not gone to pick up his load that morning, as he should have. The driver felt certain that if he had had the heavy cargo, he would have crashed into us as we swerved across the highway. This news really hit home. We all could have died.

Just then, my dad, sister, stepmother, and some friends pulled up. Boy, I was glad to see them. I ran over to them and gave my dad a big hug. "I want to go home," I exclaimed. I didn't think I was going to see them again. I would have missed my crazy dad, otherwise known as "Crazy Richard." He is always trying to show his daughters a good time. There would have been no more spur-of-the-moment trips to Ocean City, wild parties, or Sunday outings. My dad is a kid at heart, always looking out for my sister's and my best interests. He always looks for unique things to broaden our horizons and entertain us. If there is something new we want to try or somewhere we want to go, he will be the first to volunteer to help us do it. My father is a lover and a collector of antiques, or rather "toys." His vast collection has items ranging from a 1963 split-windowed Corvette and jukeboxes to a gymnast-size trampoline and pinball machines. Even if some of his ideas about raising us were sometimes questionable, I always felt the love he gave me through his heart-of-gold intentions.

After enough cars arrived to accommodate us all, we decided to go home. In the car, I explained the extraordinary story of what I vaguely remembered happening. The events were cloudy in my memory even though they had happened just a few minutes earlier. As we were driving back, I wondered what I could have done to prevent this. What if the driver of the tractor-trailer had picked up his load as planned? Maybe, if we left five minutes later or, better yet, five minutes earlier, would that have made a difference? What if the paychecks were to be delivered on Saturdays instead of Fridays? Or, even if we had left at a different time or on a different day, would this have happened anyway? Why did this have to happen to me? I was so confused. These questions echoed through my head for months to follow.

The stinging on my face was getting worse, and I could feel bruises hardening on the rest of my body. The ice pack that the doctor had given me at the side of the road had a tiny hole in it. All the chemicals inside the blue bag were oozing into the cuts on my face. This was not so good, I thought, but I would be at the hospital soon to meet my mom. I knew she would make me feel better; she always did.

Sitting in the emergency room was hell. I clearly remember the girl lying in the bed behind the curtain neighboring mine. She was wailing at the top of her lungs for the doctors to stop. Apparently she had downed a few too many bottles of alcohol and had to get her stomach pumped. She was my age, and she also had almost died that day. Looking around the emergency room, I saw sights that I had never seen before. There was so much pain. Ironically, I felt lucky to even be there. Finally, after what seemed like hours of waiting, it was my turn to see the doctor.

My mother insisted that I have X-rays taken of my face to make sure nothing was broken. I had never had any X-rays taken before and I was scared. Doesn't the radiation cause cancer? I was told to strip down to my bra and wait in a small, dimly lit room until the nurse arrived. The examining table was metal and extremely cold. There were all sorts of tools and instruments in the room that I had never seen before, and their uses baffled me. There was one poster on the wall, which I assume was for patients' entertainment. Since the doctors are never on time, to ease your tedium, do they try to educate you on the nervous system? During the lengthy wait, which all people must endure when they go to a doctor, I found myself re-reading the poster. I pondered meanings of unfamiliar words, compared my body to that of the poster's drawing, and even found myself counting all the words out of boredom. It seemed as if the nurse would never come. Maybe she had forgotten about me. When the nurse did finally come in, I wanted to tell her the torment that she had put me through, but, out of politeness, I kept my mouth closed. She draped a heavy metal-filled smock over my chest to protect my organs and then vanished into a glass observation room. If this procedure is so dangerous and they need to take so many precautions, I wondered, why are they performing this on my head? One of the large metal instruments that I had been staring at for so long was lowered over my head. The nurse called over an intercom and explained the procedure as comfortingly as possible. I motioned to her that I was ready to begin, and she then sent the radiation through me as if I were a piece of paper.

Throughout the evening that I spent in the emergency room, my mother would not stop touching me. She couldn't believe that I was alive and sitting next to her on the hard plastic chairs. She kept questioning me about exactly what had happened. And each time I would explain the unbelievable story, she would grow more and more upset and worried for my well-being. I couldn't stress enough I was okay and would be fine. I felt awful that I had put her though such grief.

After all the proper medical procedures were performed and my mother was satisfied with the results, we went home. As soon as I got home, my mother was ready to assume the role of the doctor and pick up where he left off. She changed me out of my bloody clothes and put me into some comfortable pajamas. She then rushed to make me a cozy seat on the couch, with cotton blankets and enough pillows for every part of my body. This was her procedure when one of us was sick.

My mother was a mess. She was under so much stress and would not leave me alone. She was astonished by the fact that she could have been left without me and, because of this, she eased her fear and pain by smothering me. She used almost an entire roll of film taking pictures of me. Her mother had done the same when she had been in an accident at my age and thought that it helped a lot to be able to see the damage and learn from the unfortunate experience.

That evening, my boyfriend and a few of my closest friends stopped by to check on me. I didn't want them to see me in such poor condition. I felt ugly. My face was swollen. I had severe abrasions on my cheek and bruises on my legs and shoulders. I didn't understand why I had been so badly injured. I had an air bag and my seat belt fastened. What was the problem?

I understand now that, if I hadn't had these safety devices, my skull might have been crushed and I probably wouldn't be alive. This was still hard for me to understand considering that my careless passengers, without their seat belts fastened, didn't have a scratch on them. I wanted to hide when my friends came, but I was glad to see them and needed their support. My mother had all of us sit down and passionately told us how grateful she was I had survived. By the end of the night, everyone was in tears.

This was a very emotional period for my family. Everyone was constantly touching me. My mother would check on me in the middle of the night to make sure I was still alive and well. My family couldn't leave me alone for a minute. It was as if I were two years old and needed a babysitter. I didn't think I was that badly injured. My mother later confessed to me that she cried during many of these nights. I felt awful for putting my family through such pain and misery.

When we finally located the place where the police had towed our car, my mother and I went to look at the hunk of metal. On our way to the towing company, my nose started to bleed profusely. This was a sign that it was not over yet. When it took me ten minutes to stop the bleeding, we realized that I needed to see a doctor. However, we decided to look at the car first. This was the first time I had seen the car since the accident, and it brought back emotions that I thought had gone away.

The car was totaled. My mother took pictures of me sitting on the hood with a handkerchief under my nose, and I looked just as bad as I did the day of the accident. We collected our valuables from the car and a few extra pieces from the headlights and front end as souvenirs. Then it was off to the hospital again. I hoped this would be the end of the whole ordeal, and I would be able to put it behind me. But it wasn't the end. I think about the accident everyday.

I consider this brush with death to be lucky. Not in the sense that we survived, because I owe that to God, but in the lesson I was fortunate enough to learn through this experience. I learned to appreciate life and the world around me. I now take note of all the little things I had let pass by before. At age seventeen, I was not ready to die. There was too much I hadn't done, too many places I hadn't seen, and too many experiences I would have missed. June 20th, I believe, was the most important day in my life because I learned not to take the time we have for granted but to enjoy life to its fullest. I'm going to take every opportunity to experience something new and broaden my horizons. I will not let one day go by that is meaningless. I want to accomplish a goal every day. I want to do everything I can and have as much fun as I can doing it.

WHEN TRAGEDY HITS HOME
by Adriane Helfrich

It was 4:30 a.m., and all was quiet. At home in Cherry Hill, New Jersey, my mom, dad, and younger sister Allison were all sound asleep. My cat, Chelsea, insisted upon jumping on top of the kitchen cabinet. The silence was suddenly broken when a distant knock sounded. The knock continued until my mom awakened. Half asleep, thinking it was my older sister Ashli who forgot her keys, she proceeded down the stairs to answer the door. Allison followed her.

My mom folded back the curtain, which had shielded her from whomever was outside the door. A policeman in uniform stood there with a look of disbelief written all over his face. Realizing that something was terribly wrong, my mom swung the door open. A parent's worst nightmare was about to happen.

"Your daughter Ashli has been in an automobile accident. She is at Cooper Trauma center in Camden," the policeman mumbled while holding onto a pink index card. The card contained the police department's phone number, my sister's name, and where she was.

"Oh my God! She's dead," my mom thought to herself. For my sister's sake, she tried to remain calm. Allison was an emotional sixteen year old, and more than ever she needed my mom's support.

Tears streamed down both of their faces, as they ventured to tell my dad what had happened. "Ron, Ashli's been in an accident. She's at Cooper Trauma. It doesn't look good. Hurry up and get ready, so we can go." My parents and sister got dressed and rushed to get to the hospital, preparing themselves for the worst.

My dad pressed his foot on the gas pedal until the car roared to seventy-five miles per hour. Although it seemed like an eternity since they were first struck with the news, the time was now 5:05 a.m. My dad pulled up to the front of the hospital, and my mother and sister jumped out of the car. The automatic door invited them in and closed off all contact with the outside world.

"My daughter, Ashli Helfrich, has been in an accident. Where is she?" my mom frantically asked.

"She just arrived by ambulance," the receptionist responded, pointing toward the emergency room.

My dad met up with them, and they proceeded down the long hallway toward the emergency room. There she was. Actually, there was some unrecognizable person lying on a table. Nurses and doctors were gathered around, while Allison and my parents saw a sight that would never leave their memory.

Ashli was lying there. Streams of blood trickled down her face and dripped to the floor. Glass was still sticking out of her face and arms. A long tube was inserted down her throat to aid her in breathing. Her blood-saturated clothes were sticking to her body, with various rips that displayed her bruised flesh. Blood started to flow from the gash in her knee. Ashli's face was swollen immensely, preventing her from opening either eye. Three front teeth were missing, and two bottom teeth were chipped. Her once petite nose was now broken. Her golden blonde hair looked reddish-brown because of the vast amount of blood.

Barely conscious, Ashli insisted on trying to pull the tube out of her throat. The doctors resorted to putting restraints on her wrists, and then they sedated her. She was cut off from pain for a short while, but, when she woke up, it would all come back to haunt her.

My parents, but most of all Allison, were in shock at what they saw. Allison and my mom were crying, but my dad attempted to remain strong. "Is she going to die? I can't believe this happened. Why did this have to happen?" Allison asked in between sobs.

"There is no explanation, Alli. Things like this just happen. Keep praying for your sister, and everything will be just fine," my dad responded.

My family had to leave the emergency room briefly because Ashli was getting stitched up. In the meantime, they sat in the waiting room. They were surrounded by silence, but it was occasionally interrupted by a few muffled cries. The hospital was dark, cold, and lonely. It smelled like a combination of ether, alcohol, and other medications. The doctor slipped through the emergency room door and slowly walked toward my family.

"What happened, Doctor? Do you know? Is she going to be all right?" my mom repeatedly asked.

The doctor explained that he only thing he knew at the moment was that Jodie was driving, and Ashli was the passenger. Jodie's car was lodged and crushed in between two trees, and there was very little left of the vehicle. It was too early on to be able to tell exactly what happened because both girls were unconscious at the moment. He didn't know how they ended up jumping the curb and hitting the tree, but the accident was alcohol related. Neither of them was wearing seatbelts. That is why there were so many facial injuries inflicted on the girls. The windshield flew toward them instead of popping outwards. They were extremely lucky to be alive, but Jodie was not doing well.

"What do you mean Jodie's not all right? Is she going to live?" my mom asked.

The doctor responded, "Well, she is much worse off than your daughter." Jodie was pried out of the car and flown to the hospital by helicopter. She was on a respirator because she couldn't breathe on her own. She punctured a lung and lost an excessive amount of blood. She also broke her left leg and crushed her right foot. Her face was cut up pretty badly, but she was getting stitched up. Her parents and sister were with her.

"Can we visit with Ashli?" my mom asked.

"Only for a short while," the doctor said. "She's unconscious from the drugs and needs plenty of rest. Take the elevator to the fifth floor and then turn right when you get off. Her room number is 518."

Cautiously, my family approached room 518. Ashli was lying there, while a feeding tube stuck out of her arm. The long breathing tube was removed from her throat. Her blood had saturated the white linen sheets. The swelling in her face had gotten worse. Stitches now covered the deep gashes that had surfaced on her face.

The nurse came in to check on her. She told my family that they must leave for the night, but could come back tomorrow. At home, they discussed who was going to call me at school and relay the news.

I'll never forget that call. It was Friday, St. Patrick's Day, and I had just stopped back at my dorm for a pair of slacks. As I was about to walk out the door, the phone rang.

"Hello? Hi, Mom! What's up?" I asked.

"What are you doing this weekend? Do you have anything special planned?" she asked. I thought that they were going to come up for a visit, so I anxiously said that I had no definite plans. "Hold on. Here's your father." She hurriedly put my dad on the phone.

"Ad? Hi. Listen, there's been an accident. Ashli's been in a car accident tonight."

"Oh my God! Is she okay?" I asked, trying to breathe. I felt as though someone had hit me in the stomach.

"Well, she broke her nose and lost a few teeth, but she is alive. Do you want me to come and pick you up tomorrow morning?"

At this point I started to cry uncontrollably. "Yeah, I want to be there for her," I responded.

"Okay, I'll be there around eight in the morning." When I hung up the phone, I didn't know how to react. I sat on the edge of my bed, buried my face in my hands, and started to cry once again.

The next morning, my dad arrived to pick me up. The entire car ride home was silent. Neither one of us spoke a single word. The radio was faint in the distance, and I dozed off. Two hours later, we pulled up to the front of my house.

I walked inside, and my mom and sister greeted me with open arms. Before I even had a chance to unpack my bags, it was time to hop in the car and head off to the hospital.

On the way there, we talked about what had happened. I had a lot of unanswered questions. Were they drinking? Where was the accident? What did they hit?

My parents only knew so much and could not offer the answers to my questions. Allison warned me to be prepared for the worst. "She doesn't look too good. Don't be surprised at what you see," she said. I pictured her to have a few cuts and bruises, but I never imagined seeing what my eyes encountered.

As we slowly approached her room on the fifth floor, a nervous feeling accompanied by nausea entered my stomach. Allison held tightly onto my hand, and we proceeded into Ashli's room. Her room was extremely dreary and damp because the curtain blocked any possible sign of incoming sunlight. Ashli occupied the bed closest to the window, and the remaining bed was vacant. Unfamiliar voices spoke beyond the open door and echoed down the long hospital corridors. The smell of stale urine and fresh blood was everywhere. I stood there with my mouth open in shock when I first laid eyes on her, and every time I swallowed it was a struggle.

"Oh my God! Who is that lying there? It doesn't even look like Ashli."

She was on many different medications, so she was in and out of consciousness and unaware that we were even there. I walked over to the side of her bed and stared down upon her. Her face was swollen immensely. Occasionally, she opened her left eye a crack, but the right one was completely swollen shut. Her hair was entangled in knots and had turned a reddish-brown color from the blood. Her enlarged lips hid her various missing teeth. A cut extending from above her right eye led to the base of her skull. She had a stitched-up cut above her mouth next to her left eye. Then there was her once perfect nose, which was broken.

I stood there with wobbly knees and shaking arms. "What do you think? Are you okay?" Allison repeatedly questioned. I couldn't believe this. I never imagined anything quite as bad as this. I had pictured a few cuts and bruises, but she was all mangled up. I looked over as she was starting to come to. She moaned a great deal because she was in a vast amount of pain.

"Look Ashli. Adriane came home from school to see you," my mom stated.

"Hi, Ad. Thanks for coming," Ashli mumbled and then dozed off again.

We spent the entire day in the hospital—from 10:00 a.m. to 8:00 p.m.—until visiting hours were over. I stood over her, hoping that she would regain consciousness. I desperately wanted to hold her and tell her that everything was going to be okay, but her body was very sensitive, so I could only hold her hand. Every now and then, Allison and I would leave her room to get some fresh air.

The stale odor of the hospital was enough to make a person sick. We sat outside on a park bench only to be secluded from this nightmare for a short while. We began talking about Ashli.

She had been through hell and back these last few years. First she got a D.W.I. and lost her license because of it. This was the second time she has been involved in an alcohol-related situation. Why didn't she learn the first time? Even though she wasn't the driver, she should have stopped Jodie from driving. She was so close to being killed, and it was a miracle that Jodie even survived. People always think that nothing bad will ever happen to them, but in reality it most surely can. Unfortunately, she had to learn the hard way.

We talked a while longer and then ventured back inside the hospital to meet reality. She was lying in bed with her left eye slightly open, conversing with my parents. "My teeth! I don't have any teeth left," she complained.

"Ashli, your teeth can be replaced. You're very lucky to be alive. You've got to think positive instead of negative," my mom replied.

Losing her teeth was her greatest concern because she could slide her tongue along the empty gap where her teeth used to be. She still had not gotten out of bed, so she was unaware of her facial condition. I was dreading the moment when she would see her face. What would she think? What would she say? How would she feel? Only time could tell.

A nurse periodically came in to check on Ashli. She tried getting Ashli to drink juice or eat something, but she refused. Because she had no desire to eat, a feeding tube was still necessary. "Water! Water! I need water!" she continuously shouted because her mouth was extremely dry. "Mom, I have to go to the bathroom," she said as she started pushing herself up to get out of bed.

"Oh no!" I thought to myself. She's going to see her face. I looked over at my family, and I could tell that they were thinking the same thing. My mom helped her onto her feet, and they proceeded toward the bathroom.

Ashli looked over at us and asked what was wrong. She could tell we were worried about her reaction when she looked in the mirror. We all looked extremely concerned, and she knew exactly what we were thinking, but we merely said nothing was wrong.

Gripping tightly onto the feeding tube, which was attached to Ashli's arm, they slowly headed toward the door. Allison and I looked at each other, and all we could say was "Oh, God!" The feeling I got when I first laid eyes on Ashli lying in her hospital bed returned. I watched intensely to see if she would look in the mirror. She washed her hands but did not seem to even glance at the mirror above.

She knew that her injuries were severe. I don't think she was ready to deal with seeing the reality of it all. As she crawled back into bed, a doctor entered the room. This time it was an eye doctor.

"Hello, Ashli. How are you?" he asked while pulling out many different instruments. He said that he had to check her vision to see if it was impaired from the accident. After questioning my parents about Ashli's vision in the past, he began poking underneath her eyes where fluid had built up. Ashli was yelling and crying because it hurt her. The doctor didn't explain what he was doing; this scared her because she wasn't sure what was happening. I wondered when this pain would ever end. Hadn't she been through enough already? The doctor left, and Ashli dozed off. Visiting hours were over, so we had to go home.

We planned to get a good night's sleep and return early the next morning. It was difficult to sleep that night. Visions of Ashli's distorted face constantly entered my mind. Eventually, I dozed off, and when I woke up, it was Sunday. We returned to the hospital with a card and some get-well balloons. Her room was crowded with flower arrangements from friends and family members. Pink and yellow balloons with flowers and messages scribbled across them were attached to the base of her bed and floated to the ceiling.

Ashli woke up as we entered her room. I only had a few hours left until I had to go back to school. We talked a little with her, and she seemed in better spirits. She was finally realizing that it could have been much worse. She wanted to know how Jodie was, but we didn't even know. My mom just said that she was fine, but even that was unknown.

We later learned that Jodie had undergone surgery earlier that day. The doctors inserted a steel plate in her head because she had a massive gash across her forehead. The cut was much too deep to require only stitching. Her left leg was broken and had to be put in a cast. Jodie's right foot was severely fractured, so metal pins helped hold the bones together.

Time was up, and I had to say goodbye to Ashli. It was so hard. Even though my parents were right there by her side, I didn't want to leave her. I squeezed her hand and told her to remain strong. "Everything will be all right," I assured her. I then said how much I loved her and walked out the door.

More than ever, I did not want to be back at school. The first week after her accident was the toughest week I ever had to endure. I could not focus on anything, much less schoolwork. Thoughts of her were embedded in my mind, but with the help of friends I managed to pull through. Ashli was released from the hospital that following weekend, so I decided to return home for a visit.

Her appearance had improved a great deal. The swelling in her face had almost totally gone down, and, once again, she actually looked like my sister. I was relieved to finally see the Ashli I knew and loved. She was still taking medication for the pain and was constantly tired, so she spent most of her days in bed.

I asked her what had happened that night. All she said was, "I don't remember," and changed the subject. Even to this day, neither she nor Jodie can recall the accident, but it really isn't important because they are both alive. If they were able to remember, it would only be more pain to cope with. Maybe as time goes by, they'll want to remember, and it will be easier to recollect.

Ashli's accident occurred only a few months ago. I still think about it every day, and I know she'll remember it for the rest of her life. It will be a lengthy recovery, but she's taking it one day at a time. Her spirits are high, and she knows that God gave her a second chance at life. She has daily appointments with doctors. She has gone to see eye doctors, dentists, brain doctors, and plastic surgeons. Ashli will have permanent scars and a few false teeth, but nothing compares to the gift of life. Ashli may decide to get plastic surgery in the future, or she may choose not to. Whatever her decision is, her family backs her up.

The most important lesson that I have learned throughout this ordeal is do not drink and drive. I have heard this saying many times but never gave it much thought. I knew I would never drive while intoxicated, so I figured I didn't have to worry. But now, I'll never drink a drop when I drive. It's too easy to be under the influence and not know it. It's awful seeing your very own sister cut, bruised, bleeding, with eyes that look like raw meat. There's nothing you can do for her except pray. It's the most helpless feeling in the world, and I would not wish it on my worst enemy.

I have also learned the importance of wearing a seatbelt. Ashli would have walked away from the accident without a single scratch if she were wearing her seatbelt. It takes a brief second to fasten a seat belt, but now it's going to take her years to fully recover. Every time I get into a car now, I don't even think twice about buckling my seat belt. It has become routine, and I make sure everyone else in that car follows my lead. Like many others, Ashli had to learn the hard way about the effects of drinking and driving.

SHATTERED
(Anonymous)

Before that particular December night, I was really pushing my luck. I felt as though I could get away with anything. Not once did I ever think that everything would finally catch up to me. Not me, I was too slick. I guess this feeling of mine began in my sophomore year of high school. I was enrolled in the Gifted and Talented program at my school, and my circle of friends had always evolved from that group. That is until I met new friends while at a party one Friday night in the middle of October.

At the party, my cousin showed me a world I was totally unaware of. She opened the door for me to new music, friends, places, and most importantly a new way of judging people and viewing things. Before I even knew it, I had, and still do have, a whole new circle of friends.

My close-minded, opinionated friends concerned only with money, name brands, and "the right kind of people" were left in the dust. I, on the other hand, was experiencing the thriftiness of secondhand stores, more partying than I care to remember, and raging mosh pits at local shows.

It was the first local show I went to, featuring Premonition, my friend Terry's band, that brought my boyfriend Bobby and me together. We arranged for him to drive that night of the show. He picked me up in his van, then proceeded to pick up everyone else that Terry invited, none of whom I had ever met before. Finally, after everyone was loaded in the van, we were off to the Dry Dock. Bobby and I didn't speak until we were standing around waiting for the show to begin. We hit it off at once!

During the ride home, Bobby leaned over to me and asked, "Do you smoke weed?" I had never smoked any before, but I had heard a lot about it from Beth and was dying to try it. I answered, "Yes." My drinking had already gotten out of hand; the weed was soon to follow.

By April, Bobby had asked me to "be his number one," and by May, I had lost my virginity. It took me more than six months of unprotected sex before I ever even put myself on the pill! But I'm getting ahead of myself there. It was in May also that Beth and Terry graduated.

That summer, I remember expecting my junior year of high school to be very dull. That's when I met and became friends with Caroline, and when Bobby told me he was coming back to school. He had been expelled early in my sophomore year, before the two of us had even met.

The one thing I can say about my junior year is that I went to school every day. The punch line is that it was very rare if I went to school sober or stayed in school the whole day. My days usually began by picking up Bobby or Caroline for school. It was likely that I would have a couple cans of beer, or some sort of mixture to drink. The norm? Vodka and orange juice. Bobby would supply the weed, and our day would start.

While in school—sometime, somewhere throughout my day—I would meet up with Caroline. Our conversation would go something like this, "Hey Caroline. What are you doing?"

"Nothing," she'd moan.

"Do you feel like leaving?"

"Yes!"

We normally just went to lunch. But about once a week, we'd go to the mall. That's when my fingers became sticky. For months, I wasn't able to walk in any store without taking a memento of the occasion. I was hooked. I would take anything, sometimes stupid stuff. Caroline and I were a team though. We would be in any store, in the middle of a conversation, and out of nowhere, one of us would ask if anyone were looking. If the other said no, ka-blam, something was stolen.

This did finally catch up to us; we were in Macy's when we got caught. We happened to be shoplifting, I mean shopping, for Melissa's baby shower. Neither of us had stolen anything for ourselves that day! After Caroline and I were through with Macy's and left the store, she noticed someone following us. I looked in the mirror on my left and saw him too. We kept walking. We walked into Woodward & Lothrop, and, as we were nearing the door to leave, I told Caroline to follow my lead. After doing an about-face, I confronted the man and asked if he were following us. He told us he had reason to believe we stole something. Handing him the bag and telling him that we did was the only thing I could think to do. You know what? He let us go! I mean, he shot questions at us; for instance, why we had stolen, if we had any money, and so forth. The next thing he told us was that, if we had left the mall, we would have been arrested and *would* be if he ever saw us in Macy's again. That was it. We were free to leave.

Before my senior year, I had a few more run-ins with authority figures, namely the cops. Somehow, I managed to always come out unscathed, and therefore I just wasn't learning my lesson. My senior year, up until December 15, was pretty much the same as my junior year. I'd go to school high, drunk, or tripping, and since I only had five classes, I'd still wind up with As.

But here's where my luck ran out.

I was driving home from work, around nine o'clock the night of December 15, totally straight. I mean, I had been high after school, but that had worn off by then. As I'm told, I swerved to avoid hitting a possum, but hit it and a tree anyway. My life hasn't been the same since. Apparently, I was flown to Shock Trauma and given immediate care. I suffered cracked ribs, a split palate, nerve damage to the right eye, and, the worst yet, a TBI—Traumatic Brain Injury.

The stories you see on TV are completely false. I don't even remember waking up. When I did, I wasn't talking or even aware of what was really going on. I don't remember ever being told I had a terrible car accident or ever asking. But when I was unconscious, I was frequently told this. So, when I started becoming coherent, I just knew. I stayed in Shock Trauma for fifteen days and was coherent for only about nine. You wouldn't believe how strong a support system I had. All of my family and friends came to see me. Since it was so near to Christmas, they cut off the top of an artificial tree and everyone decorated it with special ornaments.

My immediate family and Bobby were there every day. Every time Bobby saw me, he would tell me I was looking sexy. You just don't know how bad I looked. They had me hooked up to all kinds of machines. My hands were wrapped thick in gauze and tied to the bed. This was to prevent me from pulling my IVs out while I went through the agitated stage—a stage common to all victims of a head injury. There was a bolt, measuring my inner cranial pressure, sticking out from the top of my freshly, but only partially, shaved head. The reason for the shaved head was to avoid infection from the bolt. My jaw was described to my parents as having felt like mush at the scene of the accident. Because of this and the splitting of my palate, my face was so swollen that it was hard to see the girl everyone once knew.

What I recall most vividly during my stay at the hospital was when my parents walked into my room with a doctor. The doctor explained that a blood test was done on me, and traces of marijuana had been found. Now, my head may have been filled with cobwebs and my memories cloudy, but I knew what this meant. My feeling of fear must have shown on my face. The doctor asked if I'd like my parents to leave the room. I violently shook my head yes. Next, I heard my mom state that they already knew and they weren't leaving. The doctors left us alone to "discuss the matter." I now had to look into my mother's eyes. Words cannot express the hurt and disappointment in them.

After what seemed like an eternity, the questions subsided. If I hadn't already been in a hospital bed, they surely would've put me in one. Things started happening fast after this and all kinds of specialists came to see me. I was helped out of bed, taken for a walk, given a shower, and finally given something to drink.

On New Year's Eve, the wires were removed from my teeth, and I was on my way to DuPont Rehabilitation Center. Once again, I was seen by every doctor in every field, given my schedule for my stay there and then a grand tour. From the moment I got there, I insisted that I was fine, the same as before the accident. Dr. Robbins knew this wasn't the case. My therapists were all wonderful, and they all taught me a lot about my disability. Before I knew it, I was starting to like it there. Therapy was fun; hard, but fun. I began making friends with the other kids there, especially those in group with me. My parents drove to Delaware every night, and Bobby came as often as his job would permit. I had lots of family still coming to see me and quite a few friends also.

I had stayed only a week before I was freed for the weekend and allowed to come home. My first weekend home was fabulous! We had a "Welcome Home!" party. I visited both of my jobs, and even got to go out on a date with Bobby. We went to the mall and he told me that he would buy me whatever I wanted. I couldn't believe the rush that I was feeling. For the first time in a month, I really felt alive.

We had been in the mall for about ten minutes when I noticed people staring at me. I felt like a freak! Dr. Robbins had mentioned that going out into public, especially the first time, was going to be difficult. "No problem," I had said to her. "I'm aware of what I look like; I can deal with it."

Yeah, right! My eye started filling up with tears, my lips quivered, my breathing got heavy, my adrenaline was in overdrive, and my hands started trembling. Bobby took one look at me, pulled me aside, and asked if I was sure I could do this. One look into his loving eyes assured me that I could; besides, I would have to someday, right?

The doctors told me that they could not guarantee my eye would ever open, but everything else would return to normal—my hair would grow back; I didn't need to feel like I had to wear a hat forever; the swelling around my jaw would go down, and I would gain some weight.

Every weekend, I came home. Everybody wanted to see me and take me out. I was the center of attention. Friday, January 29, I was brought home as an outpatient. The novelty of my condition was starting to wear off, and I remember wondering where all my friends had gone. Now that I was home and able to go out more often, nobody, except Bobby, wanted to take me out. I was a downer; I knew it. Because of the type of injury I had incurred, alcohol, weed, and all the other drugs were no longer words allowed in my vocabulary.

The hour drive to the hospital every day wasn't so bad. It was the nights I spent home alone, without any friends, that sucked. But I kept a positive attitude. I kept thinking that once I got back to school everything would change. I only had to prove to everyone that I was not brain damaged, and that I'm still the same person. Before I was released from DuPont completely, Dr. Robbins and I had many discussions on this subject. According to her, proving that I wasn't brain damaged wouldn't be hard. The hard part would be proving that I was the same person, because I no longer was.

I wouldn't admit this fact to myself. I was still in denial when I was dismissed from DuPont on February 18. That Friday, I began my first day back in school. And you better believe I caused quite a commotion. Spending the whole day answering questions isn't what overwhelmed me; it was the two months of work that I had to catch up on that did it. My teachers weren't requiring me to make up all the work I missed; they just expected me to get a firm grip on what was happening now. Still, in order to master one concept, you have to master all the ones that come before that. Thanks to my "training" at DuPont, this didn't prove to be too hard. I really buckled down though, as I never had before.

My main goal was to prove to everyone, including myself, that I could make it and still graduate—no more skipping out of classes. Any free time I had in school, I spent working. For the first time in I don't know how many years, I actually brought homework home with me and, even more amazingly, I did it! For once in my life, I had found discipline and wanted to succeed. This new focus in my life turned off many more of my friends.

In order to catch up, I could no longer go out whenever something was happening, and I even had to give up one of my jobs. But all my hard work and sacrifices paid off in the end. Before I knew it, the Senior's Awards Assembly was being held, and I was awarded four local scholarships. Now, graduation was just around the corner.

When June 2 finally arrived, I didn't know whether I should cry or cheer. Everyone says Senior Year flies by, but considering I missed out on two months of mine, my Senior Year *really* flew by. Somehow though, I managed to push all my butterflies deep down in my stomach. I proceeded to cross the stage, shook the announcer's hand, smiled for the camera, and walked off the stage without ever missing a beat. My goal was finally reached. I truly felt my fight was now over.

These days, I realize my fight will never be truly over. Some things look like they are here to stay: the appearance of my eye bothers me; my span of attention is easily disturbed; my reading is slower; my voice has a different pitch; but, more importantly, I have a new outlook on life.

I value life more. I realize that I had always taken life for granted, as if it owed me. No more. I try to make the best of every situation I encounter and try to figure out what it is that I can contribute.

The car accident, Shock Trauma, DuPont, my family, Bobby, basically everything and everyone connected with my recovery, showed me that life is too much of a treasure to throw it away recklessly. The lessons I wish I could post for the whole world to see are believe in yourself and live life to the fullest.

A PART OF ME: Pregnancy

Turbulent,

fleshy,

sensual,

eating, drinking,

and breeding...

I speak the

pass-word

primeval...

"Since my memoir was written on a weekly basis, it was easy to forget where I left off. I found myself doing a lot of revising because I was constantly reading what I had written the previous week."

Judith Shaw

A PART OF ME
(Anonymous)

I'm eighteen years old, and already a failure. I failed myself, my family, and, most of all, my daughter. I sometimes sit alone in my room and think about how much my life changed when my daughter came into it. And then I think about how hard it is to go on now that she's gone.

The date was January 25 and the time was 9:00 a.m. For most, this would be the start of a normal day, but for me it was the start of what would be one of the most painful and unforgettable days of my life. On this day, I would place my month-old baby girl up for adoption.

I wasn't scheduled to be picked up until 2:00 p.m., but I woke up early to spend the last few precious moments with my daughter. Although at the time I was well aware that the adoption would cause me great pain, I didn't know just how deeply it would touch my soul.

I held Tiffanie in my arms and watched once again in awe as she smiled at me. Her presence brought about a marvel in me. I never thought I could love another human being with such depth in such a short period of time. I thought I could control the outpouring of my emotions up until I was to make the adoption official, but I couldn't. I looked into Tiffanie's eyes and, in my own way, tried to explain to her why I was giving her to a person who I had met only once. I started to cry. I knew that, out of all the people in the world to whom I could try to explain my decision, Tiffanie was the only one who couldn't understand.

As time went on, I began to prepare Tiffanie for her departure. She continued to look at me, not knowing that I soon would be erased from her memory. One o'clock arrived, and Tiffanie was dressed in her prettiest outfit. It was a pink baby doll dress with colored flowers and a matching headband. I wanted her adoptive mother to see her and instantly think as I did that she was the most beautiful baby in the world.

My best friend, Michelle, came to my house at 1:30 p.m. to give me moral support. I knew after the adoption was final I would need a shoulder to cry on. The whole day, Michelle and I talked about Sharon, the adoptive mother, as if she were the enemy. I was jealous. I knew that Tiffanie would soon credit Sharon, not me, with being her mother.

When it was time to be picked up by the social worker, I felt a strange tightening in my stomach. It was the feeling you get when you know something bad is about to happen. Michelle kept on asking me if I was all right. I lied and said, "Yes," but the truth was my mind was filled with the thought that I would never see my daughter again. When we got to the car, I introduced Michelle to the social worker. Michelle gave her a phony smile and immediately got into the car. My daughter sat in the back with Michelle, while I sat up front. I was silent as the social worker explained what would happen once we got to the adoption agency. I really didn't care to hear about the process. I knew what the final outcome would be.

When we arrived at the adoption agency, Michelle reached for Tiffanie. Without thinking, I pushed Michelle's hand away and said, "No, let me get her." I wanted to feel my daughter's body next to mine every moment I could. As we entered the building, two women wearing armed smiles greeted us. It was the kind of smile you develop when you help give away someone else's baby every day.

Michelle and I politely said, "Hello," and gave a quick flash of teeth. I began to get angry. I didn't want two strangers to greet me with smiles when I was about to give away my first born. As soon as we walked in, the women directed us to a small room. They said they wanted to get the paperwork out of the way before the adoptive mother arrived. I got angrier. I instantly had a vision of me signing the papers and one of the women ripping Tiffanie from my arms. The more they spoke, the angrier I became. Not really at the women, but at myself. I hated myself for being so stupid. I kept thinking, if I hadn't been so stupid in the first place, I wouldn't have to do this.

I sat there listening as the women explained what I was about to sign. After the second page or so, I tuned out. I began staring at Tiffanie. I stared long and hard. I remembered reading in a magazine how babies can sense when a person is upset. I wanted Tiffanie to look at me and see that I was falling apart inside. I just wanted her to know how much I loved her. I looked into her pretty black eyes and felt her angelic little hands, and suddenly my heart turned to dust. I felt like I could never love again.

The social workers must have noticed my inattentiveness because they asked me if I was all right. I wanted to ask what in the hell kind of question is that, but I just smiled and said, "Yes." I signed the remaining papers and noticed Tiffanie had fallen asleep. I was grateful. I didn't want to have to look in her eyes as I handed her over to a stranger.

I began to memorize every aspect of the room; it was all I could do to keep my mind off the pain. There was a large, multi-colored oriental rug in the middle of the floor, and against the wall stood an oak bookshelf that held a mini-library. An old-fashioned dark brown leather chair sat a few feet in front of the bookshelf, which was directly diagonal to a old wooden desk. There was also an elaborate assortment of baby pictures covering a portion of the wall to the left of me. I looked at the pictures and then at Tiffanie. I wondered if her face would soon be a part of the collection. My stomach was in knots with the fear that Sharon would be arriving any minute.

As I held Tiffanie in my arms, it felt like the whole world was crashing down on me. Silently I prayed that God would give me the strength to finish what I started. Suddenly one of the social workers came to report that Sharon had arrived. I trembled slightly with fear. They asked if I was ready for her to come in, and I replied, " No, not yet!" One of the women said, "Take your time; there's no rush."

I started to look at Tiffanie as if I were trying to memorize every inch of her body. Tears rolled down my face. I kept turning her from side to side, memorizing and memorizing. What I did not know was that I didn't have to memorize, because I would never forget her face. The social worker noticed my compulsive staring and said, "Don't worry, you'll see that face again when Sharon sends you some pictures." I cried harder.

Finally, I told them Sharon could come in. To my surprise, Sharon entered the room accompanied by a blinding flash of light. She had brought her best friend to take pictures of Tiffanie. I thought to myself, how could she bring someone to take pictures of my daughter without asking me? Then I realized Tiffanie was now her daughter. In my mind, a part of me held on to the hope that Tiffanie would still consider me "number one" in her life. I was fooling myself.

After the second picture, Sharon said, "I hope you don't mind."

I said, "No, it's all right," but I was thinking, "Hell yes, I mind." She then began to comment on how beautiful Tiffanie was, and I asked if she wanted to hold her. I laid Tiffanie in Sharon's arms. It felt like I had ripped out my heart and given it to a stranger. I wasn't very religious, but I knew God was the only one who could get me through that moment. I prayed for help and support. I looked at my precious little girl snuggled in Sharon's arms and knew that a part of me was gone.

It hurt so badly; a force of nature connected us. This was the child I carried for nine months. I fed her. I comforted her. I loved her. How could I ever go on with my life knowing that she wouldn't be a part of it? The devil was laughing at me. Tiffanie was the best thing I could ever create. She was perfect in every way. Nothing could ever replace her.

On that Christmas day when I gave birth to her, I spent every second I could by her side. I was mystified by her presence. To most, she may have looked like the average discolored and wrinkled baby. But to me, beauty radiated off her like sunlight off a clear blue sea.

She had enchanting black eyes and light pink skin. Her lips were so red it looked as if she had kissed the color off a cherry. Her dark strands of hair barely covered her head—the same as when I was born. Holding her in my arms seemed so unreal. It astonished me to know that a life had developed within my body. At that time, what the future held was not important. I was too busy loving my daughter.

Now, I sat staring at the faces around me with a fake smile, pretending I was all right. Sharon, who was seated next to me, was enjoying her dream come true. It amazed me how two people could be in the same room, with one so happy and the other so miserable. I wanted to tear down the walls and get out of there. I didn't want to endure their laughter and their joy one second longer.

I watched as Sharon cuddled Tiffanie as if she were her own. I wanted to scream out, "She's my baby, not yours!" but I knew somehow I had to accept that Tiffanie had a new family, and I wasn't a part of it. It was so hard to let go. I thought of the first time I gave her a bath: her eyes got as big as apples when I put her in the water. I laughed at the sight of her. Her little legs were stiff as boards, and it seemed as if she was amazed and frightened at the same time. I was filled with warmth. I had introduced her to a new experience, a new feeling—me, her mother. She depended on me, and in a way I depended on her. She gave my life purpose.

I came out of my trance and looked at Michelle. I knew she could tell that even though my eyes were tearless, my heart was crying. She had an angry look in her eyes that could have burned a hole in the wall. I knew she didn't like what was happening but wanted to support me anyway.

One of the social workers asked how often I wanted to receive pictures. I wanted to say every week and not a day less, but felt I wasn't in any position to make demands. I said, "Every three months is fine." Sharon agreed and focused her attention once again on Tiffanie. I watched her. Really watched her. She was so happy. I looked beyond my pain for a moment, and saw that this was a blessing for Sharon. She was unable to have children of her own, and adoption was her last hope.

Then one of the social workers eagerly said, "If there's nothing else you want to discuss with Sharon, we can leave so she can fill out her portion of the paperwork." I agreed, and started to gather my things. I tried to get up, but I couldn't. It was like Tiffanie was holding on to me. That same force that bonded us together wouldn't let us break apart. I loved her more than I loved myself. How could I walk away from that kind of love?

I found the strength to pull myself up and walked out the door. Michelle looked at me and waited for the tears to pour, but they didn't. It wasn't the time. I needed to be alone—alone to let the anger out and pray to God to make it possible for me to cry all my pain away.

The social worker asked if I was okay. I wasn't sure, but I smiled and said, "I'm fine," and we walked to the car. When we got in the car, I didn't want to speak. I just wanted to think about Tiffanie. The social worker turned the radio to an oldies station. They were playing "I Love You" by Lionel Richie. The words ate me up inside. As the song played, I thought of Tiffanie. The more the tears formed, the more I tried to hold them back. I didn't want to cry in front of the social worker or Michelle. I wanted to be isolated from the world, as I was isolated from my daughter.

In my mind, the twenty-minute drive dragged on for hours. I watched intensely as we passed each house on the way home. Each house represented a distance that physically separated me from my daughter. I pictured Sharon holding Tiffanie and slowly, but surely, erasing my image from her memory. Why did this happen? What did I do wrong to deserve this kind of torture? A number of questions, to which I had no answers, flashed through my mind. I had always considered myself relatively smart and often gave myself credit for my accomplishments. But at the moment I realized I had accomplished nothing but having a child before I was ready.

Finally, we arrived at my house. It took the last bit of energy I had to stop from jumping out of the car, running inside, and crying myself to sleep. We said our goodbyes, and Michelle and I got out of the car. When we got to the door, I discovered I was locked out. I could have beaten down the door with the thought that it was the only thing standing in the way of me crying myself tearless.

Michelle and I went to the telephone booth to call her mother so she could be picked up. Michelle urged me to come along, but that only stood in the way of my plan. Earlier, I needed Michelle's support, but now it was time for me to face what I had done by myself. When Michelle left, an incredible force told me that I could no longer hold back the pain. I sat by the door and cried long and hard. I cried for my daughter. I cried for myself. I cried for hope—hope that I could go on with my life and make something of myself for Tiffanie; hope that, if one day our paths crossed again, she could somehow understand why I did what I did.

GROWING UP FAST
by Ryan Bogan

It was the summer before my freshman year in college. Amy, my girlfriend, and I were routinely going about life. We both worked and spent every night together. Some nights we would spend alone in my house or hers, and had sex numerous times a week without thinking about the consequences. Our life together continued this way until we left for college together.

Then one night, Amy mentioned that she didn't know when her period was due. "I left my calendar home with all my dates on it," she said.

I said, "Call your mom and tell her to bring it with her when she comes to visit on Friday." Amy asked her mom to do that, and her mom instantly became suspicious.

Amy's mom asked, "Why, is there something I should know?"

Amy replied, "No."

Two weeks later, while talking to her mom, Amy was asked if she had gotten her period. Amy again said no, but now I began to think, what if she is pregnant? We began to get nervous, but we still thought nothing of it. And another week passed with no period.

Amy and I were in her dorm room one night when we became very nervous. I was very worried about her health. She said, "I would like to go buy a pregnancy test just to make sure." I agreed, and we took a ride down to the pharmacy. I was so nervous that my legs were twitching while we were in the store. We went back to the dorm, and she took the test with her into the bathroom. The lack of privacy in the dorm room was becoming an annoyance.

When Amy went into the bathroom, time seemed to stop right in front of me. Numerous thoughts were running through my head. "Oh God, what if she really is pregnant? My parents will kill me." Amy came out of the bathroom and said the test was positive. We couldn't believe it, so we went to the store and purchased two more tests.

The nerve-racking situation seemed nonstop. She went into the bathroom again, and this time it was without a doubt positive. Amy and I began to cry. We embraced each other to calm our fears and to put things into perspective. I kept telling her that she would be all right, and everything would work out fine.

Now we had to decide when and how to tell our parents. There was no doubt that this baby was ours to raise. Adoption and abortion were totally out of the question. The news took a few days to settle in. Somehow between the tears and the fears we managed to agree that we had to find someone to talk with. The following day we made an appointment with the clinic on campus. Amy and I went there with mixed emotions.

We were looking forward to someone answering our questions, but at the same time we were embarrassed. What was this person going to think of two adolescents who are going to have a child? We were curious to see the reaction of the nurse who was helping us. Amy and I were astonished by the kindness of the woman. She was very easy to talk to. She showed us our options and laid out our problems. Our priorities were now in focus. After this meeting, I was actually looking forward to having a baby even though we didn't tell our parents yet. That was our first priority.

Amy and I couldn't figure out how to tell our parents. What she didn't know was that she would get off easy. Amy's mom asked her, after one month passed, if she had gotten her period yet. Amy didn't say a word. Amy's mom said, "I'm coming down." Amy didn't have to say anything; her mom knew just by the way she was talking on the phone. Amy felt relieved. "The hard part is over," she said.

I wish I could have said the same thing for myself. Amy's mom came down and took her home that night. And I knew that it would be only fair to tell my parents the next day. Fortunately, my parents were coming down that day to watch me play Penn State in ice hockey. I had less than twenty-four hours to figure out how I was going to tell them. What bothered me most was that I didn't know how they were going to react.

After Amy left, I was all alone in my cold dreary dorm room. I couldn't possibly have told any of my hockey buddies. My tensions were mounting every time I thought of how I was going to tell my parents. I felt really stressed out. I was worried because I had the biggest game of my college ice hockey career against Penn State. The game didn't matter so much at this time.

All the pressure made me break down in tears. The next thing I knew it was noon the next day. I must have cried myself to sleep. I woke up to the phone ringing. It was my parents calling from downstairs. "We're here." I thought, "Oh my God, how am I going to break it to them?" It was too late now; I just had to wing it. My parents had no idea, but instantly they saw my face and knew something was wrong. I took them up to my room and just said it.

I never felt so relieved in my life. My dad asked me, "How stupid can you be? What are you, an idiot?"

My mom just broke down in tears and gave me a hug. She said, "We love you, and it will all work out." I was so nervous. I didn't know if my dad was going to kick my butt or be sympathetic. Judging by what he said, I knew he was upset.

To my bewilderment, I was wrong. He suddenly said, "I'm going to have another grandchild to see. Excellent!" I still didn't know if he was happy or mad. He made me aware of all the responsibilities involved with taking care of a baby. It was a well-deserved two-hour speech. He asked me if we considered abortion or adoption, and I said not a chance. I was taking full responsibility for my actions. The last words my dad said to me in the speech were "we love you and kick some Penn State butt."

I had survived telling my parents, but what would my friends think? I thought my friends would gossip behind my back if they found out. So, I didn't tell them. I found out from talking to my parents that my family was in full support. My grandfather, who had been ill, said, "Now I have something to live for." I guess he meant that he would fight to stay alive to see his great-grandchild.

Things had begun to settle, and it was time to get back down to reality. Amy and I visited the doctor, who told us that everything was fine. When I heard the baby's heart beat, I got excited for the first time about being a father.

The doctor informed us that we had to come back next week for an ultrasound and once a month for a monthly check up. I was very excited to see the first ultrasound of my baby. I had mixed emotions walking into the hospital and having people see two young kids who are going to have a baby, but I realized we weren't the only ones in this situation. I was very anxious to learn the sex of our baby. We sat in a dark room and saw a little fetus on the screen. After the woman checked for all developing organs, we asked her if she could tell if it was a boy or a girl. To our disappointment, she couldn't. Her answer didn't bother me, but I couldn't help imagining how wonderful my child would be. The fetus was only three months old, but I already felt attached to it. I already loved my baby.

Amy was entering her fourth month of pregnancy when we began to talk about our financial situation. We didn't know how we were going to pay for all the baby's needs. We knew we had to begin working to save money for expenses. I began working for my dad on weekends, and Amy began working at a bakery four days a week.

I began to think about getting married. Amy and I had been going out for two-and-a-half years; we had talked about marriage, but not this early in life. I thought, since we were fully committed to each other and always had been, why shouldn't we be married? I believed that if we were going to have a baby, we should be married first. I knew if I was going to propose, I would have to do it quickly. I had to ask her dad for permission first. Her dad thought it was the right thing to do. I told my parents about the plan, and they also agreed. But there was only one problem: I needed a ring. Luckily, my grandmother gave me a ring, and that weekend I proposed to the love of my life.

I had it all planned out. I took her to a reservoir near school for a picnic. I knew it was time to pop the question, but I was so nervous. I don't know why; I knew she would say yes. I poured her some nonalcoholic champagne, and I asked Amy if she would marry me. After she accepted, she asked if the ring was real. I said, "Of course it is." Still in awe, Amy began planning the wedding. We decided it would be on New Year's Day.

Amy and I quickly spread the news of our engagement. None of our friends could believe what they heard. We had the full support of our families, but not of the Catholic Church. This was a bigger problem than we had expected. The date was open in the church for January 1, but the priest told us we were only teenagers, so we must get the verification from the bishop in the diocese of Trenton, New Jersey.

This was a long, drawn out formality. While attending school, Amy and I had to drive home on Tuesday and Thursday every week for a month in Catholic services. No, this wasn't pre-Cana. Pre-Cana is a retreat-like event with a priest who teaches how to resolve problems in marriages through communication. A couple must go through this program to be married in a Catholic Church.

Our meetings were held so the Catholic Church could survey the situation of a young couple, and send this survey to the bishop for approval. First, we would meet with the service director separately for an hour. In that hour, she would ask us personal questions. For example, "How are you going to support your wife and the baby?" and "What do your parents think of all this?" Amy and I discussed how much we both bent the truth on those questions, but it had to be done. We both wanted to be married to each other, and we weren't going to let the Catholic Church stand in our way.

After a month, we met for a final session. She told us that we were more mature than most thirty- or forty-year-old adults who came in. That was a good sign for our marriage. Now, we had to wait two or three weeks for our file to go to the bishop to be approved. Those three weeks seemed like an eternity. Finally, the call came from the priest who was head of the parish at the church where we wanted to be married. The priest said, "The bishop and I have granted you permission to be married in our church." We were very excited about their decision.

Amy was exceptionally happy because she always dreamed of having a big church wedding.

With the okay from the bishop we could begin our wedding plans. Until you do it, you don't know how complicated this can be. Both our parents helped us get started. We made plans with the priest to join a class for pre-Cana, but they were already overfilled. So, we visited the priest privately once a week for a month.

Amy and I began looking for nice places where we could have our reception. We looked at four different places. They all looked very elegant, but they weren't affordable. Eventually, we found a place named Woodlake Country Club in Lakewood, New Jersey. Woodlake had a very nice atmosphere, and best of all it was affordable. We decided to have our reception at Woodlake for $52 per person. We were planning on having 125 people attend the reception. The cost was phenomenal. The reception would cost approximately $6,140. We wanted everything for our wedding day, but we had to compromise because of the price.

We had gone through the long process of mailing out the invitations, which can be tedious. We didn't know who to invite, or who not to invite, without offending anyone. After trimming down the guest list to 100 people, all we had to do was wait for the responses. Preparations were going well. We attended our first pre-Cana meeting, which was boring. The priest asked many questions pertaining to our love for each other. He kept mentioning the statistics of divorce in teen marriages. These statistics said one of every two couples married before the age of twenty end up in divorce. This statistic didn't matter much to us; we knew we loved each other, and that was all that mattered.

All the responses were returned, and most were attending. Time began to move very quickly. We found a photographer who charged reasonable prices. We had one month left until our wedding day. My nerves got jumpy just thinking about the wedding. The only cure was the length of time until the big day.

The pre-Cana meetings were well under way. Though tedious, they went by very quickly. The priest gave us a book to read to help us succeed in life. It was called "Seven Habits of Effective People." It contained helpful ideas about how to listen properly. Proper listening is meant to help communication skills, which are essential to a healthy marriage. Pre-Cana wasn't totally worthless; it provided us with the answers to basic problems in a marriage.

After the meetings were over, we had two weeks until the wedding. Between the preparation and the nervousness, I had to focus on my final exams. I felt pressure from my family, Amy, and Amy's family to do well. After all, I will have to financially support our child and their grandchild. The night before the first final, I was studying vigorously until Amy came to me with a problem. She said, "I think I have a bladder infection, and my doctor said come immediately." I was caught by surprise. I had no idea there was something wrong. I became very worried for two reasons: her health and my exam.

But somehow I managed to ask her if her mother could come and take her to the hospital. (Her doctor was two-and-a-half hours away in New Jersey.) She was disgusted with me. So I was forced to drive her home and stay with her at the hospital all night. There was no way I could study with Amy's worried parents buzzing around my head. Later around 2:00 a.m., the doctor came back in and said her urine test came out negative. Our nurse began to push on Amy's stomach.

After five minutes, the worrying was over. The doctor said, "Do you feel any better?" Amy replied, "Yes." I had lost ten crucial hours of studying because the baby was sitting on her bladder.

The next day, I took the exam at 10:00 a.m. I salvaged a "B" grade, but, I wasn't worried so much about the exam as about the health of my fiancé. And everything was back on schedule for the wedding day.

After final exams were over, Christmas was a few days away. The last-minute shopping managed to keep me from going crazy. Then Christmas day came and went. It was then that I realized that the big day was less than a week away. The last week flew by faster than any I could ever remember. Finally, the day was here.

My family woke me close to noon. The first thing out of their mouths was "Today is the big day; are you nervous?" I answered no. All night I had tossed and turned in bed, and when I finally awoke I wanted to stay in bed. I lied to my parents telling them I wasn't nervous; I was petrified. My way to avoid this awful nightmare was to sleep through it and wake up the next day being married. But in just a short period of time I realized, I must get up and face the truth.

It was a mad rush to get ready. This rush helped me to forget my fears, until the time came to leave for the church. In the last few minutes before we left the house, my brother (the best man) and I cracked jokes, which somewhat settled my nervousness. We made a last-minute check on our appearances, and we were out the door.

We arrived at the church only to find it empty. I was very glad that no guests had arrived yet. My brother and I sat in the back room in the church and watched our guests slowly march in. My brother made more jokes in an attempt to lighten my nervousness. I sat there smiling and laughing with him, but through this I thought about what was going to happen in just a few minutes. Before I knew it, the church was filled with all our guests, and word came from the altar boy that my soon-to-be wife had arrived.

It was time to go out there and face the crowd. So I did. There I was standing by the altar with 125 people staring at me. My friends and family members were sitting there, smiling and laughing. Instantly, I started to sweat, thinking that there was something wrong with my appearance, or that they were making fun of me. But as quick as this fear came on, it left when the music started. I saw everyone stand up and turn around to see the incoming maid of honor, the ring bearer, and the bride. Only one person was looking at me and that was my dad. He gave me the thumbs-up, and from that minute on the fear never returned.

I watched my wife come down the aisle. I never saw her look so beautiful. I hoped I looked that way to her. The wedding ceremony began and dragged on slowly. But finally it was over, and we sealed our love for one another with a kiss. We left the church, after greeting everyone properly, and we were pelted with rice. We entered the limousine on our way to the reception at the Woodlake Country Club.

After stopping to take some pictures, we arrived in complete happiness. We realized tonight was our night, and we were going to make the best of it. The reception went by faster than we would have liked, but we knew our "surprise honeymoon" was to Hawaii. My brothers had agreed to pay for it as our wedding present. From the reception, we left for paradise.

In Hawaii, we prayed our whole lives would be paradise together. For the one week in Hawaii, it was; but when we arrived home, reality set in. Before I knew it, it was time to return to school for the spring semester. We moved into our apartment together. Married life was great. I was never so happy. Time moved along quickly, and Amy began to get huge. She said, "I can't wait to have our baby."

When she was nine months pregnant, and our excitement had grown stronger than ever, I heard the news from my mom that my grandfather who was ill had died. There was no excitement anymore; I felt nothing but pain and anguish. There was only one thing that could change the way I felt and that was our new baby. Exactly one week after my grandfather's death, Amy gave birth to our child. It was a girl. She was eight pounds three ounces and twenty inches long. We named her Katie Lynn.

The birth of my child lightened my spirits about my grandfather's death, but I wish he were alive today to see her grow. Life and death are curious things: You lose a loved one, but God replaces that loss with a whole new life that can fit in your arms.

THE UNWANTED SUMMER EXPERIENCE
(Anonymous)

"No, that's okay, you guys go ahead. I'll catch up to you later." I found myself saying that more during the second week of August than ever in my entire life. I was tired. I figured that a summer of late nights, beer, and never getting any sleep had finally taken its toll. Being rundown was unusual because I was always the first one to work a double shift, party all night, then get up and do it all over again. I wasn't myself. I used to do it all with ease.

This summer appeared to be different. I knew I had partied too much because I could feel the beer gut slowly gaining. The end of August came too quickly, along with the constant reminder of the single thing that had been on my mind all summer: I had skipped my July period.

This had not bothered me too much because I had never been regular. My cycle lasted anywhere from a fifteen to a forty day schedule, so I did not see this as a problem. My diet was pretty stingy, maybe one meal a day and a bag of potato chips. My body was out of whack and, the summer before, the same skip in July had happened.

But now August was here and I still had the nagging feeling in my stomach that something was not right. I had been sexually active with my boyfriend for two years, so the nagging I felt could have a reason. I had an attitude of "not me, nothing like that could ever happen to me." But it did, as I found out after a pregnancy test.

"Oh my God, this can't be happening. This can't be happening. There has to be something wrong with this thing. No way, this wouldn't happen to me." I panicked. My heart raced and my throat enlarged. I knew tests like this don't usually lie, but I was ready to find fault in it.

I took two more tests only to have the same feeling of cardiac arrest and a strange throat enlargement. I knew then that I was pregnant, and nothing I could say would change that. I had heard of girls getting pregnant; in fact, it happened to one of my best friends, but I still couldn't get over the shock that it was happening to me.

After a few days, the concept worked into my brain and I slowly accepted it. You see, I am the kind of person that believes if you ignore your problems, then they'll go away. I'm not saying that this theory has ever worked, but I knew it wouldn't work now. I had to tell Ted (my boyfriend) so we could begin to sort out options.

At first, thinking about it overwhelmed me. Whatever road I chose would change my life forever. I never really thought about what the word "abortion" meant. Whenever the subject came up, I always had comments to make, but never any real basis for my argument. To tell you the truth, my argument changed with every conversation because I always changed my opinion. My friend had an abortion, and going through the experience with her made me think that it was not such a big deal. This is what she wanted to do, and she made it seem like there were no other choices. But now that I was in her shoes, it didn't seem so easy.

I understood that this was not my decision alone. Ted needed to be considered. He was just as overwhelmed as I was when he first found out. I'm sure he went through the "Why the hell is this happening to me?" phase, but he quickly came to reality. He needed to think about what it was that he really wanted to do with his life and understand that it would change forever. When I first told him, I kept apologizing. For some reason, I felt as if it were my fault, and I didn't want him to go through this. I thought, "This isn't fair to make him decide on his life so early." I wanted to deal with this problem on my own. I almost regretted telling him. I knew it was half his responsibility, but I was scared of his reaction. We never had to deal with a huge problem together. Our biggest problem was deciding who would drink and who would drive to the party. Some life, huh?

He dealt with the problem for about a day, then decided that going to bars and getting absolutely trashed was the answer. I began to see another side of Ted that I didn't want to see. I had seen him drunk about a million times, and most of those times, I was drunk with him. But now I had to stay sober. I had no choice because, even when I tried to drink, I felt sick after one beer. I realized this was because of my pregnancy, but I was infuriated that Ted would not stay sober with me. To make matters worse, Ted began to blame the pregnancy on me. He hated the idea of having an abortion. So, to him, there was no way out. Each night he stopped by around 2:15 a.m., after the bars closed, and wanted to discuss the situation. I didn't want to talk to him about anything, let alone the fate of our child, when he was trashed. It only got worse, and the last two weeks before Labor Day weekend became a living hell.

I had never hated anybody the way I hated Ted during that period. I felt lost, alone, and furious. I had the feeling that everywhere I turned the walls were caving in. There was no way out. Ted didn't talk when he was sober. He was too busy going to the beach, water skiing, and watching TV.

I really thought that this would end our relationship forever. Millions of questions ran through my mind: Was our relationship that superficial? Did he really just have the maturity of a ten-year-old at the age of twenty-one? If he could just stay sober for one night, I felt that he would see that we could get through our situation with some effort. I was at a point where I wanted to get down on my hands and knees and beg him to deal with this problem. I wanted to say, "Ted, Budweiser won't make me not pregnant anymore." This sentence ran through my head, more than the fact that I was actually pregnant.

When Labor Day weekend finally came around, I was actually excited. I wanted to get away from Ted, the shore, and the parties. Go figure. Even now it surprises me how really miserable I was. On the outside, I tried to act happy, but I wasn't. I felt that going back to school would give me some sort of a clean slate. A new environment, a different group of friends, and schoolwork would help me get my mind off things.

It seemed as though everything fell into place at the same time. Ted made a miraculous turnaround, and, the night before I left for school, we had a long discussion. This was followed by many others over the phone after I arrived at college. I hated to have a serious discussion over the phone. I wanted to talk face-to-face, but I was happy he was finally opening up.

While all of this was going on, my cousin Lisa began to play the role of a concerned parent. She had also had an abortion at one time in her life, but it wasn't by choice. Not that she disagreed with the idea, but her parents had more of a say than she did. Lisa and I kept in touch off and on during the years, but we lived far apart.

When we started to talk again that summer, we were inseparable. We talked of childhood memories, which included the endless torture she put me through as a child. She treated me like a younger sister, even though she was only six months older than I. We would play hide-and-seek; I would hide, and she would watch TV. All in all, I was glad that we grew closer again. I don't know what I would have done without her.

She was the one who made all of the arrangements at the Cherry Hill Women's Center. Since I was in school, I couldn't have a call to the Center on my phone bill for fear that my parents would see. When it was time for the procedure, I made a weekend of it by staying at Lisa's house Friday and Saturday nights.

I didn't know what to do with myself. The car ride to the clinic seemed more like ten hours instead of ten minutes. It was very early in the morning, but I was wide awake. I tried listening to music, brushing my hair, tying my shoes, but that only took up a good two minutes. I was scared, and there was nothing I could do about it. I hadn't had anything to eat or drink, not even a cigarette in over twelve hours. So besides being mentally upset, my body longed for something to do to take up some time.

When I entered the clinic, I had an eerie feeling that everybody knew why I was there. I walked up to the desk, signed in, and waited for them to tell me the procedure. Lisa tried to distract me by joking about the ridiculous headlines on the cover of "Star," but I knew why she was doing that. I'm still not sure why I was trying to act so composed, or even how I pulled it off. Lisa's comments would have been hysterical under any other circumstance, but at the time they were driving me up the wall. It's as if I didn't want the extra attention she was giving to me because I was trying my best to pretend there was nothing wrong.

The nurse called me to come behind the desk to ask about my form of payment and additional information and then said, "Proceed down the hall, first door on your left. Nurse Baker will ask you a couple of questions and then you'll be on your way." On my way? Where was I going? I realize now that I was reading way too deeply into the meaning of such sentences, but I couldn't help it. At the end of the meeting, she asked me, "Are you sure about the termination of this pregnancy?"

I said, "Yes," signed the bottom of the liability form, then laughed to myself about the euphemism "termination" and about how everyone was so politically correct.

Nurse Baker told me that the procedure took only five minutes, but I would be put under for about twenty. I couldn't understand how it could take only five minutes. Everything takes longer than five minutes. After I left her office, I had to go into the waiting room with the "other girls" who would be going through the same procedure. I hugged Lisa with all my might, told her I would be fine, and made sure she would be there when I woke up. She would.

I decided I had to go to the bathroom before I went into the waiting room, and that's when it happened. I broke down. I must have sat on that white-tiled floor for over five minutes. I started to think long and hard about what it was that I was about to do. I wanted to talk to my mom. I never had such an urge for Mommy as I did at that moment. Questions rushed at me. Was it right to make a decision so big without first consulting someone over twenty years old? Wouldn't I want my daughter to tell me? Was there something wrong with me for only asking the opinion of a few young adults? I tried twice to regain my composure, but failed. All I could do was cry. I was having second thoughts about the person I was about to become. Was this something that people would talk about? "There's the girl who had the..." and then they would say in a low whisper, "abortion."

When the crying stopped, I walked over to the shiny porcelain sink and splashed water on my face. "You're going to be okay. You're going to walk straight out of here and go to the waiting room. You're not a bad person for your decisions. Hundreds of girls have gone through this procedure." From the moment I walked out, the rest of the morning flew by. I had what seemed like twenty gallons of blood taken, then read an article about Meg Ryan's acting career. I was trying to get my mind on other things, but my mind focused on the one thing that would change my life forever.

"Here you go," said the nurse. "Put this on after you take your clothes off." She handed me a huge piece of light blue paper, which had openings for my head and arms. I had never had a GYN exam, so I felt awkward taking my clothes off. When the doctor came in, I was humiliated. I had to lay flat on my back while he gave me the ultra-sound. That's when he told me that I was ten weeks "with child." The nurse came back with the same huge smile she had on her face all morning. I just wanted to hit her. The mood I was in had no place for the nurse's fake smile. She brought me into another room. I sat on the bed, and she introduced me to the doctor who would "terminate my pregnancy." I got the regular check-up: monitoring my heart rate, checking my blood pressure, and looking in my ears. He was very nice, and I could tell he knew I was scared. He said he wouldn't be able to put me all the way under because he didn't want me to choke on the mucus in my chest.

Panic struck me like a Mack truck. I thought for sure that I would wake up, feel everything, and see what was going on. I laid down, he put a needle in my arm, and, just as the fear was climbing through my body, I was out.

I awoke in a comfortable chair with a blanket over me. I was confused. It took me a couple of minutes to realize where I was. My first instinct was to jump up, get dressed, and get out. But I couldn't move. The anesthesia hadn't worn off, and I was out of it. I dozed in and out of sleep for about ten minutes, until I finally worked up the gumption to walk to the bathroom.

It was only about ten feet away, but I had a lot of trouble keeping my balance. It was impossible to hold the cover around me, carry my small bag of clothes, and walk at the same time. The other girls in the room were in a daze also, but I felt stupid walking past them. I was walking like a drunken bum in the street. When I reached the bathroom, I sat on the toilet to steady myself before I got dressed.

When I took off my robe, I found a pad between my legs held there by surgical tape. When I took it off there was no blood, no anything. According to Nurse Baker's instructions, this was no big deal; it could be weeks before I would bleed. I got dressed, and the nurse came up to me as I was leaving and said, "Are you sure you're okay?" She must have noticed how crooked I was walking.

"Yeah, I'm fine." I couldn't see straight, but it didn't matter. I just wanted to get out of there. Lisa was waiting for me, and she had the car pulled up front. My words were slurred, so Lisa didn't get any of her questions answered. When we got back to Lisa's house, all I wanted to do was sleep. So Lisa and I took an hour's nap.

When I woke up, I felt absolutely fine. I ate dinner, then called Ted. He was concerned, but the conversation concentrated more on plans of what time he would pick me up on Sunday, rather than the procedure. The next morning, Lisa and I visited my grandmom who lives around the corner. Ted picked me up from there, and the car ride back to school was long. I was starting to feel uncomfortable. Ted didn't know what to say, and I didn't know how to act. There was the usual small talk about nothing of importance. Then he looked me straight in the eyes and asked if I needed anything. I said I didn't, but it didn't help him. He wanted to give me something to make everything all right again, but that was impossible.

When I look back on it now, it seems it happened years ago, instead of months ago. I'm not sure why, but I have a whole new perspective of the way people act. I find myself questioning people's opinions on major issues when I would have never done this before. I have come to the conclusion that people act and say what they think is appropriate for that situation. I know because I used to do the same thing. If my friends and I ever discussed the issue of abortion, I would just go along with what everyone else said. So, depending on the crowd, my opinion would change. But now I really think about things before I say them. If everyone had this attitude, the world would be better off.

It's weird because whenever I hear about abortion, I think, "God, I actually went through that." It still pops up in my mind, almost every day. I'll be the first to admit that I have second thoughts. But when I think about how my life would be now, if I didn't have the abortion, I feel more at ease with my decision. I can't imagine being five months pregnant, living at home, and not achieving my goals.

School and bettering myself are my top priorities. That way, someday, when I'm ready to have children of my own, I will be the best person I can. I love the way I live now, but I will take my past experience with me for the rest of my life.

MY CHOICE
(Anonymous)

I was scared of what was to come. I had had the appointment for four weeks: the four worst weeks of my life. On the way to the old wooden house that had been transformed into a makeshift medical center, I went over and over those four weeks in my head. Then, I thought about how I had told my mom.

I remembered that I had debated whether to tell her or not. Holly convinced me that I had to. She said that I would never make it through this alone. Holly was right. I needed to tell my mom. Thursday morning when I arrived at school, I went to Holly and asked her how I should tell my mother. I was really confused. She told me to just tell her the truth. There was no easy way out of this. I already felt so bad about the situation, and I did not know whether I could handle the pain this was going to cause my mom.

After school Holly, my boyfriend Ralph, and I went to my house. I cried the whole way. My mother saw the three of us get out of the car, and she knew something was wrong. I think she knew something was wrong that morning because I had asked her if she would love me no matter what I did. She looked at me intently and said that she would love me always. I can't explain exactly why, but the look on her face that morning made me shiver.

As we walked to the front door, I saw that look on her face again. That walk to the front door was like walking to my death. How was I going to tell her I had made the biggest mistake of my life? What I was about to tell her was every mother's worst nightmare.

I walked through the door crying. My mother ran to me, and she threw her arms around me. She asked me over and over again what was wrong. I could not tell her. The words would not come out. I cried harder. At that moment, I just wanted to die. I looked at Holly for support. Through the tears running down her face, she managed a smile. I think it was hurting her as much as it was hurting me. I looked at Ralph. He looked so small and scared. He was against the whole idea. He did not want to tell my parents. I wish he had not been there. I think it made things worse.

My mom looked at Holly and then at Ralph. She looked so upset, and I hadn't told her yet. Through the tears and the choking, I whispered "I'm pregnant." My mom started screaming, "NO! NO! NO!" She tried to push me away, but I kept holding her. I needed her to hold me and tell me everything was going to be all right. Instead, she started calling me names. She said I was a slut and a whore. The words felt like I had just been stabbed with a knife. I could not believe she was saying these horrible things, but I knew I deserved every word of it. I was such an awful child. I leaned up against the wall, and I kept wishing over and over again that I would die.

My mom was so upset. Over and over again she yelled, "How could you!" Suddenly, she turned towards Ralph and started screaming at him. She ran towards him and pushed him against the wall. My brother came out and separated them. I couldn't stop crying, and I didn't realize what was happening. The only thing I could think about was dying.

The more I kept thinking about everything, the more upset I got. I cried harder and harder the more everyone yelled at each other. I just sat on the floor by the wall watching them. The more I cried, the harder it was for me to breathe. I started to have an asthma attack, but no one noticed. I didn't care. I hoped they wouldn't notice. Holly saw me, and she came running towards me. She asked me where my medicine was. I didn't answer. My mom found my purse and got my medicine. My mom sat next to me on the floor and tried to calm me. She held me and rocked me back and forth. I wanted her to tell me everything was going to be okay. I wanted her to tell me that she still loved me. I needed my mom's forgiveness.

My mom needed my dad, so she called him at work and told him to come home. Then she called my sister and her husband. I think she needed the whole family for support. I don't remember when Holly and Ralph left because I was in a daze. I just sat on the floor staring at the wall. I kept going over and over what my mom had said to me, and the names she had called me. I didn't want my own mother to think that way about me.

I must have stared at the wall for about an hour. My mind went blank. I just sat on the floor not seeing anything and not thinking about anything. My body felt numb until the front door opened. I heard my dad's footsteps and a chill ran through my body. I didn't want to see my father's face when my mom told him, so I ran to my room and shut the door. I sat on my bed, hugging my pillow, waiting for my father's reaction.

Finally, I heard the dreadful sound of footsteps coming down the hall. My father came into my room. The look on his face surprised me. He looked more concerned than angry. He said being angry with me wouldn't make the problem go away. He hugged me and let me cry on his shoulders.

I guess I should have been relieved, but instead I began to panic. The numbness was wearing off. Now that I had finally told my parents the truth, I had to think about what was next. I knew there was only one solution that would make everyone happy.

Everyone assumed that I would have an abortion. I was not sure this was what I wanted. I had thought about it a lot. I knew it was what I should do for my family, my boyfriend, and me, but I wasn't sure it was the right thing to do. I just wanted someone to tell me that it was all right to have an abortion.

I went to Planned Parenthood to get an exam and a referral to a clinic. I was so ashamed of myself that I let the woman doctor at Planned Parenthood harass me. She made me feel like I deserved everything that happened to me. She told me I should stop crying because it wouldn't get me any sympathy. I didn't say anything back to her because I was too scared. I just lay on the examining table crying. When the exam was finally over, and I had gone through counseling, I went home. I locked myself in my room and cried.

My mom called Chestnut Medical Center to make an appointment for me. I had gotten a referral from Planned Parenthood to go there. I had to wait several weeks to have the procedure done. I hated the waiting. It gave me more time to worry.

As the van came to a stop, I was awakened from these memories. We had arrived at Chestnut Medical Center. I began to feel sick to my stomach. I wanted to wake up from this nightmare. I couldn't believe this was happening to me. I hated myself for everything I had done. I looked at my mom, my dad, my sister, and my brother. I know they wanted to support me, but I didn't want them to deal with my problems. I had already hurt them so much.

No matter what I said, they felt they had to come in with me. We walked into the old wooden house with a sign on the door that read Chestnut Medical Center. It didn't look like I thought it would. I thought it would look like a doctor's office, but instead it looked like a house. There were a lot of other people there. I couldn't believe that everyone was there for the same thing. There were about eight other girls my age, and the rest were between twenty and thirty. A few of the other girls looked as nervous and scared as I did, but the rest looked as if they had been through this before.

I stood there staring at everyone in disbelief until the nurse handed me some papers. As I filled out the forms, I started crying again. I couldn't believe I was sitting in an abortion clinic, being shipped through like I was on a factory line.

The first thing they did was ask me questions. Then I was called back to get a blood sample done. I waited for about two hours before they called my name to go back to the room. I was really nervous, and I felt sick. When they called my name, I couldn't breathe. I stood up, and I felt really faint. I started to walk to the door, ready to pass out. I reached for the side of the door and stood there for a short while before I could start walking again. A nurse gave me a paper gown and told me to put it on. Then she came back to get me and take me to the room where the abortion would take place. I felt like just another girl that made a mistake and was taking care of it. No one seemed to care about what was happening to me. I was just another patient.

I lay on the table waiting for the doctor to come back to the room. It wasn't long before the doctor came. There was a nurse with him who held my hand the whole time. I cried, and she looked at me with a smile and said, "You will be all right, sweetheart." If it wasn't for her, I wouldn't have made it through the abortion. I was in so much pain. The doctor tried to explain what he was doing, but I couldn't understand what he was saying. I was trying to keep myself from screaming. I felt like the inside of my body was being twisted around and then yanked out.

When it was finally over, the nurse carried me to the resting room, and I laid down for a short time. My parents came to get me from there. I had to lean on my dad the whole way to the car. I was still in a lot of pain. As we left the building, we had to go past some protesters. I cried and kept walking. I just wanted to go home and get away from that place.

For the next week I stayed in bed. I didn't want to go anywhere or talk to anyone. I wanted to curl up in a ball and sleep. I wanted to drown myself in the pillows and dream of a better place away from the pain.

My parents were ashamed of me. I could see it on their faces every time they looked at me. They no longer trusted me. I was no longer the perfect daughter they had always wanted. I never would be.

My grandfather went into the hospital with heart problems. The doctors did not think he would make it. I blamed myself for his condition. I thought that God was punishing me for what I had done by making the people I loved suffer. I shrank into the darkness. Everyday I became more isolated, more depressed.

By some miracle, my grandfather made it through his surgery. I was grateful that he was all right, but at the same time, I was ashamed. He did not know what had happened to me. My parents did not want any other family members to know. My parents were afraid of what they would think. I did not want them to know either, but I felt as if I were lying to my grandfather. He had always thought so highly of me. But I couldn't tell him, because I was afraid I would lose his respect.

Gradually I put myself in a dark hole. I began to have nightmares. Every time I closed my eyes, I felt the pain and sadness. I could never escape it. The same nightmare would haunt me night after night: the nightmare of the day I had the procedure done. I called it the "procedure" because I had trouble admitting what happened. When I closed my eyes, I saw the doctor's face and I heard a crying baby.

The horror of that day is inscribed on my brain for the rest of my life. Day after day, I am reminded of what I did. I can't go anywhere without seeing bumper stickers that say "pro-life pro-child" or see t-shirts that say "Of the people that go into an abortion clinic, only half come out." I can't watch TV without seeing commercials protesting abortions. The guilt will always be there.

I will never forget what happened. I will never forget the day I took a child's future away for my own happiness. I made a selfish decision. I never thought about the child. Every day, I think about what the child would have been like. I wonder what color its eyes and hair would be, or if it would have been a boy or a girl. I made a choice—it may have been a selfish choice, but it was *my* choice.

TO OVERCOME
by Jessica Simmons

I had always been very involved in school. I played three sports, was captain of the soccer team, was a member of the community service program, sang in the choir—the list goes on. My father was a community figure, known by my principal and teachers. I was at the peak of my senior year and my popularity. Girls envied me because I had a boyfriend for two years. I had just received an Air Force Reserve Officer Training Corps (AFROTC) scholarship for three years full tuition at almost any college I could get accepted to. My future was bright.

When the rumor hit the school that I was pregnant, my world came crashing down. Friends, teachers, coaches, counselors, and parents gasped at the news. "Jessica?" they said. My life seemed too ideal to them for me to suddenly become a statistic in the issue of teen pregnancy. Whispers were inevitable. Suddenly I heard my name in the hall on all sides. People walked by me to stare at my stomach in amazement. They were looking for evidence of the tragedy that couldn't happen to a nice girl. But that's what I was.

In the beginning, I didn't tell a soul except for my boyfriend, Shawn. We did a lot of crying. We were determined to take care of this situation ourselves. He was two years older than I and working full-time, so he had enough money to pay for clinic visits and ultimately an abortion. I thought that was my only option.

My father hated Shawn and had forbidden me to see him. I was so scared of his reaction to my pregnancy that I wasn't being honest with myself about how I really felt. I thought that I would just have an abortion, and all my problems would go away,

I began lying about where I was going. I took off work in order to keep my appointments at the clinic. This was effective until my father called the day care center where I worked. My boss told him that I had called in sick, and when I got home, he demanded an explanation. It became clear to me that I'd have to tell my mother. She and my father were divorced, and I lived half the week with one and half the week with the other. I thought that, if she knew, she could help me keep my secret.

I was so afraid that my mother would think that I had been irresponsible. The truth was that I hadn't been neglectful. In fact, I felt that I had approached sex very responsibly. I waited until I had been with my boyfriend a year. He agreed to go for disease testing, and I, after discussing it extensively with him, went on birth control. No one told me that taking antibiotics with the pills would reduce the effect. I figured that out on my own.

I didn't plan on telling my mother the way I did. She asked me where I had been one day when I came home from the clinic. I couldn't handle my secret anymore. I broke down and told her everything. She cried. She handled it very well, though. She told me that I had other options, and that she would help me. She said that I shouldn't base my decision on my father's opinion. We talked about adoption, keeping the baby, and abortion. At that time, my mind was still set on abortion; my life was all mapped out, and this just wasn't in the plan. My mom let me know that there were other choices, and she'd help me no matter what.

Days went by, and I still stuck with my decision. School was canceled for almost two weeks because of snow and ice storms. I sat in my room looking out at the white world and just cried. The storms were causing problems for me because I had to keep canceling my appointments on account of the icy roads. I was starting to get worried because I knew that the longer I waited to have the abortion, the harder it would be for me emotionally. I could already feel myself becoming attached to the child.

Finally, Shawn and I managed to keep an appointment. I had to have a sono-gram to determine how many weeks pregnant I was. I wasn't showing at all yet, and I couldn't remember the date of my last period. I entered a cold, sterile room that smelled of alcohol and felt a wave of nausea. The woman who per-formed the sonogram was less than sympathetic. She never smiled; she simply did her job in a business-like manner. Part of me wanted to see the screen to see the little life that was growing inside of me. Another part of me was repulsed by the idea, reminding me that I was choosing to end this baby's life. The nurse pretended not to notice my tears.

The results of the test were a nightmare in themselves. They showed that I was fifteen weeks and two days pregnant. The clinic wouldn't perform abortions that far into the pregnancy, and the nurse gave me references of hospitals that would. My mouth refused to move. I knew that if I was four months pregnant, then the baby was already formed; its little heart was already beating.

I walked out into the waiting room to tell Shawn. I grabbed his hand, and we went into the parking lot. I choked out the results. We talked and cried the whole way home and came to a decision together. We decided that we couldn't end the life of an innocent child. It was our fault that it had been created, not the baby's. Now we had to tell our parents.

The drive home seemed to last forever. Strangely, instead of feeling anxious about telling my parents, I felt a huge wave of relief. I knew that the worst was still to come, but I finally knew what it was I had to do. I could tell that Shawn felt better, too. He had never wanted me to have an abortion, but he had left it up to me. Finally, I had made a decision for myself and no one else.

When I got home, Shawn and I sat down in the kitchen with my mom. There were more tears when we told her, but she too was relieved. She was very religious and felt that having the baby was the right thing to do. We still had to tell my father. My mother called him and asked him to come over to talk with us. He refused and demanded to know what was going on. She didn't think we should talk about it over the phone, so she kept trying to persuade him to come over. Finally, he asked her if I was pregnant. The rest of their conversation was terrible. My father screamed at her. Then he hung up on her. By this time I was starting to run out of tears.

When I woke up the next morning, the car that my father had given me for my sixteenth birthday was gone. He had come in the middle of the night and taken it. He had made it very clear that I was no longer welcome in his house.

Going to school that week was hell for me. I couldn't concentrate on my work, and all I kept thinking about was my situation. I hadn't told any of my friends except for one, and every time I talked to one of them I could feel myself about to tell them everything. It just wasn't something that I could face on my own. Finally, I blurted it out to two of my girlfriends, who promised not to tell. I trusted them—they knew that this secret could ruin my life at school.

A week later, someone at my school asked me if I was pregnant. They had heard it from a friend of a friend of a friend. Of course, all of my friends swore that they hadn't told anyone. The rumor was spreading quickly, and I was starting to get tired of telling people that it was none of their business.

Even my teachers were beginning to talk about me behind my back. They would whisper in the teacher's lounge about how I had ruined my life, and it was no surprise when the guidance counselor called me into his office to discuss my dilemma. Someone had slipped my name into the counsler's "Anonymous Box." My counselor talked to me a lot about going to college, and I made it quite clear that I still intended to go. I had been accepted by Florida State University and needed to rethink which school I would attend, but I realized I needed a college education. He didn't have much faith that I wouldn't become a statistic. I wasn't the only one being hassled at school. My brother was two years younger, and people who were afraid to question me went to him. He came home every day angry with someone new. He simply told them that it was none of their business and ended the conversations. He was very emotional about the whole subject, however. In the beginning, I had sat him and my sister down and told them, so that they would hear it from me. He cried. The situation at school was very difficult for him, and I felt guilty.

Meanwhile, my senior year was passing quickly. All of my friends were having a great time; they went to parties and came home late. I didn't feel as though I could relate to them anymore. My problems were so much bigger than "What outfit will I wear today?" I felt strange whenever I went anywhere with them. I kept trying to go to senior activities, so that I would have the experiences to look back on. The senior trip was terrible—we went to an amusement park, and I couldn't ride the rides. The senior prom was embarrassing—I was seven months pregnant, and everyone kept coming up to me to feel my stomach and tell me how cute I looked. Graduation was awful—I was huge in my gown, and I spent the evening in tears because my father refused to come. All of a sudden, the year was gone, and I had none of the fond memories that the rest of my classmates would recall of their senior year. What I had was a huge stomach, swollen ankles, and a lot of stretch marks.

The summer was nothing but a test of my endurance. My house didn't have air conditioning, and the heat went to record-breaking highs. I was absolutely miserable, and I spent almost all my time "swelling" in the house. My ankles, fingers, and stomach looked as if they had been filled with an air pump.

I worked at a day care center, and I continued working throughout the summer, since I was in desperate need of money. My co-workers watched me day after day as I trudged up the stairs to get the children's snack from the kitchen, and as I sweated out on the playground in the afternoons. The other teachers were constantly asking me how I was feeling and if I was drinking enough water. I would say I was fine no matter how I felt.

By this time, I could feel every move the baby made. Sometimes it kicked so hard I would drop my lunch. The children at the center were amazed at my growing stomach. When someone explained that there was a baby inside, they couldn't understand why it wouldn't pop out if I pulled my shirt up. Every once in a while a big-eyed child would announce that she felt it kick.

I was visiting the doctor regularly, and he thought it necessary for me to have a sonogram. Girls under eighteen have the biggest chance of having low-birth-weight babies, and the doctor wanted to be sure everything was going smoothly. Shawn went with me to the office where they performed the sonogram. The doctor was very friendly, and he didn't make me feel strange about my age as so many other adults did. He told me I would feel something cold, and he squirted icy gel onto my bulging stomach. That machine changed my life.

I had known I was pregnant, but somehow seeing that tiny little being hammered the fact into my soul. I was going to have a baby! The doctor gave me a due date of July 29, and asked us if we wanted to know the sex. I was so excited that I could barely say yes. He zoomed in on the screen, and after a few minutes of chasing the active fetus around, he told us that we had a little girl! Shawn was at the bottom of the hospital bed, and I felt his hand touch my foot. I looked at him, and we exchanged smiles through identical tears. His life was changed too.

The doctor printed out some pictures and gave them to us. In one of the pictures, she was sucking her thumb. We couldn't talk about anything else on the drive home. Now that so many difficult things were done, we could begin to focus on the happier aspects of our situation. For me, this meant picking a name, buying all the essentials in pink, and telling my friends and family that "it" was now a "she." Instead of wishing this had never happened, I was becoming more excited than I had ever been in my life.

I quit working two weeks before the supposed due date, and quickly adopted a regimen of talk shows, cross-stitch, and chocolate marshmallow ice cream. As my due date came and went, I began to wonder if I was going to have the child at all. I was noticeably uncomfortable, and I began to get depressed. I cried for no reason at all. My sleep patterns were nonexistent despite the body pillow, and it seemed that I used the bathroom at least three times an hour. Each week, I went to the doctor with the hope that he would tell me I was ready to give birth. Instead, he would say he'd see me next week.

I was very afraid of the whole birthing process. Shawn and I had attended a class, and the videos were terrifying. I didn't know how I would make it through the experience. Strangely, by the time I was three weeks past my due date, any fears I had were gone. I was ready to stop being pregnant! People told me to take a bumpy ride, eat a taco, jump around the house, or go for a walk. Apparently they thought that these tricks would speed up the process for me. They were wrong.

Finally, on August 19, I began to feel a little strange. I wasn't sure what labor pains were supposed to feel like, and I couldn't distinguish them from all the other aches and pains. That evening, however, they became strong and regular. Shawn came over to my house at nine o'clock. When my mother came home an hour later, we decided to call the doctor. He asked me questions about my contractions, and by eleven we were on our way to the hospital. They connected me to a machine that gauged how strong the contractions were. Shawn stayed with me every second, and I was glad that he was there. The nurse gave me a type of sedative so that I could sleep.

When I woke up, the contractions were so strong that I could barely stand up. Shawn and I walked around the labor and delivery ward to speed up the labor process. Finally, the pain was more than I could stand. They gave me an epidural and I fell asleep again. Shawn had been up all night, too, and he was sprawled across a recliner.

At noon, the nurse woke us up and told me it was time to start pushing. She stood on one side, and Shawn was on the other. I held his hand so hard that his knuckles turned white. He got really excited, because he could see the top of the baby's head crowning. The nurse brought a mirror, and for a second I forgot that I was in pain. After forty-five minutes of pushing and breathing, I gave birth to a nine pound and nine ounce baby girl.

Immediately after birth, my family and Shawn's mother crowded in. We were so happy that we both were crying. She was so beautiful! I couldn't believe that this moment had finally come. People say that childbirth is the worst pain that you will ever feel in your life, but that when you see your baby, you forget everything.

For me, the stress of being pregnant at seventeen was combined with this special pain. I not only dealt with swelling and weight gain, I faced terrible stereotypes that unfairly label teenage mothers. Although I realized that my situation was not ideal, I was determined to make the best of things. I had to keep some semblance of order in my life.

Looking back, I can finally understand what all those women meant about forgetting the personal struggle to focus on your child. I had somehow created this perfect little being out of chaos. Ironically, it was this chaos that I had fought the hardest to overcome.

These are really

the thoughts of

all men in all

ages and lands;

they are not

original

with me. If they

are not yours as

much as they

are mine,

they are

nothing...

"Upon graduation, I packed up the stuff that accumulated in my dorm over four years. In my desk, I found stacks of papers with short paragraphs written all over them—some were sideways, some were diagonal, but they were all strange. They forced me to read them again.

"I sat cross-legged on the floor reading scraps of paper that came alive with stories. They told me things about myself. They revealed the mood I was in when I wrote the piece, as well as my view on that particular topic. I'm positive that I remained on the floor for more than two hours, but dared not move because I did not want to spoil the moment. The beauty in some of the poems brought tears to my eyes, just as the beginnings of stories begged for endings.

"I was zapped with the awesome power of my own writing, and vowed then and there that I would keep it alive."

Andrianne Gamble

EDGE OF ADULTHOOD
by Joseph Battle III

As I walked down the aisle, hearing my family's cheers made me feel special. I reached the podium and thought, I've finally become an adult. Principal Kenneth Flickinger presented my diploma, and I returned to my seat. On the ninth of June, I had finished high school.

Six disastrous months followed. Although I learned much during this time, I sometimes wish that those months had never occurred. When I was younger, my differences from others were not apparent to me. No one was black, white, or any other color. People were people.

Soon after high school though, I found racism infecting everyone: my friends, my enemies, and even my relatives. Never had such pain tormented me. My father was black, and my mother was white. Why did that make me so different and so insignificant? Why did I deserve the misery and pain of such a curse?

The next six months also taught me positive things as well. I realized being black wasn't a curse, and that I should be proud of myself. These months showed me many things I hope to use to live a better, more mistake-free life.

After I graduated, my friends and I celebrated nightly. Life was great. In mid-June, Lance Zanti called and asked me to move to Ocean City for the summer, and I accepted. I slowly realized it was hard to live on my own, especially at the beach. The sights, sounds, and smells—fights on the Boardwalk, the acrid scent of saltwater, and police officers hassling teenagers—didn't enhance the experience.

I worked at Del's Frozen Lemonade and used the money for rent. It was hard to live without money for necessities, but my roommates provided food sometimes. Eventually, I developed a method to steal money from my employer. Delicious sandwiches from Mother Cluckers, swollen with meats and drenched in oils and vinegar, filled my stomach daily. I felt guilty, but survival was more important than my conscience.

In the coming months, my immaturity surfaced time and again. Lance and the others—Barry, Jeff, Joe, and Kyle—helped me, but they caused problems as well. Rock music, which I disliked, dominated the stereo and ruined parties. I loved hip-hop music. The raw beats, deep bass, and smooth lyrics inspired me with pride for my culture. I loved booming bass, vibrating in my chest like the croak of a person racked by croup.

Our cultures clashed frequently, and we became violent a few times. Once, after we drank a keg of beer, I played a cassette tape of N.W.A. and my roommate, Kyle, began to degrade the music. He offended me, and I retaliated with verbal bombshells. He came toward me, and I rose from my chair at the brown table between us. As we stood nose to nose, spittle spraying on each other's faces, his light brown hair fell over his eyes. Suddenly, Kyle shoved me into the stereo, scraping skin off my back. I regained my feet and threw a punch at his nose. My knuckles smashed his lips, and a line of blood rolled down his chin.

Barry grabbed me and dragged me out the door. As we tumbled out, he said, "Come on, you fucking half-nigger!" Immediately, I began throwing uncontrolled punches at his head. He fell to the ground. I pounced on him and continued to swing my fists. Tears started running down my cheeks. I couldn't believe that my roommate had made such a vicious comment. From the street, to our left, someone yelled, "Freeze."

I turned my head, no longer fighting, and stared into the barrel of a gray Glock nine-millimeter. I stood, raising my hands, and thought the day couldn't get worse. A passing police officer had seen the scuffle and was now pointing his gun at me; Barry climbed to his feet and raised his hands.

Another officer arrived and suggested that we be arrested. The first agreed, and I was handcuffed. A paddy wagon, which smelled of urine and sweat, took me to police headquarters. They called my mother, because I was a minor, and suggested I attend classes for alcoholics. I resented being called an alcoholic, and it hurt, but nothing hurt as badly, nor bit as deeply into my soul, as discovering racism in supposed friends.

My emotions exploded. I feared jail, hated Barry, and felt angry and betrayed. That night, spent in a detox trailer, fanned the flames of my feelings. Confusion set in. My anger grew, and I wanted satisfaction. I wanted Barry and the arresting officer to feel what I felt when suffering such humiliation.

Though I hungered for revenge, I did nothing. I didn't want to upset the rest of my roommates, but it was too late. Our living situation was never the same.

Confrontations plagued the remainder of the summer. Frank, my employer, asked me about the missing money, and I was forced to confess. He took the money from my next paycheck and allowed me to continue working, but I had lost his trust. Once again, I was ashamed.

Weeks later, our landlord evicted us. I gladly went home to Reisterstown and began preparing for Boston University. My summer, I thought, would help me in college, and I soon found that it did, although it didn't help much. I relaxed until September, then began packing for college.

My mother gave me a large black chest with gold trim that looked like it held a pirate treasure. Of course it didn't, but I did find space for most of my valuables. The chest measured about three feet long, four feet wide, and three feet high. My stereo, compact disc player, and television went under the shelf that fit into the top. I also found room for shoes, compact discs, and cassettes. Comic books, which I had been collecting for four years, filled the shelf. When I locked the lid, I realized how valuable the contents were and became afraid of thieves and baggage clerks. I didn't want to lose all of my belongings.

The chest, along with its contents, represented my only links to my mother and my home. I didn't want to lose these bonds to home. Homesickness had afflicted me, in a small way, while I lived in Ocean City. I knew that I couldn't survive in Boston, millions of miles from home, without something familiar to rely on. Mom told me not to worry, and my fear faded. She told me that lost and stolen baggage was rampant only in movies and on television. I no longer thought some unseen stranger would steal the chest filled with my life. I continued packing my suitcases for the upcoming trip.

When I finished, I was relieved and almost forgot the paper with the address of my room. Imagine if I had arrived in Boston without my address. There would have been undue confusion and embarrassment, so I quickly put the paper into my bag.

On the first day of September, I boarded an Amtrak train at Penn Station in Baltimore, along with my mom and aunt. Nine hours later, we were in a taxi, driving to Commonwealth Avenue. When we arrived at my building, we unloaded my belongings and took them to my fifth floor room. The chest was hard to carry and barely fit into the small room, but we managed. Afterward, we walked around campus, getting accustomed to the university. At six o'clock, Mom and Aunt Minnie hailed a cab, hugged me, and left for home. I was alone, and I was scared.

I went back to my room, unpacked my things, and set up my television and stereo on the combination desk and bookshelf. I took the bed on the left side and put my clothes into the scarred, brown dresser. Hanging my button-down shirts and jackets in the closet to the right of the door, I wondered how someone was supposed to live in this small space. For the rest of the day, I lounged around, waiting to meet my roommate, Rob.

Outside my window, the football team practiced, and I heard the crack of helmets, orders from the coach, and the cadence of the quarterback. I looked down onto the field and saw maroon helmets, white practice jerseys with grass stains, and pigskins flying everywhere. As I started daydreaming about playing in the NFL, a key rattled in the lock. The door opened, and a lean, pale-skinned man with short, brown hair entered.

I knew that this was my new roommate, Rob, because we had received profiles of each other during the summer. Apparently, the university did not want boarding problems, so they gave students the chance to avoid uncomfortable situations. I soon found that I should have taken these profiles more seriously. I said hello and introduced myself.

"You're Joe? I thought you were black," he responded.

This statement bothered me, but I simply explained that my father was black and my mother was white. He then introduced himself as Rob O. and told me some of his background. His wealthy family lived in Long Island, New York, and he was an engineering major beginning his senior year.

With nothing in common—we had different backgrounds, family incomes, and ages—I knew disaster was lurking in the shadows. I was already uncomfortable and did not want to have a bad experience during my first semester. A feeling that our relationship would be disastrous overtook me, but I decided to stay and weather the storm. With this decision, I had made my first mistake of the semester.

We talked for a few minutes; then Rob showed me the key sights on the campus. I learned the location of my classes, other dormitories, and fun places to go on weekends. The next day, Rob showed me around the city of Boston. We went to malls, good stores such as Tower Records, and the Bull Finch Pub, better known as Cheers. Over the next two days, while waiting for classes to start, I familiarized myself with my new surroundings, and I began to think I had misjudged Rob, as well as the future.

My good friend from Franklin High School, Adam, attended Boston University with me. We had been friends since seventh grade and had the same classes throughout high school. I bumped into him on Commonwealth Avenue outside of his dormitory on September 3, and we renewed our friendship. He lived ten minutes away—it was a very big campus—but I was glad to have a close friend in this new city. For the first time, I began to feel at home in my new surroundings because his friendship allowed for a small bit of familiarity.

On September 5, I attended my first class, Microeconomics. The size of the lecture hall astounded me. Thirty students, at the most, attended my high school classes, but there must have been three hundred in this class. I could not believe that we, the students, were supposed to learn in such an impersonal setting.

The professor seemed to be a good teacher, although it was only my first college-level class. He kept my attention by making me laugh and speaking to me as if I were an equal. My previous teachers acted as though they were above their students. Adam was in the same class, and we sat together. We joked around but managed to pay attention to most of the lecture.

Afterward, I had two hours until my next class, so I went back to my room. Hunger caused me to go to the dining hall an hour later. I wolfed down a hot pastrami on rye with mustard sandwich, savoring every tangy bite while drinking a Coke, and then left for my second class.

Although Greek philosophy was not my forte, I thought that I could do well. But, though it was only an introduction, the first class made me sleepy. I wondered if this class would liven up at all during the semester. Socrates, Plato, and other ancient philosophers, I thought, were most likely rolling over in their graves at the way this class was being taught.

I felt happy when that endless class finally did end. After hurrying back to my room for some well-deserved rest, I took a short nap. The rest of that day was spent reading and watching television, although my television only received one channel. Luckily, I loved the old Bob Newhart show.

The next day started at eight o'clock when I woke up and showered. After dressing and brushing my teeth, I left for my nine o'clock class, Macroeconomics. I arrived just in time and sat down as a tall, bald man with a shiny, tanned skull walked through the classroom door. When he introduced himself, his foreign accent made him hard to understand. I never deciphered his name. I only knew that he was our teacher.

The professor laughed at his own unintelligible jokes, but his lesson went fairly well. I learned more in this class than in my two previous ones because the teacher didn't dwell on the introduction very long. When he gave us homework, however, I felt angry. I didn't want any homework yet. Nor did I want to worry about schoolwork. Soon I was resentful, as well as anxious, that I might not be able to handle college.

After a quick lunch, I went to Business Math. Adam sat in a middle-row, end seat; I joined him, and we talked until the teacher arrived and started class. "I didn't know you were in this class, too," I said.

"Oh, yeah, man, They stuck me in this math because I didn't know what else to take," Adam replied.

"Same here," I added.

Although the large class had about fifty students, it actually seemed friendly and personal. I found math to be an easy subject, and this class proved no different. Surprisingly, I felt contempt for Business Math because it didn't challenge me at all. My high school math classes—Algebra II, Geometry, Trigonometry, Analytic Geometry, and College Algebra—appeared to dwarf the difficulty of Business Math. The class ended, and Adam and I decided to go eat dinner. After a quick dinner, I returned to my room and slept.

For the next three weeks, things went well. I attended class, did my homework, ate, and slept. Hanging out with Adam and going to parties were my only forms of recreation, and I soon noticed that I was homesick. I wanted to see my family, to feel the warmth and comfort of my bed, and to simply be in my home town.

My college classmates, especially my roommate, began to get on my nerves. I hated to hear that they were receiving BMWs, Mercedes, or other expensive items for various special occasions. Admitting that I drove a Ford Escort made me feel inferior. I hated seeing Rob buy a new, expensive stereo system on a whim. I felt poor. My scholarships began to feel more like burdens than opportunities. Resentment of my parents' meager salaries swelled inside me, which made me feel ashamed and unappreciative for all they had given me.

The stress, disgust, and hatred soon turned to lethargy. A permanent cloud of sleep dust hung around my head. I began to ignore the alarm clock, to miss classes, and to neglect classwork and homework. I simply dropped my philosophy class because it was too early for me. When my roommate made fun of me for my study and work habits, I struck back by making fun of him. This caused much friction between us.

My two good friends from Reisterstown, Chris and Rich, came to visit me one night. Adam, Chris, Rich, and I piled into my room with two cases of Keystone beer and drank heavily. That night passed in a haze, and I remember little. After Adam left, Chris and Rich slept on the floor. They left for home early the next morning.

My hangover thumped in my head and churned in my stomach. Rob woke me that afternoon and blamed me for a tear in his Squishy ball. "How did my ball get ripped, man?" he asked.

"What the hell are you talking about?" I replied. "I don't know how your ball got ripped."

"Either you or your friends did it. You better buy me a new one," Rob growled.

Silence greeted him. My ability to seem unsympathetic infuriated him, and I loved it. I felt in control of the situation.

"You're an idiot. What an idiot," he said as he left, slamming the door behind him.

As I lay there thinking about the confrontation, I knew in my heart that I had to leave Boston University. Denying it over and over in my thoughts did not help. I could no longer wake myself for class, concentrate on homework, or live with a rich, snobby, little white boy. I hated Rob and wanted to beat him into unconsciousness, but that was not the solution. Prejudice, hatred, and violence would solve nothing. Leaving school remained my only option.

As I told my mother of my disappointing decision, I felt the cold finger of regret tapping my shoulder. My immaturity—the inability to attend class, to do homework, to deal with stress, and simply to live away from home—forced me to drop out. I stayed for my Business Math exam on December 19 because it was the only class I thought I could pass.

After my exam, Rich arrived to take me home. We loaded his car with my things, but my chest would not fit, so I had to throw it away. But I didn't care; I was on my way home. After saying goodbye to Rob and giving him a new Squishy ball, Rich and I left for home. A huge weight fell from my chest as Boston receded in the rearview mirrors.

I left Boston University with much new knowledge, but this wisdom couldn't be learned from books. My experiences in Boston and Ocean City taught me that life as an adult is much tougher than as a child, and that life as a black adult is tougher still.

UNCHARTED TRIP
by Christina Berzeler

It was my junior year in high school, and my main focus was on grades, SATs, and sports. I was the captain of the soccer, basketball, and softball teams, and class president. I devoted my spare time to train for the Empire State Soccer Games, which took place in Syracuse the following spring. My dad was my trainer, and my parents and friends supported me through the rough times. I never thought of dating until I met Jerry.

Jerry was good looking, an honor student, captain of both the football and wrestling teams, and, most importantly, a friend as well as a boyfriend. I fell in love with him instantly. I was experiencing feelings that I had never felt before.

I had always shied away from relationships because of the hardships I saw other people go through. I had a belief that friends will stay forever, but boyfriends would come and go, so I never attempted to date. I also was a daddy's girl, so the only male role model in my life was my father. He always said that, if you are going to play the game of love, be prepared to get burned.

I grew to realize the meaning of male companionship by spending a lot of time with Jerry. Our relationship was very convenient because we belonged to the same group of friends. It was easy for us to see each other even if we did not plan to. On weekend nights, our friends would meet at the group's hangout to find out the details for the evening. We knew we were bound to meet each other sometime during the night.

As months passed, we were voted prince and princess at the junior prom and were nominated cutest couple of the year. Everyone envied our friendship/relationship.

Also that year, I was named best female athlete for the school year for Long Island, and I made the high honor roll for both semesters. I was having the best time of my life, achieving all my goals, and I wished for the continuation of my success in the future.

Success followed me throughout the summer. I started on the Empire State Women's Soccer Team, and we won the gold medal at the State tournament in Syracuse. Sports and school were great, but I did notice a considerable change in Jerry. He was not as sweet and understanding as he had been. In fact, he became extremely demanding and possessive. I should have learned the first time he hit me that this abuse would last.

The first time it happened, I thought it was a mistake. People have strange reactions to stress and anger, but hitting someone you love is wrong. I was getting punished for the divorce of his parents and his father's cocaine addiction. I tried to help him with his problems, but I caused more aggravation for myself. Everyone at school noticed the bruises on my legs, arms, and face. I denied the abuse to everyone, even to my best friend, because I was so ashamed. Everyone at school knew I was an athlete and that bruises were a part of the game but not whip marks or finger bruises on my forehead. There even were days I was so embarrassed to go to school because I looked so terrible.

I was never so scared of one person in my whole life. The only person that I told was my guidance counselor. She found out by rumors in school. My teachers started complaining of absences, tardiness, and interruptions in class by Jerry. The problems in our relationship started to affect my school work and athletics.

My friends did not understand how I was feeling. I could not admit to them or myself that I was such a weak person. Also Jerry was well liked, so this did not help my situation. I did not want to put them in a position of choosing Jerry or me. Then I thought of telling my mom, but I did not want her to know that he controlled me. So I decided to go on with my life, being inferior to my boyfriend.

Staying with Jerry was the worst decision I could have ever made. I was just giving into his demands and abuse. Something so obvious to a stranger was missed by everyone close to me. I lost an enormous amount of weight. My face was drawn and pale from being undernourished. I thought I was going to admit myself to a hospital for bulimia. My stomach would not hold anything. The sight and smell of food made me sick.

My whole body was nervous. I would jump at the sound of his voice. Finally, my friends realized what was happening. They thought I had been losing weight to get back into shape. Everyone knew I was so weight conscious that they did not take notice. When I told them the truth, my friends did not associate with Jerry.

At first, Jerry thought we all were busy with college applications. College was not an interest to Jerry, since after graduation he was going into the Marines. During this period, we did not see each other much. He thought we were taking a break from our relationship because I focused my attention on college. In reality, I was trying to get away.

After a few weeks, he became very persistent and hostile. He stopped over my house at random, followed me through school, and watched all my practices and games. He would even go to the extent of sleeping in his car outside my house. My father went nuts. Jerry was harassing his daughter, and this madness needed to stop.

My father got a restraining order against Jerry, but I begged my father to give him another chance. My conscience told me to do this. God help me if I ever trust my conscience again. I got myself in the same situation again. He was happy, and I was miserable. The abuse did dwindle, and, for a while, we did get along—until the drugs came.

I have never experimented or even thought of getting involved in the drug/alcohol scene. I was the president of Students Against Drunk Driving and a member of the Alcohol/Drug Prevention Team. I counseled students on the effects drugs have on their bodies. I was an athlete, school president, and a role model for our youth, and I had an abusive boyfriend addicted to PCP, otherwise known as acid. I had heard of acid, but I did not know whether you sniffed, drank, or ate the drug. I remember seeing little white paper tablets wrapped in tinfoil. It looked like garbage to me, not drugs. Everybody knew Jerry was on acid, except me.

The effects PCP has on people is tremendous. Jerry started using acid for wrestling, so his workouts were intense. Acid makes your adrenaline pump vigorously for twelve hours. He needed this intensity to lose pounds to make his weight for the next wrestling meet. I knew, when it came to wrestling, he was psycho, but now I know it was only the drugs. I found out that he was addicted to PCP by my own personal experience.

It was the day before February break. I had a really bad cold, so Jerry went to the cafeteria to get me some hot tea. I drank the hot tea, and off I went to English class. In class, we were reading *The Crucible*. As I was reading, the words started moving all over my paper.

I looked up for a moment to clear my head; I just thought I was dizzy from my cold medicine. When I glanced back down, not only were the words moving, but so was my desk. I started to panic. My hands were blurry, and trails followed my movements. I looked to my friend for help, but everything looked like ripples in water. I thought that maybe I took an overdose of my prescribed medication. But before I knew it, I was breathing heavily and sweating. The last thing I remember was seeing a black screen and then passing out in the middle of class. When I awoke to an extremely bright light and people hovering over me, I was confused. My friend was lying next to me stroking my hair, and a wet cloth was placed on my forehead to cool me. When I realized what had happened, I jumped to my feet. Filled with embarrassment, I asked to be excused from class.

Walking down the hallway to the cafeteria, I felt as if I was in a 3-D movie. All kinds of objects were soaring past me, and the outside trees looked like they were trying to grab me into their branches. As I sat down in the Commons, a place where everyone hangs out and meets between classes, I tried to relax, but everything was moving too fast. It just so happened that Jerry got out of class early, and all I can remember him saying was "How does it feel?"

"How does it feel?" At that moment, I didn't even want to know what that meant; all I wanted to do was go home.

On the car ride home, all Jerry did was gloat. He looked as if he had just won the Nobel Peace Prize. He was gloating because he knew I felt miserable—so miserable that he took pride in seeing me in pain. The dizzy spell disappeared several hours later. I still was confused as to what bug had hit me. But gradually, I realized that it was no bug. It was acid.

Weeks later, Jerry and I were celebrating our anniversary. He took me to a cozy little Italian restaurant. Everything was perfect: an elegant dinner, flowers on the table, firewood burning, and soft music playing in the background. I couldn't have asked for anything more romantic. As we started eating the main course, I felt nauseated. I ignored my feelings until I saw something move across the table.

Was I hallucinating, or did something really move? Frightened, I stopped eating dinner and told Jerry everything that was happening. Feelings and emotions poured out of me. I thought I was seriously ill. I told him about how I felt when I passed out in class weeks before and that I was feeling the same sensations again. I even got to the point that I thought I was pregnant. Dizziness, nausea, and bad eating habits are symptoms when you're pregnant, but he immediately rejected that idea. Finally, Jerry told me the truth.

He told me to remember the day that I passed out in class. He asked me to describe how I felt. Before I knew it, Jerry took the words right out of my mouth, and he started to describe the feelings I was going through. He then proceeded to say that I was tripping on acid. All those illusions, hallucinations, and cold sweats I was experiencing were from the drug.

I ran out of the restaurant. Thoughts were rambling through my mind. How was I supposed to get home? Who was going to drive me? And, ultimately, what would my parents say? Jerry grabbed me furiously and threw me into the car. As we sped down the highway, I tried to get away from him. Fire and anger came into his eyes. I saw him clenching his fist, and then he struck me on the left side of my face.

While he was hitting me, we swerved, and I looked up to see an enormous tree coming straight at us. Jerry tried to regain control, but the car went sideways and hit the tree broadside. The total impact was forced upon me. I was not wearing my seatbelt, so gravity threw me to the back seat, where my head broke the window. I was lying unconscious and not breathing; Jerry panicked. Fortunately, a man who witnessed the accident was a paramedic. If it were not for a concerned stranger, I would not be alive today.

The paramedic rushed over to the scene. He found me sitting up in the backseat lying against the broken window. The tree was holding up my head. The paramedic checked for my pulse, but did not find one. According to the law, he was not supposed to remove me from the vehicle, but under the circumstances it was either break the law or watch someone die. Thank goodness for me, he decided to commit a crime.

As he pulled my body from the wreck, he opened my mouth only to find it filled with glass. After wiping the blood off my face and cleaning my mouth, he began CPR. Jerry was holding my head upright, and he noticed that I started to breathe again, but I did not regain consciousness. When the paramedic realized that I was breathing voluntarily, he opened his medical kit to get scissors. He then proceeded to cut strips in my pants and shirt to see if I had any visible broken bones. Within minutes, a police officer and ambulance arrived at the scene and took me to Stonybrook University Hospital. The police officer arrested Jerry. He was charged at the scene with a DWI, but later it was changed because they sampled his blood and PCP was found.

When I arrived at the hospital, they first pumped my stomach to get food, glass, and alcohol (which I did not drink that night) out of my stomach. They also took blood tests and realized that I had taken acid. This meant the doctors could not give me any medication or treat me until the effects of the drug wore off. The doctors tried to find out if I had any broken bones by poking me with a pin. However, when you're tripping out on acid, you feel no pain. So all these procedures were useless.

The accident occurred at 12:15 a.m., but my parents were not notified until 4:00 a.m. The police had found my wallet at the scene, and Jerry identified me, but the hospital needed more proof than just my license. I was listed as Jane Doe for four hours, just in case I would have died. The paramedic who saved my life stayed with me until my parents arrived. Later, he told my parents that I was not supposed to make it through the night. He did not want me to die alone without anyone at my bedside.

When the acid wore off, I was still in a coma and diagnosed as being paralyzed from the neck down. I was in the intensive care unit of the hospital. Doctors would not X-ray me or have an MRI done because they were afraid of doing more damage. My mother said that I woke from the coma four days later. All I can remember is when my father was talking to me, I tried so hard to respond, but all I could do was give a little squeeze to his hand.

After five days, the initial shock wore off. I started moving my legs. The doctors knew that I did not break my back, but they were still unsure about my neck. They say I was still in an awakened, unconscious state of mind. I was screaming obscenities and talking foolishly about things that did not exist. In the night, I would scream for my dog, Spotty, that had died a year earlier. I could not recognize people's faces except my father's, and I mixed up dates. I did not know my high school's name, and I did not remember my birthday. Doctors said it was too early to determine if there was any permanent damage.

A week went by, and I was making progress every day. I was finally diagnosed with severe head injuries, a broken neck and ribs, and a sliced liver. My left motor skills were considerably slower than my right. I started to remember people's names, but I was confused about the night of the accident. All I could remember was leaving the restaurant.

Making excellent progress, I was moved to a regular room but was under strict control. They finally took the tubes out of me, and I was actually able to consume real food. Things seemed to be turning around. As for Jerry, no one had seen or heard from him since the accident.

After three weeks in the hospital, I was still not able to stand. Every day, nurses stretched my legs. Physical and occupational therapists examined me to see if I was making improvements, but there was still no sign of me leaving the hospital. The attention drove me crazy. Everybody was fussing over me like I was a baby. I know they were all scared for my life, but the prognosis was good and there was no chance of my dying.

The number of visitors who came to see me after the accident was incredible. People that I had not spoken to in years tried to make up for lost time. Others I was hardly acquainted with were now my best friends. Family members that I despised came, and our quarrels seemed to have been forgotten. Deep down inside, I knew they all pitied me.

Suddenly, Jerry walked into the room, tears bursting from his eyes. Staring at him, I felt no warmth. At this point, I knew how foolish I had been for dating him. My life had literally revolved around Jerry, and he almost took it away from me. My future had dwindled before my eyes. My full-ride scholarship was taken away. Doctors told me that I could not go to college in the fall. Everything I had worked for was lost in one night. This time, there was no way Jerry was to be forgiven.

I checked out of the hospital exactly a month after the accident. I still could not walk very well. The muscles in my legs became weak, and I knew I needed extensive physical therapy. The broken bones would have to heal on their own, and I would find out in a couple of months if any bones were permanently damaged. I also was told that I could never play any kind of contact sports again. That meant no college athletics. For me, facing death, the accident, and all my wounds, this news crushed my heart. I was determined to prove the doctors wrong. I was going to play college athletics one day, and I did get that chance. After months of pain, sweat, and tears, I was back on the soccer field, more greedy and aggressive than ever.

I attended college that fall. I was not on a scholarship, nor was I known as a big recruit. Instead, I was accepted strictly on my academic ability. I tried out for the women's soccer program in September and made the squad. It was difficult being a walk-on, but I needed to prove everyone wrong. I realized I was not the best anymore. I was just an average player. Being average made me appreciate the abilities of my teammates and helped me identify with the word "teamwork" for the first time in my life.

As for Jerry, he was charged with attempted manslaughter, but it was dropped in court. Presently, he is a private in the United States Marine Corps stationed in California. This may seem hard to believe, but I still talk to him. He calls on weekends and holidays, expressing his sorrow about what he did. Do I feel pity? No way. I look at this tragedy as an experience. I have learned to appreciate my family and friends and my self-esteem. I fell in love with a wonderful guy who respects and treats me the way every girl dreams of. I am just grateful that God gave me another chance to live in this world and not view it from above.

SURVIVE
by Tim Schultz

Pssssssssss. The air brakes hissed and slowly fizzled into silence. The bus had finally reached its destination. It was the end of a long journey for the bus driver, but merely the beginning of mine.

A voice began to scream as a human figure scrambled up the staircase of the bus. "Gentlemen, you are now at the United States Marine Corps Recruit Training Depot located in Parris Island, South Carolina. When you are addressed by anyone on this base, wearing a military uniform, the first word out of your mouth will be 'sir' and the last word out of your mouth will be 'sir.' Do you understand?"

"Sir, yes sir!" the voices on board the bus screamed.

"No, I can't hear you!" the man barked.

"Sir, yes sir!" the voices screamed again.

"When I give the command, you will fly off my bus, and put your nasty bodies on any pair of yellow footprints on the ground outside this bus! You will not move; you will not speak. You will do nothing until told to do so. Now, get off my bus, get off now, move! Get off, get off, get off!" The man barked even louder this time.

Seventy-three bodies raced toward the open doors of the bus. My only thought was to get off that bus as fast as my legs would take me. I felt like a salmon fighting to make it upstream, as bodies slammed into mine. I pushed and shoved and drove my legs as hard as I could, pushing the men ahead of me into one another. I got closer to the stairs and the pushing faded quickly. I prepared to race down the steps, all the while thinking, God, don't fall, whatever you do, don't fall down these steps. I stumbled a bit on the last step, but, by then, I already had my mind on the pair of yellow footprints in the third row.

Oh good, time to relax as everyone else gets off the bus, I thought as I stood in formation. I wondered whether my feet were on the footprints. But I'd forgotten to check earlier. I missed my girlfriend, Kristen. It would be three months until I saw her again.

My time to relax was over. All seventy-three of us were rushed column by column into the receiving building in front of us. The doors were made of brass and stood twenty feet high. They must have been polished every day because they glistened even in the darkness. Above the doors, also in brass, were the words *Semper Fidelis*, which means "always faithful." The building emitted a regal glow as it looked down over all the young men about to pass through its portals.

As I entered the building, I was immediately told to sit down in a metal chair with a small desktop attached to it. I never got the chance to look at the men yelling at me to sit down, but I will never forget the man who next spoke to me.

All I could hear was his voice. It grew louder and louder as he approached the entrance to the room. Not only was his voice loud, it was inhuman. He sounded like an old man battling emphysema; however, he was nothing of the kind. He stormed into the receiving room one solid step at a time. He halted in the center, performed a right face, and immediately went to parade rest. The man was chiseled from granite, and his face was blacker than charcoal, which made the whites of his eyes glare like a snake. A large brass buckle adorned his webbed belt with the Marine Corps emblem positioned exactly in the center. A wrinkle did not exist in his uniform. I wondered whether it was made to fit him that way, or if he was crafted to fit the uniform.

He spoke again, this time directly at us. "I am Drill Instructor Sergeant Atkins, and I will be your drill instructor for the next three days. Once you have completed receiving, you will be sent to your full-time drill instructors, but until then you are mine, and you will do nothing until told to do so! Now get on your feet! No, not fast enough, sit down! Now, get up! Gentlemen, you will learn to move as fast as humanly possible, or you will pay with pain!"

He ordered a young man in the first seat to open all "hatch" (doors) in the back of the receiving room. Then, after his command, we shuffled like a herd of cattle through the hatch and into snake-like columns in the next room. As I stood there, huddled closely to seventy-three men I never met before, I could hear the faint buzz of a pair of barbers' clippers.

We were all doomed. Our only shred of individualism was about to be shaved off. "Next," said a recruit, who had been posted in the doorway of the barbershop. Every thirty seconds he would scream "next," and the line would slither ahead. It was my turn soon and I still hadn't seen what the shop looked like. I knew I needed to get to my seat fast because other recruits were getting yelled at for being slow. I was nervous. I felt as if my name was about to be called in a starting line-up, and I had to run onto the football field. Only this debut had no glory.

"Next," the recruit said. I knew my name was next, and still it surprised me. I jerked forward and entered the shop looking for an empty chair.

"Right here, right here, sit down," one of the barbers said.

I sat down, and he slapped a smock over my chest. One, two, three, four, five swipes and he was finished. He ripped the smock off my chest and said, "Go!"

Just like that I was bald. I solemnly walked over to the trash can, wiped the loose hair from my bald head, and got back in line. I brushed my hand over my head and looked at the recruit in front of me.

"Sucks, doesn't it," he said.

I don't know what time it was when I arrived on the Island. But, standing in line, I could see a clock through a door marked, USMC ADMIN. REC. "God, it's already 3:30 a.m.," I thought. I had been up for twenty-two hours, and all I could think of was sleep. Little did I know, I wasn't going to go to sleep for another twenty-two hours.

Forty-four hours is a long time to stay awake, especially with people scream-ing orders at you constantly—telling you to hurry up, stand still, look straight ahead. It seemed ridiculous at the time, and only later did I realize that staying awake for forty-four straight hours was my job. I was being trained to be a United States Marine.

There was no introductory level class to prepare you for this experience, and there was no tour guide at the door who said, "Hello, welcome to Parris Island." You were simply thrown into the most stressful environment known to man and expected to stay awake for forty-four hours.

The last man was finally shaved bald and, after wiping the loose hair off his head, he joined the seventy-two other recruits in formation. It was completely silent, except for the sound of the barbers cleaning their clippers.

"You better lock your body, you nasty thing," a voice screamed. I knew that voice. It was the uniformed nightmare, Drill Instructor Sergeant Atkins. No one was sure whom he was addressing, but at his command, all seventy-three of us snapped to attention. He centered himself in front of the platoon and began call-ing our names in alphabetical order. Each recruit ran from formation, when his name was called, into a line in front of a door at the medical building. My broth-er-in-law had warned me about this place. He said, no matter what happens, don't go to medical. The way things looked, I didn't have a choice.

We spent the next fourteen hours in medical. Most of the time was spent standing in lines waiting for yellow fever shots, small pox vaccinations, dental exams, vision and hearing tests, and, of course, getting yelled at. Getting yelled at in boot camp was sort of like breathing; there was never a moment without it and after a while you forgot that it was happening. Medical was even worse than I imagined it. Getting shots was very similar to running the gauntlet as each corpsman was armed with an air-powered injector. I was given seven shots in a row. After the last shot, I was told to sit down in platoon formation. I never felt faint, but three or four recruits had reactions to the shots and fell to the floor in convulsions. One young man fell to the floor screaming, and we were all told to turn around while they worked on him.

I'll never forget the feelings of hopelessness that went through my mind the first few hours I spent on the island. The thought of going home was unimaginable, and the faces of the people I loved were fading. I didn't know if I would survive this place where so many others had failed. Three had already been sent home because they couldn't handle the shots, and the drill instructors promised that there would be others. Some wouldn't be able to make the runs, while others would get stress fractures from all the hiking, and worst of all, some would not qualify on the rifle range. To make it through Marine Corps boot camp took everything you had, plus a lot of luck. The questions rolled through my mind, and every experience was making me doubt myself even more.

That night, at evening chow, I decided the only way I was going to make it was to dedicate my heart and soul to getting home. There were people counting on me to do my best and make them proud. My mother, my sisters, my brother-in-law J.P., and most important Kristen, my girlfriend. She had stood behind my decision no matter how much it hurt her. Then there was my father, the man who didn't believe in the military, the one who wouldn't say goodbye to me that morning because of foolish pride.

He was the reason I was in the Corps, and he would be the reason I survived the Corps. The two of us had been in a cold war ever since I had gone off to school and not lived up to his expectations. He had been kicked out of the Army in his early twenties because he couldn't shoot straight. Not me. I was strong, athletic, and I had hunted all my life. There was no way I was going home early. I was here to prove something, and I wasn't going to leave until I held the title "Marine."

As I sat down to eat my chow, I remembered a promise I had made to myself on the plane. It was a promise to Kristen as well. Every time I sat down to eat, I would ask God for the same thing. "Dear God, give me strength, give me soul, and give me heart; but most of all give me love so I can get home. I love you, Kristen." I knew that my ability would eventually weaken, and I'd have to turn inside for strength. Love was the only thing I could turn to.

My first day of boot camp was finally coming to an end. We marched back to our barracks, after chow, and learned how to make a military rack. Drill Instructor Sergeant Atkins showed us once and gave us one minute to complete the task. It took at least twenty times until everyone in the platoon could do it. Every time we didn't finish, he'd make us strip the racks and bring everything into the middle of the squad bay. We eventually learned some teamwork and had all the racks made in time. Once Drill Instructor Sergeant Atkins inspected all the racks, he had us sit on the floor. He began to speak.

"Gentlemen, you just learned two very important lessons in the Marine Corps: one—teamwork; two—you are only as fast as your slowest man. You may think I'm hard. You haven't even seen 'hard' yet. You are going to meet your real drill instructors tomorrow. They are big, they are mean, and they will try to break you. Half of you will not make it to the parade deck on graduation day. It is their job to see that the best half does. Those of you who apply the two basic rules you have just learned will make it. Now, on my command, you will fly to your racks and lie at the position of attention. Do you understand?"

"Sir, yes sir!" we screamed.

"Move!" he commanded.

We all ran to our racks and lay at the position of attention. A few moments later, taps were played, and then lights out was sounded. I lay in my rack and thought about home. I thought about Kristen and my family. I thought about what my father might say if he knew what I was doing. I thought about how hard my life had just become.

I graduated from Marine Corps boot camp on October 28. I was chosen by my drill instructors as one of the top four Marines in the platoon. I led second squad, platoon 1009 onto the parade deck at Parris Island. After the ceremony, I was greeted by my girlfriend, my mother, and a man wearing a t-shirt that read: "My son, one of the Few, the Proud, the Marines."

METAMORPHOSIS
by Laura Novak

I was always chubby, but in sixth grade I really ballooned. Because I gained so much weight, no one would talk to me; it was thought fat people were no fun. I was constantly teased about my weight, and always picked last for teams, no matter what the activity. There was a saying that fat people were dumb people. Children can really be cruel to those they don't like. I was the butt of jokes, had few friends, and always felt self-conscious. When I tried to make friends, the friendship lasted only a few days, before I was once again cast aside. One particular memory sticks in my mind.

In the sixth grade, the science classes would all go to Camp Greentop in the Catoctin Mountains for a week for our Outdoor Education. Once there, we'd take midnight hikes to study the stars, all-day hikes to study rock formations, field trips to local points of interest.

Previously, there were sign-up sheets where groups of eight could pick who they wanted to camp with. It was always easy for the popular kids; they'd all get together. Even the nerds had their group. When everyone was finally grouped together, there were only two of us left, Andie B. and me. But Andie was left because her friends were in another science class and were not going this particular week. We were stuck in with the popular girls because they had room for two more. It was then that I knew my week at camp would be an interesting one.

And so it turned out. The first night there, the girls all camped out on one side of the cabin, leaving Andie and me on the other side. The second night, five of the popular boys came over trying to scare the girls, but they found out that I was there and soon left. The third day, we needed to pick partners for an activity. Andie found one. But I didn't. I was isolated. Except when it was real late at night and pitch dark out, I'd be the one they'd get up to go with them to the latrine because I had the only flashlight. Life at camp was not fun. We returned home that Friday, and once again I was brushed aside.

In the sixth grade, I was separated from my friends in English. I had taken a placement exam, and it was determined that I should be placed in the advanced writing courses. So I left my friends (they felt that I was a goodie-goodie) and joined the rank of the nerds. That was too much to deal with, being fat and now a nerd. However, the nerds didn't accept me either, so I floated between the nerds and my old friends. I was in a constant struggle to feel accepted, and I was growing tired of it.

The following year, I decided to return to my old classmates. It took a while for them to accept me, but we all made amends. I took the fundamental classes like Art, Shop, and Home Ec., and was still teased about my weight. One day in Home Ec., Danny T. walked over to talk to me.

"Hey, when is skiing season? How many slopes are open?" He should talk; he was just as fat.

"C'mon, Danny, give it a rest," I complained. "Why not pick on someone...."

"Else?" finished Danny. "Someone my own size? Laura, you must've forgotten. You *are* my size." And with that he left, laughing at his witty joke. The jokes continued. If I walked by a group Danny was in, they'd move their chairs around and complain of earthquakes.

"Thunder thigh" sightings were yelled from one kid to another in the halls. His friend Mike W., too, was cruel. The two of them would gang up on me. Once they played a cruel joke by writing me a note. Danny gave it to me after school.

"Laura, here quick. Take this note. It's from Mike. I think he likes you," yelled Danny as he jogged by the side of the bus to keep up. "C'mon, take it."

"Oh Danny, don't you two ever quit?" I asked. "I don't want it."

"You have to take it. C'mon, Laura. I can't keep up with the bus."

I took the note, swearing that I wouldn't read it and that I would throw it away as soon as I got off the bus. But curiosity got the better of me. I had to read it: "Laura, I really like you, but Danny won't let me. He's my friend. I can't go against what he says. Mike."

So there it stood, someone really liked me, or so I thought. The next day Mike came running up to me.

"What did the note say?" he demanded.

"What?" I asked in disbelief. "You mean you didn't write the note?"

"Of course not," he scoffed. "Why would I write you a note? Danny was just playing a joke."

That was me, the joke. No one really wanted anything to do with me. I tried to change the kids' attitude toward me. I wore all the latest fashions, had my hair cut in a popular style, and began to hang out at the mall—for that was considered ultimate coolness. Then it dawned on me. In order to change others, you must change yourself; then the others can't help but change as a reaction. I thought about that for awhile and made plans. I was ready to strike.

In eighth grade, I decided to try out for the pom-pom squad. They performed at halftime at home football games. Although I was self-conscious about my size, I liked to dance even more, and that over-ruled my fear. For tryouts, all we had to do was perform an original routine to a three-minute selection of music. Some girls worked in pairs, others in groups of three. I decided to do a solo since the intricate steps I made up would have been hard to copy. For weeks, I practiced in my back yard, knowing that I would be awesome at tryouts.

Tryouts came sooner than I thought, and I was a nervous wreck. When my turn came to do my routine, I stood in front of the four judges: Mrs. Trimmer, a gym teacher; Mrs. Harrison, an English teacher; and the two sponsors of the pom-pom squad. The music I chose was "Digital Display" by Ready for the World. The music started, and I began my routine. As I danced, I watched the faces of the other girls. They were surprised that a fat person could dance so well. Some nodded, some gave the okay sign, and the judges looked impressed. After my routine was over, I went to sit down with the other girls who had already gone ahead. They congratulated me on my routine. As I sat there, I watched the others; I was a shoo-in.

Decisions were posted the next day. Eighteen girls—including myself—made the squad, and our first practice was the following Wednesday. The day finally arrived, and many anxious girls waited patiently while directions were given. We were also given dates of practices and games. We would officially start practices on the next Friday.

Trying to teach a lot of young girls a new routine took patience. However, a few budding prodigies—again, including myself—were discovered and really got the group going. It was evident that the sponsors also recognized us and appointed us leaders. The season went well, but I noticed myself drifting toward cheerleading, and that was when I decided to pursue cheerleading.

The winter sports season started, and with it came basketball. When the announcements were made about basketball cheerleader tryouts, I jumped at the chance. Tryouts came with big expectations and big egos. Newcomers wanted to try out, only to hear that the regulars were the ones that usually made it. I had big expectations. I'd always wanted to be a cheerleader. Besides, my two cousins were cheerleaders. Why not keep it in the family? Plus, such prestige went with being a cheerleader, and the fun part was wearing the uniforms on the Fridays that we had games.

Tryouts were to be held during one week: four days of practice and the last day for the actual tryouts. However, the coaches could cut those who were a problem or just lacked the coordination to cheer. Monday, the first day of practice, I was nervous. I looked around to see who was there. There was Julie; she wouldn't make it. And there was Jenni; her reputation was too loose to be a cheerleader. I wondered how she could even think of showing her face. Sandy had tried since the sixth grade, and she still hadn't made it. It seemed to calm my nerves to pre-cut others. There was Mrs. Porter, the head of cheerleading in the high school and the middle school. If you got in good with her, you made it all four years.

"Okay, girls, listen up. Please sit over there by the stage," she directed. "Good, I'm Mrs. Porter, as many of you may know. Over there is Mrs. Manges, and that's Mrs. Schildt. I'll be taking the eighth-grade girls; Mrs. Manges will be working with the seventh graders; and Mrs. Schildt will be taking the sixth graders. Please separate into your groups."

I got up and walked over to where Mrs. Porter was standing. I saw Gabrielle and smiled a weak hello. She motioned for me to sit next to her and asked me if I was nervous.

"There're so many new girls trying out that I doubt I'll make it," she said.

"Yeah, I am nervous," I told her. "I've never tried out for cheerleading before. I'm going to be a nervous wreck."

"Don't worry about it. Didn't you do the pom thing?"

Ah ha, someone had noticed that I was making myself visible. My plan was beginning to show some results.

Mrs. Porter came over and gave her talk about cheerleading. There would be eight to twelve girls on a squad. She had us warm up with stretches; then, three high-school cheerleaders showed us the cheers. There were two chants and one cheer. Boy, were they hard. This wasn't anything like poms.

"I am not coordinated enough for this," I told Gabrielle.

"Sure you are," she replied. "You're doing fine." She gave me a sign of encouragement.

Practice continued for the rest of the week with tryouts held on Friday. All day Friday, girls were talking about who would make it and who wouldn't. At recess, girls would gather around to watch others practice the cheers. By the way we were practicing, one would think we were trying out for the Dallas Cowboy cheerleaders. The last bell of the day rang, and a zillion nervous girls ran to the locker room to change and practice. Anxious laughter filled the room. I accidentally bumped into Gabrielle who was in front of the mirror.

"Sorry," I offered when I noticed I smeared her lipstick.

"That's okay," she replied, "I'm so nervous, I would've ended up doing it myself."

Tryouts went smoothly, but not for everyone. Sandy forgot the cheer twice, and Christine sprained her ankle. I forgot part of a cheer and had to lip-synch the words. After tryouts, Mrs. Porter mentioned that results would be posted Monday. I couldn't sleep all week: how was I to survive the weekend? I'd be a wreck.

Sunday afternoon, I got a call from Gabrielle. She was ecstatic; we had both made the girls' basketball cheer squad. It wasn't much, but it was a start. I finally felt accepted. And with this new awakening, I knew I had survived the years of being an outcast.

I had done what no fat person ever attempted before, and I became a better person because of it. I had spent three fruitless years putting up with cruel kids. I tried without success to put a stop to the maddening verbal abuse and isolation, only to be ridiculed more. I don't believe there was a time when acceptance by peers was more crucial than during the middle-school years, when approval is the hardest.

However, I made a point of becoming a better person. I realized that if I couldn't change them, I would change, creating a need for them to change. By joining the pom squad and the cheerleading squad, I broke the mold of being a "fat" person, and eventually became a real person to my peers. I wasn't made fun of or excluded from activities. Students made a point of saying "hi" or inviting me to hang out with them. I was no longer known as "thunder thighs" or "ski mountain," but as "Laura, the pom captain" or "Laura, one of the cheerleaders."

As I left middle school, I looked at a bright future, knowing that the worst was behind me. I was becoming a new person, one that few would remember as "the fat kid." The summer before ninth grade, I went on a crash diet. I lived on bread and water, literally, until I was at an acceptable weight. But I enjoyed the results of losing the weight and continued on my crash diet throughout ninth grade. Some friends were worried that I'd waste away to nothing, but I quickly explained that a person of my size could not possibly waste away. In fact, a person my size dreamed of the day when she'd have to worry about wasting away.

I was very determined to lose the weight that I had been carrying around for so long. I would finally get rid of my size thirteen clothes, knowing that I would be content at an eight. But that was short-lived. I was obsessed with losing more weight. I wouldn't rest until I could fit into a size six. Mom became worried that I was losing weight too fast, so she had the doctors prescribe a diet plan.

But I wasn't happy with it. I couldn't follow a set schedule. I hated plans and charts. I needed to do this on my own, so I could feel the control. I never had control over my body before, and I wasn't going to let someone else determine what was right for me. I was on a roll, and no one was going to set any limits on my happiness.

The first clue that I was getting somewhere happened in my ninth grade Latin class. Mike W. was in the class, and I figured he would start up with the old antics. Lo and behold, I was right; he passed me a note, and I threw it away, saying that I was tired of his jokes. But he fished the note out of the trash can and handed it to me again. "Read it," he said.

I really wasn't in the mood for his antics, but I read it anyway. In it, he wrote that he liked me (for real), and that he would like to take me to the movies. I couldn't believe it, the one person who really teased me, and he was asking me out. Well, I accepted the invitation, and later on in the year, we became really good friends. He almost asked me to the Homecoming Dance, but a friend of his beat him to it. Mike never gave up, though, and by the time of the Homecoming Dance in tenth grade, we were an item.

I continued my dieting, since I was on the cheerleading squad in tenth grade. My dieting became so drastic that my doctors began to worry, but I wouldn't listen. I was just about to reach my goal. I could wear a size three. I had gone from a size thirteen to a size three within a year and a half. I thought I had never looked better, but now when I look at my eleventh grade Homecoming picture, I can tell that I was all skin and bones. It was so bad that the strapless dress I wore wasn't held up by much. My collarbone stuck out more than anything else. But at the time, that didn't matter. All that mattered was the reading on the scale. I had gone from weighing close to 170 pounds to a lightweight 118 pounds. I felt great, I looked great, and I could wear anything that I wanted to. During my eleventh grade and twelfth grade years, I was the fashion plate at our school. I'd wear something, and later that week I'd see someone trying to copy the look. But no matter how hard they tried, it wouldn't look the same because they didn't have my body.

Along with the loss of weight, I gained my self-confidence. I was outgoing (being a cheerleader all four years in high school helped with the social scene) and knew how to tease the boys. And did I tease them. For a while, there would be five guys at a time trying to get my attention. Wherever I'd be, someone would come up and flirt. Not a little flirt either. To the guys, I was Laura Novak, the little girl who was a hot babe. It was a social thing to be seen with me. I was the party hotline person; if there was a party, Laura was the one to know. I knew people from other schools and had a network system set up. There was rarely a weekend that I was home alone. My parents never saw me, between my games, after-school activities, and dates. I had become a social butterfly. Even Mrs. Porter commented that I had blossomed into a very beautiful woman.

All my dedication had paid off. But I don't think I would've been able to lose the weight if I hadn't been picked on and had a rough go at things. I was determined to lose the weight to make the others eat their words. I did it as revenge to all those that belittled me or felt that I wasn't good enough.

To all those who used me for the flashlight, I thumb my nose. To all those who picked on me and insisted on making my middle-school years miserable, I grant you the grace of knowing me, for I'd never admit that I knew you. To all those who thought they were better, you were wrong. I am. I set a goal, and I achieved it; you only belittled and snickered. And to all those who have been in my shoes, you have the power to take over your lives. It's up to you to unleash it.

CHILDREN IN NEED
by Valeree Klunk

I was so excited as I hung up the phone. My first real teaching job. I hardly noticed the heat of the late June afternoon as I ran to my supply of books to see what materials I had that would be suitable for tutoring a sixth grader in math. I had several that I assumed would be on her level, and I quickly set about preparing a lesson.

I had entered my name several weeks before to a service that matches tutors with children in need of special help. Knowing that, after I completed college, I wanted to work with learning-disabled children, I thought tutoring would be an excellent way to get experience, earn money, and still have time for my own classes.

When Julie's mother called me, I couldn't wait to get started. We set a date, time, and fee, and I told her that I looked forward to meeting her. When we hung up, I spent the whole evening preparing Julie's lesson. Three days later, I was sitting in the Saintses' living room next to a very shy girl who would barely look at me, much less speak. When I introduced myself, she smiled at me weakly as if she were skeptical of the whole idea of being tutored. They both listened as I discussed how I planned to run the sessions. Perhaps I was overly exuberant because Julie's mother cut me off and informed me that I would have to move extremely slow because her daughter was really "stupid" in math. I was horrified and didn't know how to respond to such a comment.

Julie continued to stare at the floor. Had I been more experienced, I would have immediately been able to identify her mother's attitude as a large part of her learning disability. However, at the time, I just considered the statement harsh and moved on. We moved to the kitchen and spread out on the table. A sixth grader should be working on word problems in all four operations and long division, and that was the lesson I had prepared.

However, as we began going over the material, it was immediately obvious that she had no idea what I was explaining. A little surprised, but undaunted, I began to give her less complicated problems. Each time she looked at me with a combination of confusion and frustration. She was never able to give me an answer. Again, had I been more experienced, I would have known that I should begin on a very simplistic level and move forward until I reached her limit and begin teaching her there. This would have kept her from becoming frustrated as she missed answer after answer. But, after all, I was learning, too.

It took nearly the entire hour for me to determine that Julie was on about a fourth-grade level, unable to do even the simplest multiplication. I smiled at her as I left and assured her that next week would be better now that we knew where to begin. She didn't appear reassured and, as I started my car, I began to wonder if I was in over my head. I was under the impression that her school teacher would do the actual teaching, and I would just be responsible for reinforcing what she was learning. But now it was painfully obvious that she was very far behind even for the slowest class.

I wracked my mind that whole week for the most effective way to teach her multiplication tables. On Saturday, I stood on her front porch armed with a hundred pennies. I explained that we were going to begin to learn multiplication. While I spread the pennies out on the table, her mother stood over us and said, "Isn't it ridiculous that you have to go all the way back to multiplication for a sixth grader? If Julie ever did anything, maybe she wouldn't be so far behind." Julie's eyes immediately welled up with tears, and she stared intently at the table. I had to blink back a few tears of my own, wondering how this child had any self-esteem at all.

Carefully, I spread out two rows of three pennies. "How many pennies do I have?" I asked.

"Six," she responded.

"Great," I said. "See, I have two rows of three pennies. That's two times three. Two times three is six."

We repeated the process several times, and each time she answered correctly and looked genuinely pleased with herself. I was thrilled. My first teaching tool was a success—until I gave her a problem and told her to set up the pennies. She looked confused and arranged them differently several times, each time looking for approval. I couldn't believe what I was seeing. This twelve-year-old child was not able to arrange four pennies into five rows for "four times five," no matter how many times I demonstrated the process. Inexperienced as I was, it was clear that this wasn't a case of a girl who was lazy or bored or had just fallen behind in class.

This child had a disability. Unfortunately, with my limited training, that was as much as I could diagnose.

That was just the start of our troubles. Julie's biggest problem was boredom. She hated that hour. I couldn't blame her. Very few twelve-year-olds would be content spending Saturday afternoons sitting at the kitchen table doing something they absolutely hated. The next problem was her mother, who presented Julie with such a low self-image it was a wonder she had learned what she did. She was constantly commenting on how ridiculous Julie's answers were and how she wasn't concentrating.

Very slowly, we made progress with multiplication, but she was still falling behind in class. The pennies got old after a while, so I substituted M&Ms and made a game of it. We started with a full bag and used them for problems. The problems she got right, she kept the candy; the ones she got wrong, I kept. Soon she had many more at the end of each session than I did. This is what got us through multiplication, and she actually became quite good at it.

Then we tackled division. She was much less confident here, and we had to stop many sessions because she was close to tears. It was about this time that I began to notice a change in her. She got her hair cut like mine and began asking me where I bought my clothes. Suddenly, she was dressing like me, too. At first, I thought it was cute and dismissed it. Then I hit on an idea. I made up a test of all kinds of division problems. She and I would work hard in the next few weeks, and she would periodically take the test. When she got them all right, she and I would spend the whole day shopping together. To this day, I have never seen a child or adult work so hard to learn anything. She went through division in just a few sessions, and, although it didn't stay with her as well from week to week as multiplication had, she had the basics down. Plus, she was catching up with her class. We went shopping together and we both had a great time.

Shortly after that, her mother concluded that she was sufficiently caught up and, with the help of her parents, would be all right without our sessions. I've spoken to her from time to time to see how things were going. There is no doubt in my mind that she should have had some testing to find out the degree of disability she had. But at any rate, she is in high school now and seems to be doing well.

Working with Julie was a great experience, but Mary is the one responsible for giving me direction for a career as well as a whole new way of looking at life. Mary is one of the most influential people in my life. She changed the way that I view a lot of things, taught me enormous amounts of patience and understanding, and gave me many goals to strive for. Sooner or later everyone in life meets someone like Mary—someone who will always leave a mark on him or her. But my Mary was unique; she was three years old.

I had my first real full-time job: I was working as a teacher's aide in a local day-care center. I had always loved children and made all my spending money babysitting. Since teaching was a job consideration, I decided that gaining some direct experience was a good start. My job wasn't difficult, but at times it was trying. I prepared snacks, read books, passed out crayons, helped the teacher prepare lessons, and took over the class if she was called to the phone or if a parent needed to speak with her. The first several weeks were uneventful.

Then, early one Monday morning, shortly after I arrived, the senior teacher I worked with told me we were getting a new student. She was a little nervous; our new student had cerebral palsy, and she had no training in dealing with special children. The child's mother had to work and hadn't been able to find a babysitter to handle her daughter, who was given to extreme temper tantrums.

When Mary came through the doors of our classroom, she had as much idea of what to expect as we did—none. Within minutes, she had a tantrum (the first of many) when her mother left. Mary was an unusually beautiful child with long blond curls, rosy cheeks, and huge blue eyes that seemed not only to look at you, but inside of you. She was unable to speak and only made guttural noises. She had braces on both legs, so walking any distance was very difficult for her. At three years of age, she was not toilet trained, nor did she care to be.

From day one, Mary made it clear that she did as she pleased, and God help the child or teacher who stood in her way. Within the first week, both the senior teacher and I were at our wit's end. Every time we lined up, we couldn't find Mary. Whenever we had free play, at least two children would end up in tears because Mary hit them. She ate everything (pudding included) with her hands. Once, when we forced her to use a plastic spoon, she ate it, and we spent half an hour pulling the sharp pieces out of her mouth while she screamed and tried to bite us. By the end of the first week, our director called her mother and told her she would have to remove her. After an hour-long phone conversation, she agreed to keep her a little longer when the mother explained she absolutely had to work. Then the senior teacher and the director came up with a new plan.

When I arrived that second Monday morning, they took me in the office and informed me that I was to become Mary's personal caretaker. Too much time was being taken from the other kids in the class because of her. My only instructions were to never let her out of my sight (even while she was napping, which was rare) and to keep her from hurting herself or others. Hardly feeling optimistic about this task, I expressed my concern to my director, who assured me it was only temporary.

The first few days were unbearable. She didn't want me constantly at her side any more than I wanted to be there. Even though she couldn't speak, she never left doubts in anyone's mind about what she wanted. When she desired a toy that another child had, she simply took it. If the child put up any struggle, Mary became extremely violent. To this day, I have never met an adult with a temper that equaled hers. The children were frightened of her and avoided her.

Then one day after a particularly rough morning, she crawled up in my lap while I was cutting things out for a bulletin board and sat there very still for a long time. I didn't attempt to remove her, partly out of excitement at this small accomplishment and partly out of fear of crossing her. From that moment on, she and I were inseparable. As soon as she walked through the doors in the morning, she headed straight for my lap and stayed there until lunch. I began getting her to help me do things. She would hand me this and run to get that. I was slowly able to get her to eat with utensils and take short naps. She was still very violent when she didn't get her way, but the tantrums occurred less and less.

One afternoon, after her third toilet-training accident of the morning, I became frustrated and told her that I was disappointed that she wasn't even trying to be a big girl for me. That was the first time I ever saw hurt in her eyes. I immediately regretted saying anything and hugged her, but she was already crying. After that she had very few accidents, but I still regret the way I handled it. With all the progress we were making, my director was very pleased and informed her mother that we were considering letting her stay. For my part, I was extremely attached to her. She was at my side all day, and I admit that sometimes I showed favoritism toward her.

She was almost functioning normally (except for speaking and motor skills) when the seizures started. They were small at first and steadily grew worse. Eventually, she was completely blacking out. As a result, she had to wear a special helmet. The first day she returned to school with her helmet, she was worse than ever. She had worked so hard to become part of our class, and now she was different again.

The senior teacher and I had her show her new "hat" as a show-and-tell and then planned a Hat Day where all the children would wear something from home. She felt more accepted and got much better again. By the end of the summer, she was not hurting children at all and was saying "please" and "thank you" although she would only say it for me. Mary ended up staying for two years, and so did I. When she reached school age, they removed her to place her in a special program.

I haven't seen her in three years, but she is as much a part of me as she was then. She made me realize that I want to work with special children, although I'm not yet certain in what capacity. A lot of times when I feel that familiar "Why me?" I still think of Mary and all that she accomplished and how things will always be much more difficult for her than for the average person. Then, somehow, I feel guilty for letting trivial things get to me. I doubt she would remember me, but I've followed her through the years.

I learned a lot about myself from her. Although I'm easily frustrated when I can't do something, I have a great deal of patience with special children. Next year, I plan to do an internship at an orphanage for emotionally disturbed and abused children.

THE EXPERIENCE OF BEING ALIVE
by Laura Barnhardt

"I don't think we're searching for the meaning of life, but for the experience of being alive."

Somebody else said that, but I don't know who. I know what he meant though. My pursuit for that experience began when I entered high school. It wasn't deliberate, but high school is the time when you begin years of experimenting. They are the years of trying drugs, defying your parents, driving a car for the first time, dating different people, changing friends, and doing weird things to your hair. It's a desperate search.

Soon, you're old enough to travel alone, go to college, and drink beer. Then you experiment with philosophies, majors, and sorting out everybody's opinions about everything. They call it "finding yourself."

After that, you're still looking—just less obviously. However, if you find anything good after you turn forty, everyone will whisper that you're having a crisis. Basically, it's all the same search—the search for the meaning of life. The hunt continues throughout life, one thing leading to another. And every time a person finds something new, they think, "That's it. This is what life's all about."

I'm no different—I defied my parents, bought a car, went to college, met all kinds of different people, and found a good hair-style. Twice, when I fell in love and when I decided to be a writer, I've been sure that I had found the meaning of life. Of course, now, I know you can never be sure.

When I met Ward, I felt pretty confident. He was the first and only man I've been in love with. I loved everything about him. I loved his beer-guzzling friends and his genuinely nice parents who left their beautiful home to our care every weekend. I loved his preppy, rich style; his analytical mind; and his quiet, gentle touch.

Ward always made me feel as if I were doing some kind of charity by being with him, and that feeling was mutual. It's easy to feel like a princess when someone is making you special dinners and placing roses in your bed so, when you wake up, it's the first thing you see. For awhile, I lived a fairy tale.

If Ward wasn't the meaning of my life, he was the center of it. We did just about everything together. We cleaned our rooms together. We typed his college applications together. We grocery shopped together when we made dinner together. (He always bought salad and something he could smother in ketchup.) Together, we drank enormous amounts of beer with his friends. We set up dates for my friends with his. We carved Halloween pumpkins together. We skipped school together.

Afterwards, when we felt guilty, we did homework together. Of course, his answer for my school problems was to buy Cliff Notes, but the way he used them was plagiarism. I didn't want to get caught up in any sort of stealing. Besides, I always thought of writing as sacred, and plagiarism seemed sacrilegious.

I love all sports. This great passion probably stems from the fact that I am totally uncoordinated, incredibly slow, and will never be able to play them. However, Ward was an athlete. He played hockey and tennis mostly, but since it was such a big part of his life, it was natural for sports to be something he wanted to share with me.

Ward wasn't satisfied with being a spectator as I was.

He had to be involved to enjoy it. Sometimes, I would give in to him and let him try to teach me to play tennis. Although all I really learned was how to piss him off and laugh at his attempts, I was content with watching him play hockey and reading *Sports Illustrated*.

When he took me to my first baseball game, he touched a place in my heart he never would have been able to reach. I still remember the evening in the greatest detail. I can still smell the aromas: cheap beer intertwined with roasted peanuts, the disinfected smell of the concrete, and the awful perfume of the woman sitting three rows behind us. In fact, she and her husband were two of the few people sitting near us, probably because it was a hot Tuesday night in August. Just walking toward the giant stadium was exciting; I had never even seen it up close. What struck me the most were the fans who watched the athletes in the clean, white outfits. Everybody watching was a part of the spirit. They booed the opposition, they cheered the batters, advised the pitcher, and sang chants of encouragement in between. Even babies cried in the silence of a home-team error.

I think Ward was touched by my child-like reaction to the whole new experience of being at a game because he took me again the next week. But none of the newness had worn off. Years later, it still hasn't. People should never lose their enthusiasm for something they like. If you thought of every time as your first time, I doubt you could get bored with life.

Ward led me through a lot of first times. For one, he was the first guy I made love to. We had been together for about five months. And since he was a young and previously sexually active male, Ward couldn't wait until I gave in to him. But I had to be sure I really loved him and that he really loved me. I had to be totally satisfied with our relationship out of bed before I would commit to a physical relationship.

But when it came to him telling me how he felt about things, it was very hard for him. "But what's the point in having feelings if you can't express them?" I asked. It might be a cliché, but it's still a very good question and one I asked him often.

He always countered, "Why can't you express them in action?" I didn't have a reply to that.

Then one night, I told him he should become a lawyer, and I wanted to be his lover—kind of all in one breath. I didn't want to sound hesitant when I was finally so sure, but I was scared to death. I mean all my parents really said about sex was that I shouldn't do it until I got married. It was one of many things we disagreed on. Not only did I have an open mind about almost everything, I didn't believe that women don't need or enjoy sex. As far as I could tell, I wanted to make love to Ward as much as he did to me. Furthermore, I couldn't see how being attracted to a tall, athletic man with silky black hair and smooth tan skin wasn't natural.

Why I decided to say "yes" when I did, I admit, was probably because I love the element of surprise. It reminded me of one of those Kodak commercials. "Capture the Kodak moment." Naturally, I didn't have a camera handy to capture his jaw dropping in shock, followed by a happy and truly excited expression. And finally he gave me a serious look when he was trying to tell me with his deep and expressive eyes that he loved me. Anyway, that moment was golden, and it will remain a photograph in my head.

It turned out that that night was one of many nights and days that Ward and I were together in that way.

I know that some people let sex rule their lives and their relationships, but I dismissed that very quickly as the meaning of life. It's much too complicated. There are too many emotions involved. There are too many things to worry about: faithfulness, pregnancy, disease. But, just as quickly, I decided making love, in its true form, is one of the best experiences of being alive.

On the other hand, the worst part of life is endings. I've always had a problem with them. I always read the end of a book to see if it's happy. If it's sad, I debate whether to read the book at all. It was like that with Ward. The time was coming when Ward would leave to go away to college. College and long-distance relationships are a whole different ball game. That was one game I did not care to partici-pate in.

So I knew the ending was there, but no one could have told me that I would be hurt so badly. And most important, there was no way of predicting when that hurt would end. It's much easier to endure pain when you know when it will end. If you break your arm, in six weeks you'll have a healed, itchy arm. Knowing that makes it easier. But in matters of the heart, there's no way of knowing when you'll be healed. And that's what makes it so hard.

I hated it. I hated that he left. I hated that our relationship ended. I hated that, even though I knew his life was changing. There was no way I would be just friends. I wouldn't even accept an agreement where we could date other people.

At the same time, I had an even harder time not being able to share in his excitement; I had shared the whole getting-ready-for-college period with him. I even typed his application to the University of Delaware—the very place that was ruining my life.

I remember he sat next to me while I slowly typed his name. "Would you be careful? This is my future you're typing," he said.

I laughed and replied, "You're not paying me enough to take any criticism."

We both laughed when we got to the part where it said to list extracurricular activities because we honestly debated whether he should list me as one. He did spend the most time with me. However, when it came down to helping Ward pack up and leave me, I wasn't so cooperative. There's a big difference between leaving and being left.

The months after he left are a blur of tears. In fact, I wouldn't remember any of it if I hadn't been keeping a journal. Sometimes I wrote down some little thing he used to say or about one day we spent together. Other times, I wrote about how I was feeling about Ward at the moment. But I always wrote each word care-fully, and each one was filled with meaning. Each week, I looked over what I had written the week before. Somehow, it was comforting.

As more time passed, I began to wonder if anyone else would appreciate what I had written. At the same time, I wasn't sure if I wanted to share my thoughts with anyone else. In the end, curiosity won, and I let a few people read select por-tions of my journal. And they said they were really touched. Did that mean they felt sorry for me, or that I was a good writer?

My mom wouldn't let it drop. She was convinced that after years of paying for ballet and trombone lessons, and encouraging me each time I found some new hobby to take up or some new club to join, my true talent was writing.

She admitted that my work wasn't Pulitzer Prize material yet, but she stressed the word "yet." Besides that, writing didn't cost her a lot of money—no lessons at the YMCA. She did rush out and buy me a copy of *The Elements of Style* by Strunk and White.

Being serious about writing wasn't something I decided because it was the "in" thing to do. None of my friends wrote. Most of them didn't even read unless they were forced. English writing assignments were right up there with cleaning your room and not being allowed to watch television. Still, there was definitely something cool about having a thought even worthy of the effort it took to write it on paper. It's exciting to have a story to tell. It's exciting to choose the words to tell that story. Most of all, it's exciting when someone reads and enjoys your story.

But keeping a journal mostly about Ward became very limiting and painful. That's when my mom suggested I take a journalism class. At my high school, the so-called class just gave the newspaper staff an extra hour to work on the school's monthly news publication. I wrote a writing sample and was joyfully accepted on staff. I was greeted with donuts, welcomes from the staff, and the editor-in-chief's compliments on my writing. I was assigned my first news story on a national politician's education campaign in our county.

Having to interview important people, do research at the library, and write a coherent, informative article to be published for two thousand of my fellow classmates sure wasn't the same as scribbling in my diary. Never before had I experienced the pressure of deadlines, self-doubt, and inexperience.

Actually, writing was a draining experience. It was hard to put together the sentences. It was hard to be catchy and witty. It was hard to write facts without being boring. At the same time, when the writing started to flow, there was nothing else in the whole world except me and the written word. Nothing else mattered: not eating or sleeping, not my friends, not going out, not even Ward. Whenever my dad, who insisted he had to talk to me about something, interrupted me, my head spun. I was on such an incredible high that any interruption seemed like coffee that crashes a beer buzz. And seeing my name and the article I worked hard on and was proud of in print made me feel useful. I never felt that way before. I mean, it wasn't like I went to work everyday or ever made any contribution to society. I wasn't supposed to feel useful or important until I was grown up and had a job and voted—or so I believed. And since Ward was gone, I didn't think I'd do anything except cry for the rest of my life.

My search for the meaning of life had been disrupted when Ward and I broke up. For months after he left for college, I felt dried up and lifeless. It was like being in a fog all the time. The whole world seemed gray and ugly. I needed new ideas and fresh thoughts. When I stopped brooding about Ward, when I was forced to examine other people's lives and write about them, I stopped pitying myself. I was happy again. I could be happy without Ward. That's all people really want in life anyway—to be happy.

"And, to be happy, you have to find something to love and pursue it."

Somebody else said that, too. And again, I don't know who. It's true, though, that love can be a person, a career, a goal—just about anything. And the pursuit can be in many forms. For now, my love is writing. I pursue it in my classes. I pursue it in my spare time. I pursue it by writing for my college newspaper and by covering sports for my hometown newspaper. I continue to search for ways to make my writing better and my love more passionate.

Maybe someday someone will quote what I write. Maybe they'll even remember my name.

CONTRIBUTORS

A 1995 graduate, **Laura Barnhardt** majored in mass communications and minored in political science. Before she graduated, she took a job with *The Baltimore Sun* doing research in the newsroom. She now has a two-year internship with *The Philadelphia Inquirer*, where she covers local government. Laura reports loving writing as much now as she did when she wrote her memoir.

Joseph Battle III writes stories in his spare time. He also plays music, football, and basketball. He has not yet decided on a major, nor has he completed college. He comments, "I'm just proud to have been considered [for *Songs of Myself*]."

Christina Emilie Berzeler enjoys reading, aerobics, weight training, traveling, skiing, and mountain biking. Majoring in speech pathology and audiology, she will graduate in 1998.

Ryan Matthew Bogan works as a deck technician and a hockey coach. Majoring in geography, he will graduate from Rutgers University in 1999. He is married and has one child. He writes, "Thank you for giving me the opportunity [to appear in the book]. I am very proud of myself, and I have been bragging to everyone."

Eric Canfield majors in Business Administration. After he graduates in 2001, he plans a career in the business end of electronic music.

Dha wool Chung spent six years in American schools and six years in Korean schools, and is fluent in both languages. Her favorite sports are skiing and playing basketball. In her freshman year at college, she became an avid reader and writer. She writes, "Actually, rewriting has become my hobby. I've learned to enjoy and love writing."

Brendan Curran will graduate in 1999. He plans to work in the media industry making films or educational multimedia.

Brian M. Davis accepted a full-time position as Staff Accountant with the mid-Atlantic office of Deloitte & Touche LLP. He graduated in 1997 with a degree in accounting. He enjoys sports and web-page design.

Abby Michelle Forbes wants to work with the poor here and abroad. She wishes to open a theater for underprivileged kids. Majoring in theater and minoring in Spanish, Abby will graduate in 1998.

Andrianne Gamble works as an Administrative Assistant for the Mercantile Safe-Deposit and Trust Company. She majored in English and graduated in 1996. She is presently pursuing a second bachelor's degree in psychology. Upon completion of the program, Andrianne hopes to pursue a degree in law. She writes, "I am thankful to those who believed in me and my talents with the pen."

Valerie Gatzke is pursuing a bachelor's degree in English with a concentration in writing. She writes, "After I graduate in the fall of 1997, I look forward to exploring life and my passion for writing."

Jessica Carroll Graham majors in mass communications. She writes for "Towerlight," Towson University's campus newspaper, and enjoys rollerblading in her spare time. Jessica was awarded a fellowship to study English and writing at Oxford during her junior year. After she graduates in the year 2000, she plans to work in broadcast journalism or public relations.

Michelle Haynie attended Towson University for one year. She will graduate from Salisbury State University in 1999 with a degree in physical education. "I only write for myself—thoughts, feelings, and dreams," she says.

Emily Kathleen Hegner left Towson University to attend Colorado State University. She will graduate in the year 2000 with a degree in fine arts/ceramics. She writes, "I enjoy fishing in the Colorado Rockies, hiking, sewing, and sorting my thoughts and emotions through poetry."

Adriane Helfrich majors in psychology and will graduate in 1998. She hopes to pursue a career in psychology and do some writing on the side. She writes, "I enjoy writing stories, and hopefully I will get the opportunity to write my own book. I am extremely proud of my work, and I am excited that my memoir is being published."

Christopher Matthew Jones left Towson University to attend Essex Community College. In the fall of 1997, he transferred to the University of Baltimore where he majors in business. Christopher enjoys tennis and billiards in his spare time

Valeree Klunk (Byer) graduated in 1996 after majoring in psychology. She teaches preschool in Fallston, Maryland, where she lives with her husband. She writes, "I am very excited about this opportunity. I have loved writing for many years and have journals full of possibilities. I have often thought of freelance work—maybe this is a start."

Stacy Spring Knight will graduate in the spring of 1998 with a degree in computer science.

Describing herself as "very motivated," **Nina Lattimore** majors in mass communications. She will graduate in May, 1998, and hopes to work in media relations.

Karl Peter Malicdem majors in biology and will graduate in 1999. He plans to become a doctor. His hobbies are sports, especially basketball and baseball. He writes, "Writing about my father was probably the hardest thing I ever had to do. When I looked at my brother going through life without him, I realized this story had to be told. I did it not so much to tell of the suffering my mother and I went through, but to show how much my father meant to us."

Laura Michelle Novak (Silverman) graduated in May of 1997 from the University of Maryland Baltimore County with a degree in health science and policy. She plans to work in the health insurance industry. "Life is full of surprises," she writes.

Kelly Lynne Nyman will graduate in May of 1998 with a degree in early childhood education. She likes to rollerblade and write poetry.

Estelle Willow Petri will graduate in the year 2000. An English major with a concentration in writing, she plans to pursue a career in editing. While in high school, she received an honorable mention in the Hollins College Poetry Contest. She writes, "[Being part of] this book is an incredible honor for me. Thank you for this chance."

Charles Ramsburg, Jr., majors in English. An aspiring novelist, he will graduate in 2001.

Hollie Christine Rice graduated in 1994 with a degree in English education. She lives with her husband in Reisterstown, Maryland, and teaches sixth-grade English. Her hobbies include rock climbing, mountaineering, and writing short stories.

Timothy Schultz majored in physical education and psychology, and graduated in the fall of 1997. He enjoys all sports. He writes, "Thank you for including me."

Jeffrey Sengebusch, who has had work published in several anthologies, will graduate in the year 2000 with a degree in geography and environmental planning. He comments, "I write a lot and hope to some day have my own book. I love listening to music and damaging my hearing at concerts."

Judith Ann Shaw will graduate in the year 2000 with a degree in mass communications.

Jennifer Ann Shropshire majored in English and graduated in 1994. She works as part of the development staff for Senior Campus Living in Baltimore and sings in her spare time. She writes, "This [book] is a very pleasant surprise. Thank you for the wonderful opportunity."

Jessica Marie Simmons majors in English and plans to graduate in May, 1998. She has one daughter, Chandler. In her spare time, she reads, writes poetry, and spends time with her daughter.

Amber Tolley will graduate in the year 2000 with a degree in mass communications.

Oleg Tsygan majors in marketing and will graduate in the year 2000. In his spare time, he enjoys driving.

Alessandra Vadala majored in English and graduated in 1996. She is presently working toward a master's degree at the College of Notre Dame of Maryland. She is collecting material toward a biography of her great-grandmother.

Diana Lynn Wheeler graduated in 1994 with a degree in psychology. Studying for a degree in pediatric nursing, she works as a volunteer on the pediatric psychology research team at the University of Maryland Baltimore County.

ARTISTS

Kelly Freed is majoring in mass communications at Frostburg State University, Frostburg, Maryland. She has made the Dean's List and will graduate in the spring of 1998, and hopes to attend art school afterward. Her photograph, "Tunnel Vision: The Chance," opens the section titled "Steel Will" (p. 165) and it also appears on the book's spine.

Theresa Herlihy's untitled photograph appears as the book's frontispiece (p. vii). She is currently studying photography at Towson University and "living in the shadow of her future."

"Finding Her Wings," by **Stephanie Malanowski**, is the only painting used in the book. It opens the section on pregnancy (p. 195). Stephanie majors in painting at Dundalk Community College in Baltimore, and plans to earn her master's degree in fine arts.

Jim Mullins graduated from Towson University and works as a consultant in rehabilitation and disability studies. He explores ways visual images can increase acceptance for people with disabilities. His untitled photograph opens "On the Road" (p. 133).

Justin Ritmiller's photograph—"For a Moment, Timeless"—opens the book's last section, "Edge of Adulthood" (p. 229). Majoring in visual communications, Justin will graduate in 1998. He writes, "My work is an expression of personal thoughts and ideas that cannot be articulated verbally."

The wintry scene opening the section on illness (p. 43) was taken by **Sunny Seldin**, who titled the photograph "Sweet Dreams." She attends Boston University where she majors in art history. Sunny hopes to pursue a career in photography.

Jimmy Serkoch's photograph "Black Mass Blues" opens the book's first section, "The Interloper" (p. 1), and also appears on the book's cover. A philosophy major at Salisbury State University on Maryland's Eastern Shore, Jimmy will graduate in 1998. He wrote that the following poem goes with the photograph:

Webs of individual decisions
Spun in defiance
Often stain the soul
And become its cage
For life

Jennifer Bai Ling Yen's silver print on plexi-glass opens "Lark Lane: Travels" (p. 67). She titled it "Sink in the Past," and writes, "Time never waits for me, but photographs catch my memories and enable me to share my experiences with my family and friends back in Taiwan."

The untitled photo that opens the section on family (p. 97) is by **Ming Zhu**, who came to the United States after studying for two years at the Tianjin Art Institute in China. She is a visual communications student at Towson University, and she likes photography because it can express her emotions and feelings.

RECOMMENDED READING

Baker, Russell. *Growing Up*. New York: Signet, 1982.

Dillard, Annie and Cort Conley. *Modern American Memoirs*. New York: HarperCollins, 1995.

Paterson, Judith H. *Sweet Mystery: A Book of Remembering*. New York: Farrar, Strauss, and Giroux, 1996.

Zinsser, William. *On Writing Well, 5th Edition*. New York: HarperCollins, 1995.

"Writing and talk do not prove me, I carry the plenum of proof and everything else in my face. With the hush of my lips, I wholly confound the skeptic. Now, I will do nothing but listen, to accrue what I hear into this song...."

Walt Whitman